SCHOOL WARS
THE BATTLE FOR BRITAIN'S EDUCATION

MELISSA BENN

VERSO
London • New York

First published by Verso 2011
© Melissa Benn 2011

The moral rights of the author have been asserted

1 3 5 7 9 10 8 6 4 2

Verso
UK: 6 Meard Street, London W1F 0EG
US: 20 Jay Street, Suite 1010, Brooklyn, NY 11201
www.versobooks.com

Verso is the imprint of New Left Books

ISBN-13: 978-1-84467-736-8

British Library Cataloguing in Publication Data
A catalogue record for this book is available from the British Library

Library of Congress Cataloging-in-Publication Data
A catalog record for this book is available from the Library of Congress

Typeset by MJ Gavan, Cornwall
Printed in Sweden by ScandBook AB

MELISSA BENN is a journalist, novelist and campaigner. She has written for the *Guardian*, the *New Statesman*, *Public Finance*, *Cosmopolitan* and the *London Review of Books*, among many others. Her writing on education includes *Education and Democracy*, co-edited with Clyde Chitty, and *A Comprehensive Future: Quality and Equal* *for All Our Children*, written with Fiona Millar. A regular broadcaster and speaker, she is a founder member of the Local Schools Network, set up to support local schools and to counter media misinformation about their achievements and the challenges they face.

Also by Melissa Benn

Non-fiction

Death in the City (with Ken Worpole)

Madonna and Child

A Tribute to Caroline Benn: Education and Democracy

(co-edited with Clyde Chitty)

Novels

Public Lives

One of Us

For Dad—the great encourager

Contents

Introduction

A View from the Ground

In the mid 1990s, my partner and I made the unremarkable decision, as do thousands of parents every year throughout the UK, to send our children to local schools. Living in an inner-city area, where the question of education is often so fraught, while we did not unduly agonise as parents, we did make a conscious and considered choice based on a deeply held belief in what constitutes a good education. Of course, it is important that our daughters should learn and do well, but we also wanted them to discover how to take their place in the real world. In the lyrical words of pioneer educationalist Alex Bloom, we wanted them 'to experience just relationships with persons'.

We were lucky in many ways. Our elder daughter started school at the local primary soon after New Labour came to power; her sister joined her there two years later. In their younger years, then, they were 'Blair's children', benefiting from the visible public passion of an eager new government with a clear mandate to improve the nation's schools—and, in time, generous increases in education funding. Primary-school class sizes were kept under thirty; there was renewed emphasis on literacy and numeracy. It was a time of relative economic buoyancy and cultural openness, and, looking back, one of several missed political opportunities—when a popular young government with an impressive majority might have made some important reforms, that not only improved our schools, but expanded the possibilities of comprehensive education itself. Sadly, the political story was to unfold in a different direction.

We discovered then, as so many parents do, that state education is in much better shape than a hostile press, TV and radio will usually allow. Our local primary school was filled with exceptionally committed and hard-working teachers. The school put appropriate emphasis on the building blocks—reading, writing and maths—but there was also plenty of history, geography, science, art and design project work, and a wide range of extra-curricular activities including drama and music and many out-of-school day and residential visits. An on-site refugee centre—the only one of its kind in the country—which worked hard to help migrant families integrate into both society and school, and a counselling service, The Place To Be, were just two examples of the thoughtful and realistic way that the school handled potential obstacles to learning amongst its pupils. Dozens of languages were spoken, and cultures represented, within the school community, and rich use was made of this unique facet of an urban primary like ours—in Brent, North-West London, one of the most ethnically diverse areas in Europe.

Watching regular class performances and special assemblies in which children from an extraordinary spread of social, ethnic and religious backgrounds lined up shoulder to shoulder, it felt as if we had stumbled across—or held the key to, at least—some kind of practical utopia. I was moved by a profound sense of possibility, the honest belief that all our children could be educated together, successfully, the common good confirmed and extended by a mix of state resources, staff commitment, and parental and community engagement.

I had not reckoned on the fraught process of secondary transfer, in which parental ambitions and anxieties, particularly in inner-city areas, are so powerful. Going through this experience —twice—and watching many parents endure it in the years since, has confirmed for me that schooling remains one of the key ways in which class identity is formed in modern Britain. It was striking how many of the middle class, happy to support 'all-in' primary schools, departed from local comprehensive education at secondary level, and quite how desperately a few sought to secure, by whatever means lay open to them, the right school place for their child. 'Place' is a particularly apposite noun here. After all, the word ranges in meaning from social station to locality, a suitable setting or occasion, high rank or status, and finally job, post or position.

This experience made me profoundly distrustful of the concept of parental choice, in all its varieties. To state the obvious: what choice can a family on a joint income of £20,000 or less exercise to apply for a school that charges £12,000 a year—before the inevitable add-ons—not to mention the difficulties their child might well face trying to integrate in a social environment where the majority of families can comfortably afford such fees? How many families even know of the existence of, let alone are able to access, the shadowy world of tutoring and exam preparation that powers children into the highly selective grammars (and private schools) thickly dotted around our major towns and cities?

State-funded faith schools are a particular provocation to many parents. Every year, one can comfortably second-guess which children will win a place at one of the more prestigious Anglican or Catholic schools, pupils selected on the occasionally dubious grounds of their parents' long-held religious practice or their children's artistic or musical 'aptitude', one of the criteria by which schools select a percentage of their pupils. Clearly, the higher-achieving of these schools are choosing families and pupils as much as the other way around, thus creating for themselves a highly favourable pupil mix—what Professor Tim Brighouse would call a 'comprehensive plus' intake—and in the process contributing to a small but crucial narrowing of true comprehensive intakes in many local schools. Enabling faith to be played as a school advantage card has been increasingly criticised, most recently by John Pritchard, Bishop of Oxford and Chair of the Church of England's Board of Education, and it manifestly undermines the claims of these affiliated institutions to embody genuinely inclusive values.

*   *   *

Once again we chose the local community school, a brisk twenty-minute walk from our home. At the time, exam results were average, there were no rousing speeches about Oxbridge entrance, the school had no rugby team. Like so many comprehensives in inner-city areas, there was a far higher percentage of children on free school meals and children with special needs, and far fewer middle-class children, than lived in the surrounding area. But we admired and warmed to its friendly, open spirit, its determination to do well by every child and to keep improving. It looked like the London in which we live now, not a cosy recreation of the city I grew up in. There was a great deal of nervousness, and prejudice, among local parents but we decided to trust our instincts, helped by the fact that we knew a number of older children who had successfully made the transition. Several years on, our faith in something other than raw league tables, covert social snobbery and urban myth feels more than justified.

Yet despite their many strengths and successes, as well as their evident challenges, comprehensive schools like ours are routinely denigrated in the wider world. It may be bad luck, or a reflection of the tendency of national journalists to conduct research in locations easily reachable from their Central London offices, but over the past decade both our local primary and secondary schools have been subject to media 'sting' operations. In the first case, an experienced *Evening Standard* reporter, Alex Renton, who had already written a highly praised undercover piece about what life was like at an NHS hospital, was looking around for an opportunity to write a similar exposé on education, and pitched up at our local primary. Posing as someone interested in becoming a teacher, Renton was assigned to spend a week with a class of eight- and nine-year-olds. According to a subsequent report in the *Guardian*, Renton 'is a personable chap and the kids like him, as do the teachers. He notes that there are children with special needs, that there is a teacher shortage, that a classroom window is broken. On day three he observes a class of six- and seven-year-olds and remarks that "disruptive children ... spread chaos around them." Next day he witnesses a session designed to deal with bullying in which a teacher coaxes children to understand inappropriate behaviour. Renton is also told about a boy who is suspected of having been a victim of sexual abuse.' When Renton asked the class teacher, whose own daughter was at a private school, to speculate on the relative achievements of children in the two sectors, she intimated that the brightest children would rank somewhere nearer the middle in her daughter's class.

Renton was positive about many aspects of this inner-city primary. But the double-page spread was published under the alarmist headline: 'There was such a staff shortage, the security system had to be put in the charge of two eleven-year-olds', a story that the school subsequently claimed to be untrue. The school and parents were angry at the paper's deception, the distorted picture that was presented and the intimate details that were revealed. According to the *Guardian*, children in the playground 'are discovered trying to break Renton's name code in order to find out who he had written about. [The school] realise that one clue to the identity of the possible sexual abuse victim was too revealing and are concerned that the child will suffer from taunting or even bullying.' After receiving a number of complaints, and conducting its own investigation, the Press Complaints Commission severely censured the paper. Editor Max Hastings later told the *Guardian*, 'It was a considerable cock-up, a seriously misconceived exercise. One still asks oneself how, after all these years in the business, could we get it so wrong, a collective moment of madness.' Yet the paper never issued a formal apology to the school.[1]

By then, of course, the harm had been done. Readers of the *Evening Standard* would, on their tube ride to work or back, have perused yet another casually negative article about an ailing state school and the sad lives of the creatures that populate it: a complete misrepresentation of the day-to-day life of this remarkably hard-working, stable primary.

In April 2005, Channel Five broadcast *Classroom Chaos*, a programme claiming to tell the dark truth about our schools. A qualified teacher—who had not taught for thirty years, according to a later BBC news report—signed on as a supply teacher at a number of schools around the country. With a camera smuggled into her handbag, she filmed her unsuccessful attempts to control a number of classes. No school was named but in a short, relatively harmless sequence at the film's outset, one class in our local comprehensive could be identified by its uniform.

The film caused a national outcry. Executive Producer Roger Graef went into battle claiming that 'as their classes spiral out of control, teachers face at best indifference and rudeness, at worst taunts and threats and chaos … The worst sufferers are the 15,000 supply teachers … Successive reports and teachers' unions bear out the widespread nature of this problem. It sounds like a profession on the edge of a collective nervous breakdown.'[2]

Tory politicians promised that should they come back to power, they, of course, would do better. Labour politicians spluttered defensively and the National Union of Teachers (NUT) criticised the underhand methods of the documentary makers. But the real victims in this trial by media were the schools themselves, deceived and demoralised by the entire exercise—though pupils at our local school reported interesting conversations in class about the documentary, and the questions it raised—and the nation's parents, passive recipients of a dangerously undifferentiated message about the state of state education. A teacher with rusty professional skills, to put it mildly, a clear agenda and a hidden camera is clearly not a typical member of even that most battered wing of the profession, the supply-teaching force. Once again, the casual viewer was left with a lingering—and, in the case of our local comprehensive, mistaken—impression of bleakness and blanket chaos.

Stories such as these give credence to the claim that our system is 'broken', our children's education a mere 'factory school' experience. My objection to the objectors, my scepticism about their scepticism, is based in the first instance on the evidence of my own eyes: our daughters' evident enjoyment and sense of safety throughout their school years, the many excellent, and some truly inspirational, teachers they have encountered, the range of academic achievement within the school (including results that match any school, state or private, in the country), and the numerous concerts, plays, workshops, debates and sporting events. I remain impressed by the determined, friendly and modest atmosphere of our school epitomised by our head teacher, who has steered the school through a period of dramatic change and improvement by dint of consensual debate and continual encouragement. All this has confirmed it for me: comprehensives work. Given an increase in resources and greater political will in relation to school structures, and particularly selection, they could be world-class. And we are simply crazy, as a nation, to permit the dismantling of what has so far been achieved, against all the odds.

At present, however, most state schools occupy an uncomfortable space between public and private; they are neither business enterprises, working to a market model, nor a robust public service, sustained by a mix of state, community and third-sector effort. Under increasing pressure from a competitive ethos, driven by league tables, schools like ours are expected to deliver ever higher standards and improved results without the necessary resources, judged against far more selective or far better resourced schools, despite vastly differing contexts. It is plainly ridiculous to compare the results of a secondary modern in a deprived part of Kent with those of an elite grammar in Birmingham, let alone those of an expensive private school. One is not comparing like with like on any single measure. This is one of the reasons I have become so impatient with those parents who behave, in the words of radical educator Michael Fielding, like 'querulous consumers', stamping their feet at every discrepancy in provision between the so-called best and worst schools, wilfully ignorant of political and economic structures or pressures.

On the other hand, many comprehensives still draw on an extraordinary communal wealth that remains invisible to most measures of accountability, including league tables and public comment. This explains the often puzzling strength of parental attachment to a school that has only average or even poor results. A good local school is a mix of self-interest and shared interest that transcends, and nullifies, the values of profit and consumption, commerce and customer. Given the strength of these values, it is no surprise that some parents feel angry and even betrayed when other families trade the compromises of shared interest for the clear gains of self-interest, or that many a friendship eventually founders on the rock of school choice. More positively, it explains the extraordinary loyalty that even more affluent parents, who could easily have chosen the private or selective route, feel towards a local comprehensive as the embodiment of the vital ideal of common citizenship.

One of the most impressive aspects of our school is its powerful sense of community; the myriad, informal ties that bind so many different individuals and families together in a common purpose. Hundreds have contributed to the life of the school over the years, be it through fund-raising, standing for an hour or two behind a stall, painting faces backstage for a production or, in my own case, helping to create a visiting writers and speakers programme. Parents are encouraged into the school, and even welcomed to add something to the curriculum, in both small and substantial ways, if they have the time and expertise. A school community can also think out loud collectively about the often unexpected problems that arise. When, tragically, a young child was killed on a dangerous crossing near a local primary school, one of several serious local traffic accidents, a group of parents and school staff, clothed in black, marched through the neighbourhood demanding traffic safety measures from the council, something we won almost immediately.

An active and strong school community benefits all parents, whether they are involved or not, because all instinctively feel part of a common and successful enterprise. The greater the mix of children in terms of social class and levels of achievement, the greater the sense of collective possibility, the easier the job for the school. At parents' evenings I am always moved and impressed by the warmth, detailed attention and sometimes appropriate sternness shown by teachers towards every child, whatever their family background, whatever their academic progress or lack thereof.

I have seen, up close, that there are no quick fixes. Education, particularly in 'all-in' schools like ours, is about constant encouragement, over days and weeks and years, particularly for those children who lack support from home or who have difficult or disrupted lives, although there is a limit to what we should expect schools and teachers to be able to rectify. It is also not just about exam results but about fostering all kinds of interests and talents.

Still, it would take a hardened cynic not to be moved by our latest GCSE celebration evening, and the sight of so many students proudly walking up to the stage to receive their certificates to the audible and generous congratulations of their peers. I could not help thinking how many of those same young men and women would have been written off, under the old selective system, before they reached puberty—losing their intellectual and personal confidence, maybe for good. But we were also that night celebrating the stellar results of children who would have sailed through the eleven-plus. To enable the education of all children, side by side, seems to me a far richer definition of success, for both our education system and our society as a whole, than to take only the apparent winners, most of them from relatively affluent backgrounds, and educate them in separate, privileged enclaves, while condoning second-class facilities and resources for the unlucky majority. We may have a long way to go in genuinely equalising resources within our education system but I remain grateful that I, and millions of other parents, have not had to educate our own children within such a brutal and unimaginative framework.

Given all this, I find it hard to take seriously the accusation made by critics of existing state education that middle-class parents who send their children to comprehensives are deluded, or disingenuous. Or, most damagingly, that they are—in the words of teacher and free school founder, Katharine Birbalsingh—'disguising the failings of state schools in the inner cities'. The charge of conspiring in the provision of second-rate education to poorer children is never, I notice, put to parents who support private schools, grammar schools or the more socially selective church schools. Often, it is local families, in partnership with staff and school leaders, who have turned schools around in the most difficult circumstances, and made them remarkably successful.[3]

State education has never commanded the same loyalty or sense of affection from the British public as the NHS. In this book I will explore some of the reasons why this might be, including the divided way which universal education was imposed after 1944 and the consistent refusal of politicians to consolidate the changes first foisted on them by popular parental demand. High-quality comprehensive education was never presented to the people as a democratic ideal; indeed, it was never presented in any coherent form at all.

This absence of a binding ideal, combined with a lack of the resources necessary to furnish it, ensures that 'education, education, education' remains a national obsession, rather like a mildly unhappy, forever unresolved relationship. Much tinkering by successive governments has done nothing to help the matter; in fact, it seems to make it worse. The nation continues to agonise over the related issues of school choice and school quality. Almost every day, TV, radio and newspapers supply some new story on the subject, be it parents failing to win their first choice of school, violence in the classroom or the impending crisis in further education, including rising tuition fees. Public debates, private seminars and grandly titled conferences on some aspect of schools or learning take place virtually every week.

It was not always the case. Writers about education in the 1960s and 70s frequently remark on the muted nature of political and public interest during this period. One reason for this, I would suggest, is that despite the transformation during this period from the selective to the comprehensive model, the system as a whole was more stable, with far stronger local government. And it is no coincidence that anxiety about comprehensive education really took off around the time of the oil crisis in the early 1970s. Worries about education and the economy are bound to be connected: the more perilous the national finances, the quicker pundits and politicians are to locate the problem in our schools, and to propose yet another radical overhaul of the system. This has now become an ingrained cultural habit.

This book comes at a pivotal and highly dangerous point in the story of state education. With manic zeal, the new Coalition Government is advancing the 'choice and diversity' revolution begun in the Thatcherite years and pursued with ambivalent vigour by New Labour. It comes accompanied by the deepest cuts seen for a generation, a high-risk strategy that has angered large sections of the educational community and whose wider impact will soon be felt by the public. While in England the fear is of further fragmentation and division, Scotland and Wales, both of which have comprehensive systems, are also convulsed by debates about how to improve standards and, in particular, how to address the gap between schools serving different communities—while also trying to deal with the shock of slashed public spending.

Even so, are the latest school wars really a battle over the substance and soul, the fate and future, of Britain's education? Yes: at this point in history, we can say that they are. Even commentators sympathetic to these reforms describe the current government as the 'breakneck coalition'. The scent of battle is everywhere in the air. A recent feature in the *Spectator*, accusing pro-comprehensive campaigners of bullying tactics, was entitled 'Revealed: the secret war over England's schools'.[4] Writing about abolition of the grammars in his *Daily Mail* online blog, Peter Hitchens justly affirms: 'The reason why this controversy has run for so long is that it matters so much, and says so much about those who take sides in it.'[5] The writer James Delingpole has even gone so far as to describe the actions of those who oppose free schools as 'actively evil'.[6]

But the metaphor of war and battle resonates at another level, too. The current clashes over government plans represent the intensification of a struggle that has been going on, in different forms, for nearly fifty years. There has been a long and harsh battle between supporters of comprehensive schools and those who want to retain selection in some form, whether through the restitution of the grammar schools or through more subtle means.

In his calm, clear analysis of the recent history of state education, *State Schools Since the 1950s: The Good News*, Adrian Elliott compares the ideological divide over the grammar schools to a long-running Sicilian blood feud. It's a good image. In his autobiography *The Great Betrayal*, Brian Cox, the chief figure behind the notorious Black Papers (a series of interventions from the political right that lambasted progressive developments in education, from comprehensive reform to more child-centred teaching methods, published in the 1960s and 70s), describes how he found himself 'the most hated professor in the country ... nicknamed the Enoch Powell of education.'[7] The battle over how to organise our schools, and what to teach in them, has a long, bitter and tangled history.

Part of this political story inevitably involves a parallel and broader struggle over whether our public services are to be run by a democratic, devolved state, or whether they are to be put out to tender. In the United States over the last twenty years, privatised state schools on the so-called Charter model have gripped the imagination of everyone from hedge fund billionaires to the liberal elite; yet they have also posed a real danger to America's much maligned public (state) schools. As the American educator and former adviser to the administration of George W. Bush, Diane Ravitch, says: 'There is a clash of ideas occurring in education right now between those who believe that public education is not only a fundamental right but a vital public service, akin to the public provision of police, fire protection, parks, and public libraries, and those who believe that the private sector is always superior to the public sector.'[8] Without an active, well-resourced and democratically accountable state, particularly at local level, we are in danger of throwing away the tools we need to ensure both high quality and equality in education; in a nation as economically and socially divided as ours, it is vital that we pursue both. At this political juncture, the case for the state and its benign potential seems particularly hard to make.

There is a third, equally vital strand to the battle for Britain's education. We are immersed in culture wars, those bitter arguments that have raged in various media over the decades about everything from the merits of grammar schools to the legitimacy of private education and, of course, the aims and success of comprehensive education. Beneath the headlines hovers an often unarticulated anxiety, and frequently raw prejudice, about ethnic and religious difference, and a thinly veiled terror of downward mobility that fuels the frequently acrid, highly personalised clashes over school choice. Now, more than ever, we are subject to relentless coverage of our allegedly 'dumbed-down' state schools and the 'curdling' of the comprehensive experiment. Its purpose, I believe, is to soften up the public and justify further unhelpful reforms.

It is with keen awareness of all these different levels of battle that I have laid out my argument. I begin with an analysis of the politics of the Coalition and its more prominent and powerful allies. I then move back to consider the impact of the seminal 1944 Education Act, and to track the development of—and setbacks to—comprehensive education from the 1960s through New Labour's time in office. I go on to analyse some of the key issues in schooling today, from the entrenched politics of selection to the development of the new 'independent state' schools, and the substantive changes seen in the more established private sector. In the final section I speculate on how the current schools revolution might develop, ending with an outline of an alternative vision for the coming century.

I write this book as someone deeply involved in the school wars. I hope that I convey this battle with the vividness that I have directly experienced as an engaged combatant, parent, writer and campaigner: a member of the steering group of Comprehensive Future, the campaign for fair admissions; and co-founder in 2010—with fellow activists and parents Fiona Millar, Francis Gilbert and Henry Stewart—of The Local Schools Network, a web-based campaign designed to debate the impact of the new school revolution and to provide a forum for the many thousands with positive experiences of state education who want to find ways to improve it, rather than disparage or dismantle it. Both organisations are part of an impressive wider network of campaigns and individuals who continue to press for a fair schools system for all our children. Even though the LSN is not yet a year old, I was proud to see it referred to more than once in parliamentary debates concerning the 2011 Education Bill.

This book is written partly out of anger and frustration, but mostly from a powerful sense of hope. I am myself a product of comprehensive education. I am fiercely proud of that inheritance, and grateful to have been able to give my own daughters a similar start in life. On a political level, I want to contribute to the creation of a genuinely non-selective system and the enrichment of education for all children, not just the lucky minority. Few have put it more eloquently than Michael Morpurgo, the writer and former children's laureate, when he recently reaffirmed his passionate belief that 'At the heart of every child … is a unique genius and personality. What we should be doing is to allow the spark of that genius to catch fire, to burn brightly and shine.'[9] There is so much more to do. In the words of Robin Pedley, a forensic analyst and imaginative supporter of comprehensive reform in its early years, what is at stake is the encouragement of 'a larger and more generous attitude' within society and within us all. I hope the reader finds evidence of that spirit in this book. It represents my attempt to confront the realities of our divided school system, and to help bring the necessary forces together to remake it in a more inclusive, open-hearted and effective form.

I
THE PRESENT THREAT

Chapter One

Understanding the New Schools Revolution

Sometime in February 2010, rumours began to circulate that the American actress Goldie Hawn had flown into London for talks with Shadow Education Secretary Michael Gove on how she might help improve Britain's schools. Hawn's Foundation Charity runs a group of schools in the USA and Canada that emphasise Buddhist techniques of meditation and breathing. The prospect of a meeting between the would-be minister and the famous comedy actress was irresistible to the press. It felt like one of those quirky Orange cinema advertisements you get before the main film: Gove and Goldie practising enlightenment in a curtained House of Commons office, deep-breathing their way to intellectual excellence. In fact, the two never did meet in person, as Hawn rather huffily revealed later that year. 'I'll tell you exactly what I did. I had a meeting with an aide of his ... in some lobby at one of the parliament buildings down there by the river ... just in the place where you get the coffee from the vending machine.'[1]

But if the 'vending machine' discussions came to nothing—or not yet—Hawn's surreal entry onto the UK education scene was a clear sign of the impending sea change in public service reform.

New. Free. Choice. Innovation. David Cameron's rebranded party worked hard, when in opposition, to project itself as a fresh, engaging voice on education, to bury memories of the Tories' miserable record on schools when last in office during the 1980s and 90s. In the months running up to the election, Gove and Cameron gave a number of press interviews revealing the fact that they shared the school run to a Church of England state primary in Kensington. Cameron's Tories were close observers, and admirers, of Tony Blair, eager to learn from the former Labour leader's triumphs as well as his errors, and their energetic, almost evangelical approach to education reform clearly echoed New Labour's early spirit as well as its main theme.

The Tories were particularly keen to build on New Labour's academy programme, extending it far beyond the impoverished inner-city areas that it was originally intended to serve. Academy status was natural conservative territory, with its freedom from local authorities, from national agreements on teachers' pay and conditions and from an often constricting curriculum, imposed, incidentally, by the Conservatives when they were last in power. But, in a crucial political twist, the Tories planned to use this special status to the advantage of the already advantaged. These freedoms were now to be offered to existing 'outstanding' schools, with the ultimate aim of creating a network of 'independent state' schools to sit alongside, and appear to outshine, the maintained sector—that is, schools funded through and supported by local authorities.

Initially, at least, academy conversions attracted less publicity than the alluring 'free school' idea. In terms of their legal status, free schools were to be virtually identical to academies; publicly funded but independently run, they had the added ideological appeal of appearing to emanate from the combined dynamism and desperation of parents and teachers up and down the country. A few parent-sponsored schools had opened under New Labour, but the more successful of these, such as Elmgreen School in West Norwood, South London, worked closely with its local authority. The academy model, however, enabled a complete break with local democracy.

A Tory Green Paper on education, published as early as November 2007, had already floated the idea of parent- and philanthropist-promoted schools and claimed that, if elected, a Conservative Government would seek to create 220,000 school places over the next decade. Now, in the immediate pre-election period, Gove and Cameron were keen to create an impression of unstoppable momentum. Gove spoke of the 'hundreds' of parents and groups of teachers who had contacted the Tories expressing an urgent interest to start their own school: not just the 'yummy mummies with sharp elbows', but also 'the Gateshead mum ... a no-nonsense working-class woman passionate about her kids', or 'groups in Birmingham who have strong representation among the Afro-Caribbean community, some of them with links to churches ... desperate ... to set up schools.'[2] Cameron promised 'to bust open the state monopoly on education and allow new schools to be established'.

The Tory free school model was far from the original free schools, a distinct, libertarian tradition within English private education in the twentieth century that stressed genuine intellectual freedom, unfettered creativity and vigorous school democracy. The Tories had nothing like this in mind. They looked instead to neoliberal experiments within the Swedish school system, instituted since the 1990s, and the US charter school movement, which now educated a million and a half children, many of them from low-income homes, outside the public (state) school system. Taken together, these international examples of pedagogic experimentation helped project a public image of a party finally at ease with the diverse, modern world. According to Cameron, these were important models, 'making sure there's excellence, there's competition, there's innovation'. It was several months before serious doubts began to be aired more publicly about the effectiveness and wider social impact of both the Swedish and US models.

In the period running up to the May 2010 election, there was considerable media interest in a number of free school campaigns. These could not easily be yoked together in terms of their demands, as many of the groups arose from distinct and inevitably complex local factors. They ranged from the efforts of journalist Toby Young, who had rejected his local comprehensive in Acton, West London—a school judged by Ofsted to be 'good with outstanding' features—and gathered a bunch of well-heeled parents to explore the establishment of a free school, to a band of parents in Kirklees, Yorkshire, who wanted to convert an existing middle school, serving a number of villages, into a local secondary school. Inevitably, all were lumped together in media reports as state-school parents 'fed up with their educational options'. However, as writer Geraldine Bedell perceptively observed, although 'the tone of the argument is often angry ... everyone wants the same thing: a good, free, local school for all.'[3]

Suddenly, proposals put forward by comprehensive reformers over several decades—from smaller class sizes, to more resources for poorer children, to greater freedom for teachers—had apparently been hijacked overnight by the new right. It was striking how often Michael Gove employed the term 'comprehensive'—an attempt, perhaps, to link his party with fairness in the public mind and to banish some of the lingering images of elitism, arrogance and class partiality it displayed during the 1980s. In the winter of 2009, in the promisingly entitled *A Comprehensive Programme for School Reform*, Gove set out five priorities for changing our schools. But the 'c' word was used here in its blandest sense, to mean 'of large content or scope'. A year on, the department deflected criticism of unfair admissions practice by referring to government plans for 'a comprehensive programme to make opportunity more equal'.[4] In the run-up to the election, David Cameron visited the free school advocates in Kirklees and signed his name on the parents' outdoor campaign wall, adding: 'Let's support parents who want great state schools for their children. I salute your courage and dedication, and we will not let you down.'

At the same time Cameron worked hard, if not entirely successfully, to present himself as an ordinary, averagely sharp-elbowed, middle-class parent, 'terrified' of not finding a good state school for his young children.[5] It was a sign of changed times that an Eton-educated Tory leader felt obliged to send his children to state schools, although other front-bench figures, out of the direct line of fire on the schools issue, chose an expensive private education for their children. Cameron's close ally, George Osborne, withdrew his two children from a state primary in 2008 in order to send them to a non-selective preparatory school in West London. In an interview in March 2005, shortly after he was made shadow chancellor, Osborne said: 'I hate that kind of tokenistic politics where the politician uses his private life to illustrate some broader point. When it comes to choosing a school, we will make a decision on which school, state or private, we feel is best for them.'

But the Tory trump card was Michael Gove, one of the very few senior front-bench figures who could credibly front an education revolution based on apparent popular discontent. The adopted child of an Aberdeen fish processor, Gove had won a scholarship to private school and then gone on to Oxford. Gove clearly represented a different educational trajectory—and social class—to that of Cameron, Osborne and other leading Conservatives. If he was not—quite—the poor boy made good, he was certainly one of Alan Bennett's *History Boys*. Clever, witty and personally charming, Gove also had, as one feature writer observed, the faint air of vulnerability of the man who has risen far and fast. At times, however, his mission on education has seemed largely focussed on getting more people like himself—the naturally brilliant who were not born to rule—to an elite university: the classic grammar-school narrative that still obsesses our nation. Gove liked to speculate in public about what would have happened to him if he had been obliged to attend some poorly performing local school.

If a general alliance between entrenched privilege and aggressive, yet ultimately deferential, aspiration has powered so much of recent British education policy, the confident, gilded Cameron and the restless, brainy Gove perfectly exemplified the mix in human terms. There were echoes of the close political and personal partnership between the privately educated Tony Blair and his educational mentor, Andrew Adonis, the brilliant son of a Greek Cypriot immigrant, who won his chance to shine with a scholarship to a state boarding school.

From the outset, the Coalition ruled, not as if it had come to power as a result of a carefully crafted cross-party consensus, but as if it had won a massive popular mandate for fundamental transformation. As lead partners in the Coalition, the Tories were clearly determined not to commit Blair's mistake and wait before pushing through radical change. When an ebullient Gove rose to introduce the Queen's Speech debate on education, in late May, sitting to his right was a faintly dazed-looking Sarah Teather, the new Liberal Democrat minister of state for children and families. Any political discomfiture on Teather's part was understandable. After all, the Liberal Democrats had fought the general election on a platform of direct opposition to both free schools and the extension of the academy programme—principles overwhelmingly affirmed at their autumn 2010 conference.

Michael Gove's first year in office was marked by a number of embarrassing errors and U-turns. Early estimates of the number of schools that wished to convert to academy status were overblown: not over a thousand, as Gove first excitedly suggested, but a mere 153—although the numbers would later climb. Then, in a gleeful speech to the House of Commons in early July, Gove announced the cancellation of Labour's school-building programme, Building Schools for the Future. The new minister waxed lyrical on the 'massive overspends, tragic delays, botched construction projects and needless bureaucracy'. A total of 706 projects were considered too far advanced to be abandoned, 719 projects were to be axed, while 123 academy schemes were under review. Within a few days Gove was back in the Commons, forced to issue a grovelling apology; having announced that building projects would still go ahead in Derby, the West Midlands, Northamptonshire, Peterborough, Doncaster, Greenwich, Staffordshire, Wiltshire, Lancashire and Bexley, in fact all these were to be axed.

Normally mild-mannered head teachers and loyal backbenchers were roused to real anger at the brutal speed and apparent carelessness of the government's handling of the cuts in the school building programme. Tory MPs in Croydon, West Yorkshire and Kent, facing cancelled building projects in their constituencies, made special representations to the new minister. Heather Duggan, assistant head teacher at Liverpool's St John Bosco Art College, told the BBC: 'We were just floored.' When Liverpool's cabinet member for education and children's services, Councillor Jane Corbett, visited the school to try to soften the blow, the students asked her: 'How could the government be allowed to do this, to destroy young peoples' futures?'[6] On a sweltering day in July, a packed Central Methodist Hall in Westminster, London, heard impassioned speeches from parents, trade union leaders and politicians. The message on one placard—Building Schools for the Favoured—neatly encapsulated the mood of the moment.

Before the end of May, Parliament was presented with a new Academies Bill that, in the words of the BBC, presaged 'the most radical overhaul of schools in England for a generation'. England's secondary and primary schools were to be offered the chance to convert to academy status, with institutions already judged 'outstanding' by Ofsted to be fast-tracked through the process without consultation with staff, parents or the wider community; free schools could be set up on the same independent basis. 'Not since the Dangerous Dogs Act 1991 has legislation other than that intended to counter terrorism, or deal with economic crisis, been rushed through all parliamentary stages in quite this fashion', teachers' union leader Christine Blower told her party conference later that year. There was widespread criticism of the Bill, particularly its limited provision for consultation.[7] Liberal Democrats in the House of Lords, uneasy at the pace of change, pushed through some minor amendments on consultation, safeguarding provision for children with special educational needs and freedom of information.

Spending cuts were to prove a key part of the school revolution jigsaw. Clear parallels were emerging with welfare and health, where government policy was developing a similarly toxic mix of radical, fast-paced, structural change and slashed spending. In the summer, the government had already announced swingeing cuts to local authority budgets which were soon to filter through to schools. In the October Comprehensive Spending Review, while the dedicated schools budget was marginally increased by 0.1 per cent (not enough to keep pace with inflation), and an additional £2.5 billion was pledged for a new 'pupil premium', an extra sum per pupil for children from low-income families, the overall Department for Education budget fell. Some of the main savings, like the 60 per cent cut to the school building programme and the abolition of a number of education quangos, including the General Teaching Council and the Qualifications and Curriculum Development Agency, had already been publicised, as had the axing of the Child Trust funds and one-to-one tuition. The government now announced that it would also scrap the Educational Maintenance Allowance (EMA), a subsidy of up to £30 a week that allowed many students from poorer homes to stay on at school, and cut £162 million from the School PE and Sports Strategy that had up to now been ring-fenced, to fund 450 schools sport partnerships.

There was public dismay at both these abolitions. Getting rid of the schools sport partnerships was 'an act of gross stupidity', one partnership manager told the *Daily Telegraph*. Under public pressure, Michael Gove restored most of the budget for school sports; but there were reports that he had partly funded this U-turn by deciding instead to abolish Bookstart, an imaginative scheme to offer free books to nearly 3.5 million children at three key ages, from pre-school to the end of primary. A fresh bout of outrage greeted the Bookstart announcement in December: Carol Ann Duffy, the Poet Laureate, accused the government of behaving like 'Scrooge at his worst', and best-selling author Ian McEwan declared himself 'appalled' at the move. In response, Department of Education officials were dispatched on Boxing Day to meet with Viv Bird, CEO of Booktrust, which administers the Bookstart scheme, to announce the continuation of funding.[8] In March 2011, Gove restored a third of the budget for EMA, although this did not stop the Organisation for Economic Co-operation and Development calling on the government to restore the whole amount in the interests of fairness.[9] The November 2010 vote to triple tuition fees, despite explicit pre-election promises by the Liberal Democrats to oppose such a move—and widespread, sometimes violent, street protests—contributed significantly to the darkening of the public mood, and the mounting fear and cynicism about public sector reform.

Nothing, however, would stop the Coalition as it steamed ahead with a White Paper, *The Importance of Teaching*, most of whose proposals were later enshrined in the 2011 Education Bill. University-based teacher training was to be scaled back in favour of practical experience in the classroom via a new network of Teaching Schools, some to be located in the private sector. All new schools would now be either academies or free schools, and, with the Kirklees example in mind perhaps, central government gave itself the right to purchase school land from local authorities to hand straight over to the new ventures. Schools that were not meeting the new 'floor target' of 35 per cent GCSEs including English, mathematics and a science (but not to include vocational qualifications like BTEC, which many thought were artificially inflating school results) could be forced to convert to academy status. Schools that wished to convert were now required only to consult when they deemed it 'appropriate', and this consultation could be delayed until after an academy order has been made, rendering it virtually meaningless. Free schools could be set up in a number of locations including empty shops, office space or even ice rinks. Local admissions forums, important area-based committees created to scrutinise the fairness of school admissions, were to be abolished—just as a raft of new schools, with enhanced powers over their own admissions, were to be created. The School Adjudicator could no longer make changes to a school's admission policy in response to a complaint or a referral. These changes may have precipitated the decision of the existing School Adjudicator, Ian Craig, to announce that he would stand down in October 2011, six months before his contract expired.

Meanwhile a fresh row was brewing over the introduction of a new measurement of school quality, the English Baccalaureate, known as the E-Bacc. In order to qualify, pupils had to have a good GCSE in maths, English, two sciences, a humanities subject (but this did not include a GCSE in Humanities), and an ancient or modern foreign language. Many heads were furious to discover that their schools were to be judged retrospectively on the new measure—that is, on GCSEs taken in the summer of 2010. Many were now faced with unpalatable decisions concerning whether to switch pupils halfway through existing GCSE courses to make sure their school performed well in future league tables, or to ignore what many saw as Gove's arbitrary rulings over what subjects now counted, and stay at the bottom of the pile. Many deplored the absence of subjects like music, art and religious education from the E-Bacc.

A new partiality seemed to have crept into government policy-making. Critics questioned the high number of academy heads and leaders represented on a major review of teaching and learning, announced in March 2011—particularly since academies and free schools were to be exempted from so many government strictures on the curriculum and standards. There were also raised eyebrows at the appointment of ex-Blair adviser Sally Morgan as Chair of a newly slimmed-down Ofsted, given her close links both to ARK, one of the powerful new academy chains, and to the New Schools Network, a government-funded body for facilitating the establishment of free schools. On the curriculum review, announced in early 2011, Gove made plain his preference for 'a traditional education, sitting in rows, learning the kings and queens of England, the great works of literature, proper mental arithmetic, algebra by the age of eleven, modern foreign languages. That's the best training of the mind and that's how children will be able to compete.' Later he told teachers that 'the great tradition of our literature—Dryden, Pope, Swift, Byron, Keats, Shelley, Austen, Dickens and Hardy—should be at the heart of school life.' But over half this list were already being taught within schools. English teachers also questioned the fact that the only expert in primary-level literacy on the committee overseeing the national curriculum review was Ruth Miskin, the most public advocate of the controversial 'synthetic phonics' method of teaching children to read, and whose company Read Write Inc. sells training programmes to schools. Both of the primary heads also appointed to the committee were vocal supporters—and users—of Ms Miskin's training programme.

There were further embarrassing setbacks for the 'break-neck Coalition'. Following a judicial review launched by six councils including Nottingham City, Luton and Kent, challenging the legality of the government's precipitate abandonment of the Building Schools for the Future programme, the High Court found Gove's failure to consult on BSF cancellations 'so unfair as to amount to an abuse of power'. Gove dismissed the judgment as a minor technicality. A few weeks later he told Parliament that a college in Doncaster, a new school-building pilot project, was agreed by the government in an impressively short ten weeks. Not true, pointed out Rowan Moore in the *Observer*: in fact, it took 22 weeks. In the same trenchant piece, Moore, an architectural journalist, observed: 'If Michael Gove were a building, he would leak. He would crack and crumble on faulty foundations. He would be windy, but also overheat. Behind a pretentious facade, he would be shoddy in design and execution.'[10]

Rowan Moore's metaphor was a sound one. Behind the glitzy shop-window dressing of the Coalition's school plans, with their relentless harping on novelty and freedom, there was a deeper and darker agenda. While a British Social Attitudes survey published six months after the 2010 election found that public satisfaction with both health and education had improved dramatically over the past twenty years,[11] elements of the Coalition Government set out ruthlessly to undermine public confidence in public services. In order to justify rapid and widespread change, it was vital to the new right that it paint an apocalyptic picture of state education, and project an image of the nation's schools as places of intellectual mediocrity when not given over to anarchy and indiscipline. Here, it was building on an often dishonourable national prejudice that stretches back decades. Adrian Elliott worked as a head for over twenty years, and found that the public message on schools remained remarkably unchanged over that period; state schools and those who worked in them were a disaster. 'If anything, the portrayal of state education in England by the media, politicians and business leaders has become more negative. Criticisms [now] appear almost daily in books, newspapers, journals and the broadcast media.'[12]

In a piece for the *New Statesman* in 2010, Fiona Millar and I looked at the typical image of state schools presented in the press. We found a consistent picture of despair: 'discarded needles, enforced mediocrity, petty bullying, too much political correctness, not enough Jesus or competitive sport: a distorted picture put out daily by a press and broadcasting media, few of whose leaders use the system they so relentlessly traduce.' We highlighted a piece in the *Sunday Times* by one of the paper's war correspondents, Christina Lamb, who asked the question, 'What's wrong with winning?' In it, Lamb explained in anguished prose why she had to move her son from a state to a private school. The main problem, according to Lamb, was the lack of any competitive drive within what was, by her own account, a happy primary school, led by a 'firm headmistress and young, dedicated teachers'. Forced to resort to 'subterfuge' in order to find out her son's overall ranking in the class, Lamb was later dismayed to find that on sports day, 'instead of racing against each other, the children were put into teams with a mix of different ages ... with each team doing different activities.'[13]

Such worrying experiences forced Lamb to apply to the nearby oversubscribed private school, where she was deeply reassured by the head's boasting about everything from sporting achievements to A grades to Oxbridge entrance successes. Lamb makes much of her own state education and avowed abhorrence of the 'two-tier' system of education in this country. This theme of reluctant conversion is a common one, with minor variants. A piece by Will Self in the *Evening Standard* in October 2009 was headlined: 'I'm a diehard lefty but my son is going to private school'. Having described the reasons why he had to take his son out of a state primary, Self concluded that he could not be accused of hypocrisy, on the apparently watertight grounds that he had never actually believed that state education *was* an engine of social change. One of the sadder stories in this genre was by William Miller, the middle-aged son of the writer, television presenter and theatre and opera director Jonathan Miller, who, in the *Mail on Sunday* in February 2009—under the banner headline 'Atrocious lessons and daily bullying ... why I won't send my children to a state school'—castigated his father for propounding a 'a mistaken ideology'. According to Miller, he and his two siblings were 'the victims of the most cavalier of social experiments': they had been sent to a comprehensive. William Miller was at school in the 1970s. State schools are very different places today. No tales of bullying or poor teaching in a public school over thirty years ago would be used to condemn private education today; they would more probably be filed away under Interesting and Irrelevant Social History, or used to demonstrate the many improvements that have occurred within the sector in the years since.

Every story of this kind relies on often unchallengeable anecdotal detail. Little place is given to the part played by parenting, personality or other behind-the-scenes factors or tensions. According to these writers, and dozens more like them, it is the school and the school alone that causes a child's lack of achievement or unhappiness. The reader also has no way to address the clear contradictions that arise between these stories. Lamb's son was in an admittedly happy, co-operative primary where, according to his mother, his ruthless edge was not being sufficiently sharpened. Self's son was allegedly bullied and tested to the extreme. Miller blames his lack of an academic education on his middle-class parents, while other newspaper features will regularly castigate the middle class for claiming that the state education system, rather than their own privilege and efforts, enabled them to achieve good results. Parents who send their children to inner-city state schools no longer appear vaguely daring so much as disingenuous and dishonest, as Martin Samuel in *The Times* has argued, because they ruthlessly exploit their own affluence and connections to cover up their children's poor education.

The real politics of education is never openly discussed in such articles. Lamb declares herself impressed by 'the astonishing range of facilities and activities' on offer at the private school she finally chooses for her son. Yet the resource argument, central to the privilege and achievements of the private sector, is treated as a marginal element in her decision, rather than being woven objectively into the story. Even the smallest private school spends about twice what the state sector spends on each pupil, currently around £6,000 a year in England. At the top end of the market, fees are £30,000 a year for boarders. Many private day schools will charge half that.

Similarly, stories of struggling state schools are presented out of context, as if a set of teachers and local authority officials got together and deliberately decided to create a bad school, to prove beyond doubt that comprehensive education really is the engine of mediocrity. Only passing reference is made to the extraordinarily complex issues of school choice, admissions policies, funding or the huge impact that poverty has on the ability of so many children to learn. Part of the fresh attack launched by the Coalition and their allies on state schools involves the claim that poverty is used as an excuse, not by the poor themselves, but by the do-gooding middle class, who actively prevent rigorous learning from taking place; whereas in 'good' schools, home background would, of course, form no barrier to learning.

It is not just newspapers that misrepresent our schools. Comprehensives get a rough, sensationalist ride from modern TV. *Waterloo Road*, the prime-time soap opera, features the popular actress Amanda Burton as no-nonsense super-head Karen Fisher. While Fisher is appealing, her school is not. It has, over time, been both set on fire and demolished by a digger; its lockers are sprayed with graffiti, its students peddle drugs, and its often raddled-looking teachers have the temerity to belong to a trade union.

Two best-selling novels of recent years reinforce this general picture of an out-of-control pupil population in league with the politically motivated, professionally incompetent, or both. The North London school featured in Zoë Heller's *Notes on a Scandal*, published in 2003, is a den of chaos and appallingly low standards where 'last year we had 240 pupils sit their GCSEs, and exactly six of them achieved anything higher than a grade E pass.' Not, then, a fictional representation of Heller's own North London comprehensive, Haverstock School, which educated among others Oona King and David and Ed Miliband. Mercilessly lampooning the comprehensive school staff as either cynical and weary or sentimental and naive, this supremely English novel reads less like satire than a prolonged act of casual, conservative vandalism.[14]

But St George's, Heller's fictional school, seems like bliss compared to the hellhole featured in Sebastian Faulks's best-selling state-of-the-nation novel *A Week in December* (2009). Radley Graves, an alcoholic, internet-addicted teacher works at a chaotic South London comprehensive in the 'Lewisham/Catford overlap' where 'the kids were allowed to come in late to lessons ... to talk pretty much unchecked through a class ... not to work if they didn't fancy it.'[15] The school football team even plays a fixture against St Michael and All Angels, a real school which achieved notoriety when teacher Katharine Birbalsingh spoke publicly about some of its pupils at the Tory Party conference. It has since been announced that the school is to close, following a sharp drop in applications.

Published in spring 2011, Birbalsingh's thinly fictionalised account of her teaching life, *To Miss With Love*, immediately became a best-seller. With its string of unappealing caricatures— anxious heads, cynical white liberals, slick, clipboard-toting edu-preneurs and mouthy teenagers, insufficiently challenged by a complacent education establishment—the book did its bit in undermining confidence in state education and softening up public opinion in favour of government reforms.

Gove's agenda fitted perfectly with this cultural and political backdrop. As a new minister, there he was on the platform at the autumn 2010 Tory Party Conference, nodding along as Katherine Birbalsingh made her impassioned speech declaring, to huge applause, that the system was 'broken'. During his own Conference speech Gove lamented how this 'waste of talent, this squandering of human potential ... this grotesque failure to give all our fellow citizens an equal chance is a reproach to our conscience.' Launching the Education Bill in February 2011, he said: 'I would love to celebrate a greater level of achievement, but I am afraid that this is the dreadful inheritance that our children face.'

*   *   *

Two key themes shaped Gove's assault on the nation's schools. The first touched on the apparent sharp drop in the performance of UK schools in recent years, as judged by the findings of PISA—Programme for International Student Assessment: a series of tests of fifteen-year-olds across the globe, in developed nations, in maths, English and science. The release of this sort of cross-country information had become, in the words of education academic Stephen Gorard, a kind of annual 'education Olympics' although, until recently, discussion of PISA results had been largely confined to academic and educational circles, with occasional comments by government ministers, usually regarding rising trends. PISA results for 2006, for example— which showed a slippage from 2000—had received very little coverage.

Intensive press coverage of the 2009 results, boosted by regular negative commentary from Gove, gave the impression of startling educational decline under New Labour. Inevitably, it was not that clear cut. Of the sixty-five nations that took part, England was an above average performer, coming in sixteenth in science, twenty-eighth in maths, and twenty-fifth in literacy. The position was further complicated by a recent increase in the number of participating countries, bringing in some of the ferociously competitive new 'tiger economies', and questions concerning the validity of the 2003 UK sample. Some questioned the legitimacy of the entire exercise. According to Stephen Gorard, 'International comparisons also have a downside. [They] encourage policy-makers to concentrate on improvements relative to other countries rather than absolute changes over time. Above all, they seem to encourage glib remedies.'[16]

Gove put the PISA 2009 results down to a lack of traditional rigour in the nation's schools under New Labour, so justifying his argument for further market reforms. But there is an alternative, almost counterintuitive, explanation, that has been put forward in recent years by experts like Professor Peter Mortimore, former director of the Institute of Education. Might the UK's apparent decline be, at least in part, the *result* of intensive teaching to the test, so reducing pupil's broader knowledge and skills, and their ability to make the kind of independent intellectual judgements that help them to do well in evaluations, such as PISA, which actually cannot be prepared for? And what of the growing gap between the highest and lowest achieving UK students? More competition, and increased testing, might only make it worse.[17]

At the same time, Gove conveniently ignored information which presented a more complex picture of school achievement. In 2007 England finished in the top seven countries in all four Trends in International Mathematics and Science Study (TIMSS) tests, taken by 425,000 pupils worldwide, leading the *Times Educational Supplement* to state that 'England joins the elite for maths and science.'[18] Jon Coles, director-general for Education Standards at the Department for Education and chair of the National Curriculum Review Advisory Committee, told the Advisory Committee on Mathematics Education at the Royal Society in March 2011: 'Over the last ten years, just looking back at the figures, we have an awful lot to look at that suggests progress, and that's good and positive.' The number of people coming into maths teaching over the last ten years had doubled, he said, while the number passing the subject at GCSE had grown very significantly, and had doubled at A level. The take-up of further maths A levels had also increased markedly in recent years.[19]

Another favourite theme of Gove's was the tiny number of children on free school meals who made it to Oxbridge. He constantly referred to these figures, using different comparators, depending on his opponent of the moment. In the Queen's Speech debate, he pointed out that more pupils went to Oxbridge from St Paul's girls' school in London in one year than from the entire cohort of children on free school meals—a snide dig at acting Labour leader, Harriet Harman, an ex-St Paul's pupil, who was sitting opposite him. By the second reading of the Education Bill in early 2011, several MPs commented during the debate on the frequency with which Gove referred to this single aspect of the education system, using it to hammer home his broader point that social mobility had stalled under New Labour.

Jenny Chapman, the Labour MP for Darlington, challenged him on his narrow definitions, observing that 'the secretary of state often speaks about social mobility in a way that might lead people to think that he understood it.' She pointed out that he only referred to statistics on free school meal take-up and admission to Oxford and Cambridge, whereas in her own constituency of Darlington, she said, 'five or six years ago there were one or two wards where a young woman of eighteen or nineteen would be more likely to be a mother than to be a student in higher education. I can report with great pride that that is no longer the case. Teenage pregnancies are reducing, and participation in higher education in those wards is improving. That needs to be taken into account when we discuss social mobility in the House.'[20]

Chapman's argument was an important one. There were clearly schools in difficulty all around the UK, particularly in areas where poverty, unemployment and social problems disfigured neighbourhoods; family background remains the single most important determinant in a child and a school's success—or lack of. But there had also been significant improvements in state education, particularly in previously low-attaining schools. GCSE results in 2009 were the highest ever for London. There had also been a marked fall in the number of children leaving primary school without reaching the expected levels in English and maths; by 2010, 60 per cent of pupils had five 'good' GCSEs, more than three times the proportion that left school with five O levels in the so-called golden age of the grammars. And as Jenny Chapman had suggested, more higher education places were being taken up by young women and men from low-income families. Even Gove's ministerial colleagues presented a more nuanced, complex picture of school achievement. Lord Hill, leader of the Coalition in the House of Lords, told a conference in January 2011, just after the publication of the Education Bill, that 'there is much to admire and build on in the current system: hundreds of outstanding schools, tens of thousands of great teachers, the best generation of heads and leaders ever.'

*　　*　　*

The new school revolution was not just happening in government. Gove had powerful allies, keen to promote, both politically and professionally, the new strategy for schools. In the autumn of 2010 it emerged that Gove had granted half a million pounds to one of his former aides, 25-year-old Rachel Wolf, to set up the New Schools Network, an advisory body for parents and teachers who wanted to create their own schools. For Rachel Wolf, 'parents know what is best for their children, so if they are unhappy with what is on offer, why shouldn't they be free to set up alternatives?'[21] Wolf is, as it happens, the daughter of prominent academic Alison Wolf, who produced a report on vocational education for the government in spring 2011. Another voluble, occasionally vociferous, contributor to the debate was the journalist Toby Young, who led a high-profile campaign to set up the West London Free School in Hammersmith and Fulham, where the Conservative council gave him a warm welcome. Katharine Birbalsingh also became a public champion of the new schools policy. In May 2011 she announced plans to open a free school in Lambeth, apparently with the help of Anthony Seldon, Master of Wellington College—a PR marriage surely made in heaven. For Seldon, private-school involvement in free schools would 'not only profoundly enrich the lives of many children from less advantaged backgrounds, it would also give the independent school, its teachers and pupils much, because state schools in significant ways have forged ahead of independent schools, over the past ten years in particular.'[22] Seldon's view of the public sector is not one expressed by most private-school heads, nor, in fact, does it chime with much of what he himself has written on the rise of 'factory schooling' and a general lack of pedagogic imagination in state education.

When the new educational evangelists bemoan the current condition of the nation's state schools, they invariably argue that the comprehensive 'experiment' has failed. Once, the charge from the right was that comprehensives let down bright, poor children who could only truly succeed in grammar schools. Now the argument has subtly shifted—or crudely widened—and comprehensives are accused of failing all children on virtually all fronts, through low academic standards and poor vocational provision: the central finding of Alison Wolf's report in spring 2011. This position chimes with the right's broader refusal to recognise any significant correlation between family background, poverty in general, rising economic inequality and school outcomes. Almost a third of British children live in poverty, and UK children regularly score badly in international league tables in terms of general well-being and happiness; but the idea that low incomes might still form a significant barrier to learning is now dismissed as a moral frailty of the left, or soppy middle-class posturing.[23] Such arguments lay behind the Coalition decision in early summer 2011 to abolish the publication of Contextual Value-Added measures in league tables, one way in which government was able to track the relative achievement of schools with high numbers of children from deprived backgrounds, but now apparently deemed patronising to the poor.

Critics from the new educational right regularly imply that the entire edifice of state education is rotten and requires demolition rather than steady improvement. Toby Young uses his blog for the *Telegraph* and column for the *Spectator* to launch regular attacks on so-called low standards, political correctness and comprehensive reform—and reformers—while Katherine Birbalsingh, in a clear echo of Tony Blair's remarks about 'the soft bigotry of low expectations', frequently lambasts poor discipline, limited intellectual ambition and a 'culture of excuses' that 'keeps poor children poor'. Virtually, all problems in state schools are laid at the door of poor teachers, middle-class liberals and an ineffectual and yet over-controlling state. A highly sympathetic interview with Birbalsingh in the *Observer* suggested that the ex-teacher articulates a 'sense of frustration and despair felt by many people across the political spectrum at the variable and frequently poor quality of state education in our large cities and towns ... Most of the schools she has worked in have been adjudged "good" or "outstanding" by Ofsted, as are 60 per cent of all schools. She wanted to write the book, she says, to show what "good" or "outstanding" can mean in the inner city.' The interviewer, Andrew Anthony, concluded with a flourish: 'It's safe to say that "mediocre and poor" would seem a more appropriate verdict.'[24] If parents who sent their children to local schools weren't in despair before reading the *Observer* piece, they certainly might be afterwards.

For the new educational evangelists, therefore, only the new schools can act as a genuine engine of social mobility, another sign of how the education debate has subtly shifted. For decades, the issue at the heart of the school wars concerned grammars versus comprehensives. Support for the grammars has in recent years gone largely underground. Now, the academies and free schools are presented as the new face, or necessary modernisation, of the comprehensive ideal. Some of the new school providers feel a strong sense of mission, tinged with an almost religious fervour, to improve the lot of the 'disadvantaged'. As the director of one chain of academies told me, 'We are all really fighting for the same thing.'

Yet there is a glaring contradiction at the heart of this position. On the one hand, there is a strong emphasis on the non-selective, inclusive character of free schools and academies. A rigorous education should be available to all, regardless of class or ethnic or religious background. Toby Young continually uses the term comprehensive, albeit illogically: the West London Free School was, originally, designated a 'comprehensive grammar' (although as one debating opponent put it, this was rather like talking about a vegetarian butcher). On the other hand, as Young's position implies, the new school revolutionaries strongly support academic selection. When, during the debate on the Education Bill in May 2011, Nick Gibb, the minister for schools, refused government backing to an amendment put forward by Graham Brady MP, a grammar-school supporter, proposing that private schools that come in under the free schools umbrella should be allowed to continue to academically select, observers of the debate thought Gibb's rejection of the amendment flat and unconvincing. After all, the Tory party and its allies clearly celebrate, and confirm, academic selection wherever they find it. Grammar schools that have converted to academies have maintained their right to academically select. And Gove told a Friends of Grammar Schools parliamentary reception, in the autumn of 2010, that 'my foot is hovering over the pedal' concerning the expansion of selection within the state system. Clearly, the new education evangelists believe in non-selection—but only for all those who have not *already* been selected.

The new school revolutionaries regularly swing in behind Gove and Cameron in their attacks on the 'educational establishment' or 'the forces of resistance'—echoes, once again, of Tony Blair and his attack on the 'forces of conservatism'. Before the 2010 election, Cameron told *The Times* that Tory school plans 'will mean some big battles with forces of resistance. Some Local Education Authorities might not like it, some of the education establishment won't like it.'[25] (In fact, there have been no Local Education Authorities since 2006, when Blair abolished them.) It is not quite clear who or what was meant by the amorphous term 'the education establishment', but it almost certainly embraced university-based teacher training, local authorities and trade unions, all of which have found their roles severely constrained by the new government. Cameron's war cry was reiterated a few months into government when the *Sunday Times* claimed he was preparing to take on the teaching unions rather as Margaret Thatcher faced down the National Union of Mineworkers in the 1980s. Coming out of *Waiting for Superman*, the film about US charter schools, in late November last year, Toby Young tweeted, 'Just saw *Waiting For Superman*. Spellbinding indictment of teachers unions. Made by director of Inconvenient Truth. Oh happy days.'

Claims that it is the teachers' unions who use bullying tactics were a little strained by one revelation in January 2011: it emerged that Lord Hill, the minister responsible for academies, had strongly hinted to schools interested in converting to academy status that the government might turn down their request, if the school chose to abide by national pay agreements for teachers—prompting the unions to consider legal action.[26] 'It's like tanks rolling over your lawn ... while government ministers are polite and charming in private,' observed Mary Bousted, general secretary of the

Association of Teachers and Lecturers in spring 2011. 'There's never any ceasefire; there's never a chance to map out the lie of the land—they just carry on, and they are going to be left with many unintended consequences.'

There are some important silences, however. Probably the most significant development in the new schools revolution is the massively expanded role it will give to the private sector, a path partially cleared under New Labour with its city academy programme, encouraging private sponsors and charitable bodies into state education. Several companies already run schools in England, and many more provide important services to them. With the new free schools and academies, the door is wide open to the expansion of the market. Yet one would scarcely know it from public debate on education. Unsurprisingly, little reference is made by any of the new school celebrities or politicians to the growing private control of public education, or to the cost of this to the taxpayer who is, in effect, underwriting the latest round of privatisation of state education.

The government has continued, if with rather less conviction, to promote the idea that free schools represent the authentic voice of the people. The Department for Education website broadcasts a number of videos promoting the educational aims and vision of successful bidders. These short, artful films project a compelling picture of ordinary, decent parents and teachers working hard to create good schools, denied to them by a mix of local state bureaucrats and egalitarian ideologues. What these films do not dwell on is the role of the private sector in much of the free school movement, nor the extent to which many of the new school campaigns are dividing communities. Increasingly, free schools are like the educational equivalent of fireworks: random, concentrated explosions that appear to come out of nowhere, startling and polarising communities, alienating as many parents, teachers, school leaders and governors as they attract.

A new free school planned for Wandsworth, South London, the Bolingbroke Academy—sponsored by ARK, the academy chain—quickly became known as the 'bankers' free school', as its supporters included a number of bankers working for various City firms including Morgan Stanley and Barclays. Plans for the new school were strongly opposed by many local parents and teachers as well as by local representatives of the GMB trade union who, in an unusual intervention, accused the free school group of deliberately excluding one of the local primaries that served a markedly less affluent community, as a 'feeder school'—that is, a primary with special links to a local secondary. The Bolingbroke conflict was given the deceptively light-hearted tag of The Battle of Nappy Valley. Eventually, the whole intractable matter was put out to 'consultation'. Similarly, a planned free school in Stoke by Nayland in Suffolk drew protests from a local head who believed it was being designed to siphon off the wealthier families of the area. Mike Foley, head of Great Cornard Upper School, said: 'The suspicion is that parents in that [free school] group don't want our children mixing with oiks. Whatever the motivation, the impact of it is to create this division. Although we have children from diverse backgrounds, they flourish here. The view here is that children shouldn't be educated in a bubble.'[27]

Meanwhile, several ailing private schools, and ambitious religious groups, were clamouring to come under the shelter of the state's umbrella. In January 2011, it was announced that 25 Steiner schools, whose curriculum has a humanistic, artistic emphasis, were in talks with the government about becoming free schools; but elements of the Steiner ideology remain highly controversial, and the decision was thus delayed.[28] Seven out of ten free-school applications register a faith-based ethos. The Everyday Champions Church in Newark, an Evangelical church in Nottingham which intends to teach creationism as part of its science curriculum, handed over its plans for a 625-place school on the day before the first ever free school conference in January 2011, where Gove declared that 'applications' from creationist groups would be considered, with each judged on its merits. But only a few weeks later, after insistent representations from the British Centre for Science Education, Gove appeared to back down, claiming that it was 'crystal-clear that teaching creationism is at odds with scientific fact'.

Free-school development has been increasingly constrained by practical factors. As many had warned, setting up a school is a major venture; those who have made it through the various stages have mostly done so with the backing of a charitable body or an existing education provider, although occasionally an individual like Young, who wields unusual political and public influence, appears to manage it alone. By May 2011, a year after the formation of the Coalition, only four groups had entered into a funding agreement, or contract, with the secretary of state—the West London Free School in Hammersmith and Fulham, Eden Primary School in Haringey, St Luke's Church of England Primary School in Camden, and The Free School in Norwich—giving the lie to predictions that between ten and twenty would open in September 2011. Altogether, 323 groups had applied to start free schools. Of these applications, forty-one had been approved to the business case and planning stage, and seventeen to the pre-opening stage. Early criticisms of the apparent ease with which free school applications were approved had forced the government to slow down the process. Andrew Nadin, for example, an energetic opponent of a free school proposal in Bedford and Kempston, had persistently raised questions concerning a petition the Bedford and Kempston group had presented to the Department of Education claiming to show widespread support for the establishment of another school in the area. In the early summer of 2011 rumours began to circulate that Gove was trying to persuade school leaders in one London borough to back the establishment of a new free school, instead of another academy—a sign, surely, of the minister's realisation that his flagship policy was faltering.

And who was paying for the new schools? There were rumoured plans in the summer of 2010 that the free school meals budget was to be raided to pay for free schools. Not surprisingly, this proposal was soon ditched. The government then suggested that free schools were to be largely funded from a special IT fund. The cost of free schools and the new academies became a more pressing issue as cuts announced in the Comprehensive Spending Review started to bite. The entire project began to look decidedly less exciting, and potentially offensive, as existing state schools battled with leaking classrooms and cuts in one-to-one tuition. Many teenagers were facing a bleak future, without the financial support of EMA in the sixth form, and the prospect of soaring tuition fees. According to a report on Radio 4's *Today* programme in early 2011, the Department had set aside £50 million in capital funding when the policy was first announced. But *Today* revealed that Bolingbroke, the planned free school in Wandsworth, was costing a total of £28 million in public money: £13 million from Wandsworth Council, to buy the building, plus £15 million of public money to refurbish it. According to Toby Young's own estimates, the capital costs of the West London Free School were to be £12 million. While parliamentary questions and Freedom of Information requests did not elicit much hard information, it was revealed in April 2011 that the government had spent £21 million in its first year alone to private consultants to help launch the free school policy; at the same time, almost 100 civil servants were being directly employed on the policy. According to Labour's shadow education secretary, Andy Burnham: 'Pledges are being made; ministers are going round the country waving cheque books at people wanting to set up their pet projects. When the Government have cancelled Building Schools for the Future, it is unacceptable that they are not prepared to answer parliamentary questions to tell us how much money has been committed to these new schools. It gives the impression that, shamefully, ideology and not need is driving the allocation of capital to schools.'[29]

They may have attracted a lot of media attention, but increasingly free schools began to look like a distraction from the main show: the hundreds, and potentially thousands, of schools that were being enticed to become independent of local authorities. This was, indeed, the silent revolution, as one magazine article named it. The government's initial offer to 'outstanding' schools to convert to academy status had been extended to 'good' schools;

it was rumoured that conversion would soon be possible for those with 'satisfactory' status, if they were willing to work in partnership with other schools. Plainly, the aim was to create a majority of privately managed institutions, including many primaries, leaving a rump of struggling schools within the ambit of local authorities, themselves undermined by savage budget cuts.

The government was clearly playing up schools' anxieties about funding in an age of austerity. And it seemed to be working. In April 2011 a survey of its members conducted by The Association of School and College Leaders (ASCL) found that 46 per cent had either already converted or were planning to do so, with a further 34 per cent undecided. Only 19 per cent said they would definitely not go down the academy route. In May the government announced that over a thousand schools had applied to become academies since June 2010: 647 applications had been approved, and 384 had already converted. The total number of academies, including those opened under New Labour, now stood at over 650. As the government press release boasted, 'schools are becoming academies at a rate of two every day.'

At the heart of the strategy was money. Opponents of the 'conversion' plans became increasingly suspicious of the government claim that the new academies would enjoy no funding advantages, and that the move to so-called independence was all about the wish to be free from the mythical stranglehold of local government. In early January 2011, every Local Authority suffered a top-slice from their general grant to help fund the academies programme, irrespective of how many academies they had in their area. The national top-slice for 2011–12 was £148 million, rising to £265 million in 2012–13. This reduction in the budget, in addition to cuts announced the previous year, was justified on the grounds that the schools would have received the money anyway, in terms of services provided by the local authorities; now they were merely being given the budgets directly, to buy in services themselves. But the decision left many academies far better off than they would have been if they had stayed with the local authority. The question was, for how long?

Nigel Gann, chair of governors at Stanchester Community School in Somerset, resigned when the school decided to convert to an academy. He wrote to his local paper in April 2011, 'Why the rush? Well, it's money, of course. There's a substantial incentive on offer—a sum per pupil for secondaries that are able to convert before September this year; about half of that for those that follow shortly after ... Since the only extra money available for schools that opt to become academies will be taken from money the local authority holds centrally for support services, how might the movement of secondary schools out of the authority affect funding for primary and special schools and others remaining?' Gann was not a lone voice. There were growing protests at the high-handed, unnecessarily hasty manner in which academy status was being rushed through.[30]

Even some of the heads of new academies declared themselves surprised at the amount of money they had gained through the move. As one head teacher in Cheltenham told the *Guardian*, 'The increase in funding has been dramatic.' The *Guardian* was shown a number of documents by newly converted academies, including four grammar schools; all showed that the schools had become significantly better off as a result, with net benefits ranging from £150,000 a year to £570,000 in one case. The schools were supposedly being given money that would allow them to buy back the additional services, including behaviour support, school improvement and central administrative staff, that they would have received from the local authority, a funding stream known as Lacseg (local authority central spend equivalent grant). But once the schools had calculated how much it would cost them to buy the services back, some found they were incurring a clear profit of up to six figures.[31]

Over the course of a year, I talked to several head teachers, many of them leading outstanding inner-city schools. Most were opposed, in principle, to the policy of taking good schools out of the local authority, but with severe cuts looming, the government offer was a poisoned chalice. The word used most often was 'bribe'. There was also considerable uncertainty over conversion financing, and how long it would last. Schools interested in converting to academy status were encouraged to use a 'ready reckoner' on the DfE website to see how much better off they would be if they chose to go down the academy route. According to a governor of an 'outstanding' secondary in the north-west of England that has chosen to convert, 'the figures are very unclear, but it seemed from the ready reckoner that at first the school would get an extra two million over five years, which was very tempting. Then it went down to 1.5 million. And then down to a million ... The problem is, we don't yet know the extra costs. We are going to have to hire a finance director, more staff. We are going to have to buy in office services that were provided by the local authority and get an audit done, sort out our own pensions liability.' According to Peter Downes, a former head teacher, funding expert and Liberal Democrat councillor, who tabled a successful motion against the academy and free school programme at the party's annual conference in 2010: 'The dice are massively loaded in favour of academies, in terms of funding. But my thesis is that this is simply not sustainable.'

The long-delayed implementation of the pupil premium in December did little to allay schools' fears. For each of its pupils on free school meals—that is, from a household with an income of less than £16,000—a school was to receive the 'pupil premium', an annual additional amount of £430 per pupil, with head teachers deciding how it was to be distributed. Gove promised £625 million in 2011–12, increasing to £2.5 billion by the end of 2014–15. 'It's not going to mean anything for us, once you take the rest of [the cuts] into account,' one head teacher told me, shaking his head despairingly. Andy Burnham called the premium 'a con ... what was meant to be additional money for the most deprived, will simply recycle funds from one school to another. It is robbing Peter to pay Paul.'

Into this anxious and uncertain atmosphere over school funding, the government decided in January 2011 to release a mass of figures into the public domain—in the name of transparency in government—on individual school budgets in England. While this revealed that the average figure per pupil per year is £5,547.13, it appeared that some boroughs and schools were spending far more, and some far less. Ryeish Green School in Wokingham, which had closed in August 2010, had spent a staggering £32,937.91 pounds per pupil in a year, while All Saints Catholic Centre for Learning in Knowsley, Liverpool, had spent only £1,529.81. The local authority with the highest average spending per pupil per year—£8,528.50—was the East London borough of Hackney; the local authority with the lowest—£4,310.05—was Knowsley in Merseyside.[32] While some heads protested at the dumping of what they thought to be dangerously undifferentiated data into the public domain, presenting school budgets out of context, the Coalition used the publication of the figures to argue that it was not government funding that mattered so much as how schools used it.

By the close of its first year in government, the full extent—if not yet the full implications—of the schools revolution was becoming evident. It was clear that one of the principal aims of the Tory-dominated Coalition was dramatically to dismantle the role of local authorities in relation to education. A democratically accountable public service, nationally directed but locally admin-istered, was fast being replaced by a state-subsidised and centrally controlled quasi-market. Under proposals published in late May 2011, successful schools were to be allowed to expand—despite serious questions concerning the practicability, not to mention desirability, of such a plan—and so-called 'poor' schools were to be allowed to wither and die. In July, the *Guardian* confirmed that civil servants privately advised ministers that schools should be allowed to fail, if government was serious about reform.[33]

Schools policy was increasingly rigged in favour of the acade-mies and free schools, that were granted a range of special freedoms and funds. While six local authorities awaited the government's verdict on its earlier decision to axe their school building pro-grammes, Michael Gove announced £800 million worth of capital funding to refurbish dozens of academies around the country. A footnote to the new draft admissions code intimated that academies and free schools—but not maintained schools—were to be allowed to prioritise children on free school meals in their admissions policy. Predictably, this proposal was represented in the media as a bold and innovative move towards greater fairness. But if implemented, it would not only hand the 'new' schools valuable extra revenue—via the pupil premium—but might open the door for some schools to 'cherry pick' higher-attaining children on low incomes, further destabilising the intake of neighbourhood maintained schools. By May 2011, the Department of Education website did not even list community or comprehensive schools as one of the chief school types in England. Only faith schools got a mention. From being the great reviled, they had become the officially disappeared.

At the heart of the new schools revolution was a canny political con trick: the swift but steady transfer of resources from the needy to the better-off, in the name of the disadvantaged. While the government was not yet facing the kind of opposition that its proposed changes to the NHS had by now provoked, there were many, including some from within the Coalition's Liberal Democrat partners, who were angered and dismayed by the speed, range and brutal consequences of the government's education policy. These included Councillor Peter Downes who declared of the new funding arrangements for the academies: 'This is directing resources to the most privileged. In this way, life gets harder for schools at the bottom of the heap.' Faced with reductions in both central government grants and with further money clawed back from the Dedicated Schools Grant, now used to fund academies, Downe's own authority, Cambridgeshire County Council, had to make significant reductions in services to black and ethnic-minority groups, disabled children, early years services, teenage pregnancy programmes, special needs teachers, and sports and hobbies grants for vulnerable young people; further cuts were planned in music programmes, services to disabled children and early years work. Cambridgeshire's share of the 'top-slice' cut was £1.7 million. The Cambridgeshire Cabinet took the decision to protect funding to the Children and Young People's Services area for the year 2011–12. According to Peter Downes, 'Had they not done so, the service reductions would have been even more severe. But we hold our breath for next year when the Cambridgeshire top-slice rises to £3.1 million.'

'Savage' was the summing up of former Children's Commissioner Sir Al Aynsley Green, who claimed that society's most vulnerable—those in care, disabled children, young carers, young offenders and those with mental health issues—would bear the brunt of a decline in services that were already inadequate, following further cuts to the Connexions career advice, Future Jobs fund, Youth Opportunity Fund, Youth Capital Fund and Working Neighbourhood fund. His conclusion was chilling. 'We are witnessing the destruction of many of the building bricks of support for children and young people to achieve their full potential in life. It is desperately worrying. I see little in their place to inspire confidence that this generation will be looked after by government. It could spell the end of hope and expectation for many of them.'[34]

II
HOW WE GOT HERE

Chapter Two

The Piecemeal Revolution

Let's get the most damaging myths out of the way. The move towards comprehensive education was not some rash act of anti-democratic statist zeal, nor was it, in the astonishing recent words of Tony Blair, 'pretty close to academic vandalism'.[1] Far from it. Early comprehensive reform was bipartisan, slow and uneven in pace, with change occurring over many decades. The first comprehensive opened in Anglesey, Wales, in the late 1940s, while most of the transformation towards a comprehensive system occurred in the 1960s and 70s—and still the reform remains incomplete. A number of local authorities retain use of the eleven-plus to this day.

It may have been halting and fragmented, but it had a profound impact on post-war Britain. For to make real sense of the intense opposition that the comprehensive ideal provoked, we have to acknowledge the radicalism inherent in the idea of universal education; the idea that every child, of whatever background, is deserving of a serious education; that all the nation's children might learn from a broadly common syllabus, enjoying matching resources and similarly high expectations; and, possibly the most threatening idea of all, the suggestion that at some points, in some places, the nation's children—Muslim, Christian or Jewish, upper-class or impoverished, girl or boy, black or white—might actually be educated in the same classrooms together.

Here, then, were the key ingredients of what I call the piecemeal revolution, a moderate, rational plan for educational reform that still shakes us to our roots. As a nation, we are more connected to our pre-World War II and indeed nineteenth-century assumptions, prejudices and modes of social organisation, than perhaps we realise. Class stratification remains the default position, even in the twenty-first century.

That the British public has never developed the kind of affection for, and loyalty to, the idea of universal state education as it has to the National Health Service might in part be due to the crass divisions and base prejudices that shaped the 1944 Education Act. The Act was a Tory one, and so predated the reforming Labour administration elected in 1945 and led by Clement Atlee that set up the welfare state and created the NHS. Yet, in many ways, it anticipated and shared in that postwar spirit. For the first time in the history of England and Wales, the state underwrote a universal, compulsory free education system for all, which represented a tremendous leap forward. Yet written into this progress was an a-priori separation of the country's children into winners and losers by the age of eleven—a division that predictably shaped itself along class lines.

Things could have been very different. The pre-war 1938 Spens Report had 'considered carefully the possibility of *multilateral schools* … the provision of a good general education for two or three years for all pupils over eleven-plus in a given area, and the organisation of four or five "streams", so that the pupils at the age of thirteen or fourteen years may follow courses that are suited to their individual needs and capacity. It is a policy which is very attractive: it would secure in the first place the close association, to their mutual advantage, of pupils of more varied ability, and with more varied interests and objectives, than are normally found in a school of any one type.'[2] Ultimately, however, the report rejected the option of multilateral—comprehensive—schooling.

After the Spens Report, the war years saw intense consultation and negotiation between politicians, civil servants, the churches and the private schools, as well as another report—the 1943 Norwood Committee on educational reorganisation—which recommended the establishment of three distinct types of secondary school. During this time, it became widely acknowledged that if Britain won the war it would be impossible to go back to the pre-1939 situation, when nearly 90 per cent of young people left school at fourteen, only 10 per cent achieved passes in public examination and fewer than 5 per cent went on to higher education. It was vital that the country educated more of its citizens and to a much higher level.

In many ways, education had not radically altered from the fragmented patchwork of nineteenth-century provision, particularly in its tendency to assume, in the words of Matthew Arnold, that 'the education of each class in society has, or ought to have, its ideal, determined by the wants of that class and by its destination.'[3] Although a number of pieces of legislation from the mid nineteenth century onward began to implement a national system of elementary and secondary schools, locally controlled, its administration was frequently deemed 'chaotic'. While the upper classes tended to be shipped off to the great public schools or elite day schools, and the middle classes were educated in the competitive grammars—which based their curriculum upon the public school model—the working class received a wildly uneven elementary education, its quality dependent on which regional school board or church was in charge. These arrangements, more or less, continued up to 1939.

World War II was an important turning point, as it confirmed concerns that Britain was producing an under-educated workforce unable to hold its own in wider markets. Many schools had been closed in preparation for evacuation, but one million children were not in fact sent away, causing scenes of delinquency and chaos as they roamed the streets. Ministers were criticised for their ignorance: 'they did not know what had happened to state education because they educated their own children elsewhere.' Even senior officials at the Board of Education admitted that full-time schooling for most of the country's children was in many ways 'seriously defective', and that for 90 per cent of them, it ended too soon. 'It is conducted in many cases in premises which are scandalously bad.'[4]

The 1944 Act, then, embraced two vitally important principles: free secondary education for all (some state schools had charged fees prior to the war), and a clear distinction, and path, between primary and secondary schools. A young Tory reformer, Quintin Hogg—later Lord Hailsham—thought the Act 'an elementary piece of social justice'. Soon, however, it was clear that in many ways it reproduced the fragmented legacy of the earlier period.

Firstly, it wholly failed to address the problem of the private sector, which at that point was severely weakened both morally and financially, making it ripe for reform and possible incorporation into a new universal state system. But no action was taken to deal with the public schools, as we shall see in Chapter 6. Secondly, Rab Butler—appointed by Churchill to consider and draw up plans for education reform, despite his initial reluctance—and his chief civil servant, Chuter Ede, came under huge pressure from the Anglican and Catholic churches to retain their religious influence and involvement in the school system. At that time the churches ran half the schools in the UK. Although by the mid twentieth century England had become a less religious society, the idea still prevailed that this was a 'Christian country' and many thought that Christianity would temper a 'peculiarly democratic bill'.[5] A compromise was found in the conversion of church schools into two main types: 'controlled' or 'aided'. In the case of controlled schools, the state would take over their costs, appoint staff and governors, etc., but the schools would follow an agreed religious syllabus. Voluntary-aided schools retained more independence and power. The state paid for their running costs, but the Church kept buildings under its control, with help from a government grant, and continued to appoint staff and governors. The third problem with the 1944 Act was its fatal flaw: the enabling of a pernicious three-tiered school system, based on the idea that children had very different talents and aptitudes and should therefore be educated separately. Both the 1938 Spens Report and the 1943 White Paper had considered the idea of multilateral education. In fact, the latter had explicitly declared: 'There is nothing to be said in favour of a system which subjects children at the age of eleven to the strain of a competitive examination in which not only their future schooling but their future career may depend.'[6] Butler himself was not hostile to the idea that all children should be educated in the same schools. But the 1944 Act was heavily influenced by what Caroline Benn and Brian Simon called the 'wordy circumlocutions' of Sir Cyril Norwood, the chair of the 1943 committee and a strong supporter of grammar schools—and, therefore, of the idea of selection. While the Act itself, permissive but not prescriptive, did not set down how schools should be organised, Norwood called upon a 'general educational experience' to support his recommendations that different types of children should be educated in different types of school.

Many of the assumptions underlying the setting up of the tripartite system were based on the IQ research of the 1920s and 30s. A prominent place was occupied by the work of Sir Cyril Burt, who drew heavily on the ideas of the eugenics movement of the early twentieth century. Burt's research and experimentation were later to be discredited once it was discovered that he had fabricated evidence to support his theories. His arguments, however, were taken very seriously indeed in the 1930s and 40s. Burt believed that social class correlated with intelligence: the higher up the social scale you were, the greater your natural fund of intelligence. Accordingly, environment—including education—had a negligible impact on a child's intellectual development; it was what you were born with, or rather, what you were born into, that counted. Education thus became an exercise in 'sorting' pupils into the correct compartments, at any given age. As late as 1950 Burt would write, 'Obviously in an ideal community, our aim should be to discover what ration of intelligence nature has given to each individual child at birth, then to provide him with the appropriate education, and finally to guide him into the career for which he seems to have been marked out.'[7]

Not everyone agreed. One civil servant of the period was later quoted as saying that Burt held 'a general belief, I believe totally false, that children were divided into three kinds. It was sort of Platonic. There were golden children, silver children and iron children.'[8] Golden children were, broadly speaking, interested in learning for its own sake and could grasp an argument; silver children were talented at applied science or art, but lacked subtlety in language construction; iron children could only handle concrete things, for abstractions were beyond them.

From 1944 onwards, local authorities were supposed to assign children to one of three kinds of schools. The more intellectual among them were to be sent to grammar schools; the more practical and vocationally inclined to the new technical schools, and the rest were to be educated in secondary moderns. In fact, the technical schools—the ideal destination of the so-called 'silver' caste—never seriously took off, and secondary education in the post-war period quickly became a matter of grammar or secondary modern, all decided by the eleven-plus exam. Thus did the crude eugenicism of Burt and his disciples unduly influence—and warp—the lives of countless children, as the state took on the arrogant task of dividing them into winners and losers before even the onset of puberty.

The 1944 Act was an undeniable improvement on the glaring pre-war gaps in provision. For some, it opened a window on a new future; but for the majority, once again, an education system ruled in which class divisions were, in Sally Tomlinson's words, 'created, legitimised and justified'. As Brian Simon writes, 'Even under a Labour Government elected with a massive majority, the mediation of class relations was still seen as a major function of the education system.'[9] A very similar charge would be laid at the door of a future Labour Government, also headed by a privately educated leader and elected with an equally impressive majority, some fifty years later.

Long after the 1944 Act, its chief political architect Rab Butler wrote of how important it was 'to ensure that a stigma of inferiority did not attach itself to those secondary institutions ... which lacked the facilities and academic prestige of the grammar schools'. But how could it possibly be otherwise? Grammar schools had, in general, three times more money spent on them; they had the best teachers, the best facilities, offered public examinations and a secure route into higher education. Secondary moderns—even the many which offered more academic courses—could offer none of these things.

Almost every family in the era of national selection was caught up in the drama of the eleven-plus exams. The crisis was intensified for one pair of twins, who sat the exam in the mid to late 1960s:

After my sister and I took the eleven-plus (along with the rest of my class at St Mark's Primary School) nothing happened for several weeks. We forgot all about it and then, I remember, a teacher came into the classroom and read out a list of about eight names of boys and girls in the class. We had to go the Headmistress's room. Miss Simpson was long and lean like Joyce Grenfell, with a bluey-green woollen suit, and flat shoes, and we knew it was important—either good or bad. We trooped out—including me but excluding my sister—to be congratulated and told that we had 'passed the eleven-plus'. Thereafter all the attention was on me. Which school would I go to—the local grammar, or another selective grant-maintained school out of the borough? Would I wear box- or knife-pleat skirts? Blue or yellow shirts?

My poor sister meanwhile was to go to the local girls' secondary modern school. No forms coming through the post and discussions about uniforms, books, travel. She took it very badly—she was the 'failure', I was the 'success', and she never recovered from that feeling. Even today, 48 years later, she refers to me as 'the clever one' and to herself as the 'thick' one. It was not true, of course, but the education system reinforced a sense of worthlessness from then on.

I completely squandered my grammar-school education, and took ages to settle into any job until my mid-twenties. She left school at fifteen and has worked ever since. Her education in fact wasn't bad—and I am not sure which of us came off worse. The experience made my father ensure that my little sister went to a comprehensive, which were just being introduced. She really enjoyed school and it being co-ed meant she 'got on with boys—as friends' much better than her three older sisters. [Source: private communication.]

All of which meant that, as before the war, the twin threads of class anxiety and class ambition were woven right through the school organisation. According to the journalist Peter Laurie, 'To have been consigned to the limbo of secondary modern is to have failed disastrously ... and very early in life.'[10] For middle-class parents, a grammar-school place was often a make or break matter: failure was not an option for children sitting the eleven-plus exam. But while to figures like Edward Heath and Alan Bennett the grammar schools were comparatively easy to get into, and offered a chance to compete with the privately educated elite at Oxbridge and other top universities, the genuinely poor had barely a chance of passing the eleven-plus. In the district of St Anne's in Nottingham, for example, only 1.5 per cent of the district's entire school population attended grammars; in neighbouring middle-class suburbs, 60 per cent of children did. There were wide regional variations too. Only 10 per cent of children in Gateshead and Sunderland were educated in grammars, compared to 40 per cent in the affluent county of Westmoreland.

More generally, the education system retained its hierarchical and differentiated character. In fact, there were five or six levels to the post-war set-up: the public schools; the direct grant grammars, which offered some free places; the grammars; the technical/ trade schools; the secondary moderns; and the all-age elementary schools, pre-war relics that took twenty years to disappear. The complete lack of a national curriculum meant that teaching in many of the less resourced schools could still be of a poor or patchy standard. In many church schools, the curriculum was left entirely up to the discretion of the head teacher.

During this period, a lot of school buildings were in bad repair and the raising of the leaving age meant that many teachers faced 'huge classes, in crumbling, sometimes dangerous buildings'.[11] Whether in the grammars or in the secondary moderns, there were often low expectations of poor children. Discipline could be barbaric and there was little pastoral care or careers guidance, such as is common today. While the teaching in most schools was satisfactory, the percentage of poor teaching, in all sectors, was much higher than today. The curriculum was far narrower, opportunities for girls were very limited, maths teaching was often mediocre and there were vast tracts of uninspired, rote learning. Inspectors of the period had serious concerns about the quality of teaching of English, while a case study of science teaching in the post-war period in Swansea found it 'unsatisfactory in all the town's secondary moderns'. It was not just the secondary moderns; many grammar schools conducted 'dull and arid' lessons too.[12] Low standards were a widespread problem. According to the 1959 Crowther Report, on the education of fifteen- to nineteen-year-olds, 38 per cent of grammar-school pupils failed to achieve more than three passes at O level. Of the entire cohort of sixteen-year-olds, only about 9 per cent achieved five or more O levels. In his careful study of exam papers of the period, Adrian Elliott has unearthed numerous examples of unchallenging English papers and examples of basic miscomprehension of questions in maths, evidence which successfully challenges the claims made so frequently today that the increase in the number of exam passes is solely the result of 'dumbing down'. In 1961 the Ministry of Education even raised concerns about the deficiencies in general education of Oxbridge candidates.

There were of course exceptions, schools that challenged the conventions and constrictions of the time. One such phenomenon was St George's-in-the-East, a post-war secondary modern run by the remarkable Alex Bloom, and the location for one of the most famous education-related narratives of the post-war period: *To Sir With Love*. While the film concentrates on the trials and tribulations of its protagonist, a black teacher played by Sidney Poitier, the original book put more emphasis on the innovations of the school itself.

Alex Bloom was, in the words of radical educator Michael Fielding, 'arguably one of the greatest figures of radical state education in England'. He was certainly considered hugely significant by equally important figures such as A. S. Neill, the founder of Summerhill, one of the original free schools. Bloom opened St

George's-in-the-East Secondary Modern School in Cable Street, Stepney, on 1 October 1945. From the start he discarded many of the conventions, restrictions and taboos associated with schooling of the period, including corporal punishment, excessive regimentation and competition. He had a stated abhorrence of 'marks, prizes and competition.' He was dealing with children living in an area of extreme poverty, in bombed-out streets, with little hope for the future. Many were 'lonely and bothered souls', for whom school was their only experience of human warmth and structure. He also believed that most of the children emerged from primary school with the sense that they were failures. Two of his guiding principles were that the children should feel that they counted, and that the school community should mean something.

While most secondary moderns and their pupils suffered from the thin curricula, poor resources and consequent low self-esteem that usually accompanied the education of those who failed the eleven-plus, St George's pioneered collaborative, student-centred learning, in which pupils were encouraged to make up their own curriculum, and to be involved in active debates about what they were going to learn and had learned. St George's school council facilitated discussions between staff and students about the life of the school, and Bloom staunchly supported the right of students to say what they felt 'without reprisals'. A range of pupil committees took responsibility for everything from midday dancing in the Hall, school meals and sports, to the appearance and social life of the school, including concerts, parties and visitors.[13]

Former pupil Abraham Wilson has written of his life at St George's:

> Our classes were introduced to the way democracy worked by having annual elections, when each class elected a boy and a girl to represent them at regular meetings, that were chaired by the head boy or head girl, where decisions were made concerning some aspects of running the school. It was from such meetings that we chose to have ballroom dancing during the lunch break, which was very popular with the pupils in their last year at school. It was also

by a similar suggestion that we were able to have a canteen, with cakes bought from a local bakery.

Each morning the Headmaster, Mr Alexander Bloom addressed the school assembly with the head girl and boy seated each side of the headmaster. The assembly began with a piece of classical music being played. It was my first appreciation and introduction to composers such as Brahms, Beethoven, Strauss and many others. I still have very clear memories of our headmaster and remember his strong outlook and some of his views. He was a small man no more than 5'3". He had a thing about noise and would often tell us to keep our foot on the 'Soft Pedal' when he thought the volume of noise throughout the school was too loud.[14]

To Sir with Love provides some brief, but deeply felt, sketches of life behind the closed doors of London's East End at that time. The main character's respect for the hardship he witnesses among the families of his students is very moving, as is the story of their growing attachment to him. *To Sir with Love* also gives us a unique insight into the pioneering educational methods of Bloom, and his ability to engage the students. Early on in the novel, Rickie, the main protagonist, describes an assembly in which the 'Head read a poem, La Belle Dame Sans Merci. The records which followed were Chopin's Fantaisie Impromptu, and part of Vivaldi's Concerto in C for two trumpets'. Watching it from the outside, the novel's protagonist is struck by the sight of 'those rough-looking, untidy children; every one of them sat still... and attentive, until the very echo of the last clear note had died away. Their silence was not the result of boredom or apathy, nor were they quiet because it was expected of them or through fear of consequences; but they were listening, actively, attentively listening to those records, with the same raptness they had shown in their jiving; their bodies were still, but I could feel that their minds and spirits were involved with the music.'[15]

More widely, challenges were beginning to emerge to the insidious eleven-plus divide. Education researchers Brian Jackson and Olive Banks revealed the sham of claims by grammar-school supporters that there was 'parity of esteem' between the grammars and secondary moderns. Jackson's work forensically analysed how children were sorted into different streams, along class lines, early in primary school. Teachers were already deciding who was potential grammar-school material. As one teacher told Jackson, 'In the training of racehorses and athletes, we are most careful to cream and train; why not with children?' This same teacher held that 'streaming gives middle-class children the chance their parents had in private or prep schools, now that state schools are more widely used', an argument that has echoed down the years.[16] Jackson's research also examined in detail how different social groups fared within the grammar system. Very often, upper-working-class and lower-middle-class children languished in these schools and left as soon as they could, while upper-middle-class children prospered.[17]

According to Ross McKibbin, the working class lost out to the middle class in the competition for grammar-school places, which tended to go 'to the sons and daughters of professional business men/women'.[18] Those working-class children that did win places often left school much earlier, and didn't progress to further education. Grammar-school life often disrupted family routines: a new 'posh' accent and uniform was ridiculed at home; it was hard to do homework. For some, says McKibbin, 'The deliberate adherence to a local accent often meant wholesale rejection of the grammar school and its values; cultivation of BBC English represented an acceptance of those values and preceded a sometimes heartfelt adieu to class and neighbourhood.'[19]

A series of official reports, published in the late 1950s and early 60s, built up a powerful argument against selection. In a 1957 report, the British Psychological Society criticised intelligence testing and streaming; in the same year the NFER (National Foundation for Educational Research) came out against selection. It argued that the eleven-plus contained serious errors, a claim backed up by the increasing numbers of children who were achieving academically in some of the secondary moderns. The 1959 Crowther Report on education of fifteen- to eighteen-year-olds argued that 'it is not only at the top but almost to the bottom of the pyramid that the scientific revolution of our times needs to be reflected in a longer educational process.'[20] Four years later the Robbins Report on higher education concurred, rejecting the idea that only a select number of children had talent worth cultivating; the Newsom Report of the same year, looking at the education of children of 'average' intelligence, was bold enough to declare that 'intellectual talent is not a fixed quantity with which we have to work, but a variable that can be modified by social policy and educational approaches ... The kind of intelligence which is measured by the test so far applied is largely an acquired characteristic.'[21] Even Rhodes Boyson, Tory, headmaster, and champion of the grammars, later acknowledged that the eleven-plus 'makes considerable mistakes'.[22]

In the end, though, it was parental opposition that politically defeated selection. Particularly vocal were protests from middle-class families who found their children rejected by the grammars. The NFER report of 1957 claimed that 'politicians [were] beginning to find that to defend selection was a sure means of losing support.' Simon Jenkins recalls:

> At political meetings at the end of the 1960s, the then education spokesman, Edward Boyle, was torn limb from limb by Conservative voters infuriated at their children who had 'failed' the eleven-plus being sent to secondary moderns, along with 70–80 per cent of each age group. They had regarded the grammars as 'their schools'. The eleven-plus, they said, lost them the 1964 election and would lose them every one until it was abolished. Margaret Thatcher recognised this as education secretary after 1970, as has the Tory party in practice ever since.[23]

The grammar/secondary modern divide may have defined the post-war education settlement, but there were signs of change from early on. Britain's first purpose-built comprehensive, in Anglesey, opened in 1949 although it owed its existence to practicality rather than politics; it was simply impossible to sustain a two- or three-tier structure in an outlying rural area. While, according to Benn and Simon, the Tory government in power from 1951 to 1964 never said anything positive about comprehensives, it was prepared to sanction such schools in poor or outlying areas—but not in more affluent areas, where a comprehensive might detract from the status of a grammar school. Some local authorities, such as Coventry and London, pioneered the introduction of comprehensive schools, and, as popular disillusion with the selective system grew, evidence of their success was beginning to filter through.

Tory minister Edward Boyle had understood the extent and strength of parental rejection of the eleven-plus, but it was not until Labour's election in 1964 that the new education secretary, Michael Stewart, announced that the grammar/secondary modern divide was to be officially jettisoned. Many local education authorities began to send deputations to different parts of the country to examine the plans and practices of others: Coventry, for instance, became known for its use of an innovative 'house system' within its own comprehensive schools. Even before the government issued any guidance on reorganisation, a large number of local authorities had already put forward their own plans, among them Liverpool, Leicestershire, London, Manchester, Blackburn, Wigan, Bolton, Preston and Sheffield.

It is too easily forgotten that comprehensive reform was initially, at least, bipartisan. Some of the earliest counties to reorganise were Conservative, such as the West Riding, where local conservatives had opposed the eleven-plus from 1945 onwards. Here as in many other authorities, it was the county's chief education officer, the inspirational Sir Alec Clegg, rather than elected councillors, who played the leading role in drafting and revising the plans. Stewart Mason, chief education officer of Leicestershire, was another pioneer of progress in a county where there was a strong desire to sweep away the eleven-plus. By 1964, 90 out of 163 local education authorities had submitted plans to reorganise. Bradford became the first English city to abolish selection at eleven-plus for its maintained schools.

Within the Department of Education itself, there was fierce debate as to whether the government should 'request' or 'require' local authorities to reorganise their education system. In the end, Circular 10/65—circulars were a form of directive issued from Whitehall to local authorities—merely 'requested' change, although a subsequent directive, 10/66, was firmer, stating there would be no money for new school buildings unless local authorities could fit in with reorganisation plans. But for many, this permissive rather than forceful approach to change, combined with the Labour Government's lack of leadership and political direction, added up to yet another missed opportunity, an unsatisfactory halfway house.

Benn and Simon's *Half Way There* provides a detailed analysis of the relationship, or lack of, between the centre and the regions; of how local grammar schools and their resistance to change often dominated local education committees. In case after case, for example, the chief subject under discussion in LEA documents was Latin. As the authors note wryly, 'A visitor from another planet reading this through would imagine Latin must be the single subject for twentieth-century survival.'[24] Who could have foreseen that Latin would remain a potent symbol of educational and social status well into the twenty-first century?

The lack of a lead from the centre meant that change was indeed piecemeal, happening on a school-by-school basis, with some retaining streaming while others planned for mixed-ability teaching. Local authorities came up with a wide range of plans. The overwhelming favourite was for the eleven to eighteen, all-through schools of the kind pioneered in London and Coventry. However, no extra money was given to local authorities to help them with their reorganisation, while several Conservative authorities ignored requests to submit plans for phasing out the eleven-plus.

After her appointment as education secretary in Edward Heath's Conservative Government of 1970, Margaret Thatcher became notorious for cancelling free school milk and imposing entrance charges for museums. She was less well known for 'signing off' a large number of further plans for comprehensive reform; under her aegis, Circular 10/70, which overrode the hesitant directive of

10/65, simply left local education authorities free to go comprehensive. Margaret Thatcher was a strong supporter of grammar schools, but she recognised that the eleven-plus had probably lost the Tory party the 1964 election, and she did not want to risk provoking the same public reaction by flouting the wishes of powerful local education authorities, and popular feeling. By the end of her term as education secretary, Thatcher had overseen a doubling of comprehensive schools. By 1974, 60 per cent of secondary-age children were attending them.

During this period, the anti-comprehensive juggernaut was already starting to roll. Rab Butler, architect of the 1944 Act, described comprehensives as 'soulless education factories' that let down the bright child, ignored the ordinary child and promoted unhelpful forms of social engineering. Grammars that were facing closure mounted vigorous campaigns, using often inflammatory language. They were, they claimed, being 'annihilated', 'assassinated', 'wiped off the map'. Those who advocated the end of selection were compared to zealots in Nazi Germany, and when the Queen visited a comprehensive, the 'c' word was not mentioned in her presence.[25]

The emerging comprehensive faced many formidable obstacles: lack of finance, lack of central co-ordination, a hostile press, and an implacable foe in the form of the 'preservationists'—those who passionately supported the grammar-school policy. It did not help, as Benn and Simon drily note, that 'the comprehensive school as a positive policy seems never to have been fully campaigned for by either the Labour government or the department.' This ambivalence towards comprehensive reform was to become an issue under subsequent Labour Governments, with far more dramatic results.

But an account of the slow and convoluted pace of change does not do justice to the widespread excitement generated by comprehensive reform. Enormous energy and hope were invested in some of the new schools, such as Willesden High, where Max Morris, later president of the NUT, worked tirelessly to create a vibrant new institution out of a former grammar and second-ary modern school.[26] Observers of the early comprehensives admired the 'handsome, well-equipped secondary schools built on comprehensive lines' in big cities like Birmingham, Bristol and Coventry, but could see that their successful growth and full academic flourishing was impeded by the continuing existence of nearby grammar schools and independents, 'which has meant that the comprehensive schools receive few children of very high intel-ligence, and these are mainly late developers.'[27] Where there were no selective schools nearby, it was a very different story. Thomas Bennett School in Crawley was, to all intents and purposes, a true comprehensive which had already attracted plaudits for its high academic standards, 'its scholastic work, the vigour of its societies, and the conduct and deportment of its pupils'.[28] With an uncreamed intake—a unique phenomenon in a town—a large number of stu-dents had taken O levels in six subjects. Another successful venture was Ashlyns School, at Berkhamsted in Hertfordshire, where, it was noted, 'already five of its pupils who failed the eleven-plus have entered universities'.[29]

In many areas of the country, then, comprehensive reform was both uncontentious and successful. Inevitably, press interest in new 'all-in' schools was trained on neighbourhoods and schools where rich and poor lived cheek by jowl, and where the hitherto privately educated might be drawn to experiment in the showcase schools. The very possibility aroused a kind of 'edu-voyeurism', a longing to find fundamental weaknesses in the broad educa-tional aims of the comprehensive, and a new awkwardness in relations between those who had not traditionally been schooled together.

Serious reformers of this period were also concerned that some progressives might seek to capture the comprehensives for various misguided social objectives, and so turn the new schools into useful targets for the enemies of reform. As Clyde Chitty has observed, it was easy to ridicule the concept of the 'social mix', where 'the Duke lies down with the docker and the Marquis and the milkman are as one'.[30]

My own old school, Holland Park, attracted its fair share of edu-voyeurism over the years, obscuring many of its more everyday and solid achievements. One of the earliest comprehensive schools to be established, by the forward-thinking London County Council (LCC), a great deal was riding on the success, or failure, of this shiny new school whose pupil intake was drawn from both the tough Notting Hill slums (made notorious by landlord Peter Rachman in the early 1960s) and the exquisite crescents of Kensington and Chelsea. The school opened in September 1958, at the end of a week of attacks in Notting Hill by whites on West Indian immigrants.

The school itself is sited on a hill, in eight acres of grounds. On one side is Holland Park, with its woods and lawns, on the other stand the luxurious mansion houses, family homes and private flats of Kensington. The school buildings—large, glass-plated, with open staircases—were designed by the LCC's chief architect, Leslie Martin, who had planned the Festival Hall. The site included Thorpe Lodge, former residence of the governor of the Bank of England, and was used for sixth-form teaching, giving classes the air and atmosphere of a university tutorial.

The school opened with over 2,000 pupils. The land for Holland Park had been requisitioned by the LCC in the face of powerful opposition from some of the area's wealthy residents. Some of them were so opposed to the idea of the school that they had formed the Campden Hill Preservation Society, a lobby group which included the South African high commissioner, the widow of a former governor of the Bank of England, and the future Poet Laureate John Betjeman. For several years after the school opened, students were expressly forbidden to use the entrances that bordered the road of the South African high commissioner's residence, where he would hold his garden parties.

In its earliest years, Holland Park was run along quasi-grammar-school lines. Visitors in the early 1960s were surprised to be greeted by senior staff in flowing black academic gowns who ate at an Oxbridge-style high table, served by domestic

science students. There was rigid streaming, a system later abandoned for mixed-ability teaching. While most of the wealthy of
Kensington boycotted it, the school did attract some well-known
liberal names, including the children of film director Ken Russell,
of blues musicians John Mayall and Alexis Korner, and of several
Labour ministers, who traditionally educated their children in
the private sector. When my parents, Tony and Caroline Benn,
chose to support the emerging comprehensive school movement
by sending myself and my three brothers to Holland Park, ten
minutes' walk from our home, press interest escalated. Caroline,
co-author of some seminal research studies on the national
implementation of comprehensive education, was a governor
at Holland Park for thirty-five years and chair of governors for
thirteen, remaining closely involved with the school long after
we had left.

Early visitors were impressed by the highly confident and vocal
student body, well-stocked library, immense range of cultural
activities, and skilled and inspirational staff. But press coverage
of the school was hostile. A typical piece, published in the *Daily
Telegraph* in 1963, focused on the unhappy experiences of three
former pupils. When another group of former students objected
to the piece, they were invited to meet the editor—but the paper
never published their riposte. Tabloid reporters came into the
school and offered pupils money to create disruption.

Educationally speaking, Holland Park achieved considerable success, particularly for the hundreds of children branded
as failures under the old eleven-plus, or those for whom private
schooling had not worked. At a recent talk, one of the school's
most talented history teachers spoke movingly of children who had
been rejected by other schools, and for whom Holland Park was a
chance to enjoy learning and gain confidence in their intellectual
abilities. The school offered access to a wide range of knowledge and—perhaps the most crucial ingredient in educational
success—hope and self-belief. From the outset, academic results
were promising. Of the 200-plus students who entered the school
in 1962, only twelve had passed the eleven-plus, and yet sixty-six

of them went on to get 129 A levels between them. The school was proud of its record of university entry, and Allen Clarke, its first headmaster, spoke, perhaps a little optimistically, of fashioning students 'into fully integrated citizens, with no racial or class differences'.

The school changed direction rather dramatically during the 1970s, a period when progressive aims and methods were introduced into many comprehensives, with varying levels of success. Derek Rushworth, former head of Modern Languages, became head of the school in 1971 during a period of radical ferment. Under his headship, student democracy, new forms of teaching and a more open-minded regime flourished. Corporal punishment was abolished, along with uniforms. Mixed-ability teaching was introduced. Jane Shallice, later deputy head of the school, remembers Rushworth 'doing the assembly after having been to Sartre's funeral. When he returned he gave a whole school assembly on it, and every child listened to every word.'[31]

Shallice describes the nervousness and excitement among the teaching body at the abolition of streaming and the introduction of mixed-ability teaching, and the 'fever of discussion and debate' among students and staff. 'Many teachers felt passionately that old assumptions had to be challenged, past practices questioned and new alternatives developed ... there [was] continuous debate about teaching methods, about the content of courses, about the rights of students, about the organisation of the school and its relationship to the community outside.'[32]

During this period, Holland Park had a highly committed teaching body. 'Tutors ... were expected to make home visits, a practice virtually unheard-of today. There were annual visits to France, plays and concerts, an activity week at the end of the summer term when large numbers of children went on school journeys.' At the same time, staff were trying to develop a more liberal education in which knowledge was considered 'seamless', transcending traditional subjects and disciplines. 'Group work and more interactive forms of teaching flowered. Teachers also made an attempt to understand the culture into which a child is born and raised [and how this was] paramount in their intellectual and emotional development.'[33]

There were other, more radical school experiments in this period. Jane Shallice mentions the progressive experiments of A. S. Neill's Summerhill, and 'Michael Duane's depressingly short period as head of Risinghill' (a bold but brief educational experiment in an Islington comprehensive in the early 1960s), as important influences on her and other likeminded teachers.

Duane had in fact resigned in 1965, but the lessons of Risinghill still inspired many. Rather like Alex Bloom twenty years before, the charismatic Duane had pioneered a new approach to secondary education, including intensive and individual pastoral care, close ties with parents, student democracy, the encouragement of individual creativity, and, in a school with nearly twenty nationalities, an early form of multiculturalism. He refused to use corporal punishment or to expel children, on the grounds that, with compulsory secondary education, this gave them nowhere to go. Duane clashed with his bosses, the LCC and education inspectorate, and was finally forced to resign over the publication of an account of the school's sex education lessons. A hostile inspection report recommended the reintroduction of corporal punishment and expulsion, but Duane refused. In 1965, the newly formed Inner London Education Authority (ILEA) closed the school down. According to one observer, 'Risinghill closed quietly, with crowds of children talking in Mr Duane's study, and the toughest kids of all crying in the lavatories.'[34]

Duane had some passionate supporters, among them the writer Leila Berg whose lyrical account of the life and dramatic closure of the school, *Risinghill: Death of a Comprehensive*, was written as if in the direct voices of the children, parents and teachers, and repays reading today.[35] Others saw the school as an epitome of progressivism gone mad, fostering chaos and poor standards—although many of these same critics were not overly concerned about the abysmally low expectations institutionalised in so many secondary moderns.

Progressive methods in education were by now becoming a fresh battleground, part of the general reaction building up against the comprehensives; in fact, these were two distinct issues. And if Bridget Plowden's stately and moderate report on primary education courted controversy, more radical experiments in certain state schools caused apoplexy. Possibly the most dramatic example was the 'William Tyndale affair', as it came to be known. During the mid 1970s, head teacher Terry Ellis and his deputy Brian Haddow ran a highly progressive regime in this Islington primary. According to Gerald Haigh, writing about the affair many years later in the *TES*, 'It was essentially a system, much debated at the time, called the integrated day. With hindsight, it's clear that while it could work well with gifted teachers and good leadership, in the right sort of building, [without these elements] it could just as well be a recipe for chaos.'[36]

Chaos, it seems, was precisely what ensued. The children were allowed to wander freely; they could eat sweets whenever and wherever they wanted. There were few visible rules. Disgruntled parents and teachers made common cause and the press weighed in with lurid headlines like 'The School of Shame'. Enrolment plummeted. The ILEA commissioned a report on the affair from Robin Auld QC, but given a lack of clarity about the role of the local authority in terms of the management of schools, at that time, there was remarkably little Islington could do.

William Tyndale was the spark to a flame of impending crisis in the education system. Since the 1944 Act, an entirely new secondary-school structure had been set up, with no formal curriculum and no means of assessing teacher performance. When things went seriously wrong, as at William Tyndale, there was a vacuum of authority.

The Labour Government of the period felt it had to take a stand. Publication of the Auld Report in 1976 prompted new Prime Minister James Callaghan to intervene in the great debate. To many, Callaghan's Ruskin speech of October 1976 was one of the key turning points in the history of modern education; the post-war consensus was breaking down under the pressures of economic and political turmoil; the storm clouds of the new right were gathering; comprehensive reorganisation was well under way, but many unresolved questions hung over what kind of comprehensive school and what style of learning the nation wanted for its children. In many ways, they still do.

Chapter Three

The Long Years of Attrition

You could call what happened next 'the war after'. Comprehensive reformers were taken aback by the vitriol of the attack on 'all-in' schools from the late 1970s onwards. Later, they felt they had seriously underestimated the power of their opponents, whose ideas were slowly seeping into mainstream thinking.[1] But the real story of those years was not the fire and brimstone of irate traditionalists denouncing all things progressive, but the ambiguity and aggression of governments, both Labour and Conservative. Having equivocated over early comprehensive reform, and still afraid of its potentially radical implications, governments of both the right and the left facilitated a return to selection, albeit by covert means: a war of attrition that was 'indirect, complex and continual'.[2] At the same time, under cover of the language of choice, diversity and freedom, government reasserted its grip from the centre. Local government, whether proudly independent or weakly ineffectual, was perceived to be as great, if not more of an enemy, than the comprehensive ideal.

Where did this leave the piecemeal revolution? Never openly repudiated, never truly acknowledged, but certainly never celebrated. Comprehensive evolution had altered the political context for good: there was no serious attempt to restore the eleven-plus. To my knowledge, not a single lead article or mainstream politician has ever called for a return to the blighted secondary moderns. There's a real story of waste here too, of opportunities thrown away by political leaders, persistently haunted by the grammar-school narrative.

And yet, the attempts by one government after another to lure local schools away from local authorities, through bribery or browbeating, have never been as successful as their instigators hoped. The original conception of education as a 'national service, locally administered' clung on through the Thatcher years and halfway through New Labour but, as so many predicted when they were first introduced, the move towards city academies paved the way for potential private control of large numbers of our schools, with consequences we are only just now beginning to grasp.

By the early 1970s, comprehensive schools, now attended by the majority of children, were becoming more firmly established. Unhelpfully limited and limiting ideas on individual talent, and what constituted good teaching, were also being challenged. Labour returned to power in 1974, and in subsequent years education spending reached its highest level ever, amounting to 6.2 per cent of GDP. Local education authorities were now required to organise along comprehensive lines and to be more inclusive in terms of children with special needs. In 1975 direct-grant schools were abolished; two thirds of them went private.

But, at the same time, the comprehensive ideal and practice was under pressure from a number of separate but related economic and political developments. Social innovation has always flourished either in times of economic buoyancy or in the aftermath of large-scale catastrophes. The welfare state was the child of the privations of World War II—the realisation that if a nation can plan for war, it can surely plan for peace—and its implementation was borne along on a tide of relative economic calm. But the oil crisis of the early 1970s, the three-day week and the general sense of economic insecurity of that period, led many to question the price of equality.

The centre ground, that had facilitated the comprehensive reorganisation of the education system, now split apart, with the political right moving towards market theory in terms of public services, and the left turning towards a more radical politics. Only the new right, however, enjoyed direct access to a mainstream political leader. As education secretary in the early 1970s, Margaret Thatcher gave the go-ahead to more plans for comprehensive organisation than any preceding education secretary, but during her period as premier, Thatcher and her ministers became far more active and interfering in education, albeit in a highly contradictory fashion.

One of the most significant reactions to the advance of egalitarian education were the Black Papers, a series of articles written by educationalists, historians and novelists, published between 1969 and 1975. Deliberately playing on the idea of government White Papers, the Black Papers became synonymous with a prolonged all-out attack, not just on progressive methods, which they believed to be more widespread and damaging than the media would acknowledge, but on comprehensive education itself. A mix of academic critique, journalism and the odd bit of knockabout comedy, the Black Papers proved irresistible to the press; they got a wide and often sympathetic hearing, and their two founders, academic Brian Cox and Tony Dyson, a shy English lecturer, frequently featured in radio and TV debates about the problems of the nation's schools.

The immediate stimulus for the first Black Paper was the student unrest of 1968 and the Plowden Report, a report into primary education that had proposed moderately progressive ideas about childrens' learning. In his autobiography *The Great Betrayal: Memories of a Life in Education*, Brian Cox describes how the idea first came about when he and Tony Dyson were out on a walk on Hampstead Heath in 1969. Both were 'angry about the student sit-ins which were headline news at the time, and which we believed were causing harm to the status of universities and to freedom of speech'.[3] Initially, at least, comprehensive schools were not in their line of fire. It was some weeks before they decided to include any articles on comprehensives in the collection they decided to put together, which included contributions from Kingsley Amis and Philip Larkin, the historian Robert

Conquest, and Walter James, then editor of the *Times Educational Supplement*.

That first appeal for papers excoriated 'the revolutionary changes [that] have taken place in English education—the introduction of free play methods in primary schools, comprehensive schemes, the expansion of higher education, the experimental courses at new universities. There are powerful arguments in favour of such changes, but particularly in the last year or two, many people have become increasingly unhappy about certain aspects of the general trend.'[4] Reflecting on this early period many years later, Cox recalls that

> Tony and I ... regarded ourselves as moderate progressives; we were reformers opposed to a rigid selection system at eleven-plus, and in the forefront of new teaching methods in sixth forms and universities .... At the same time we ... believed great damage was being inflicted on education at all levels ... my difficulty was to balance the invective of intransigent traditionalists with a sympathetic and generous attitude to some progressive reforms. I was not always successful.[5]

The Black Papers received enormous and approving coverage. Labour was thrown, according to Clyde Chitty, 'by the sheer ferocity and scale of the right-wing attack on its education and social policies'. Such was the shift in the political mood that by May 1976, Rhodes Boyson, a comprehensive school headmaster, later Tory MP, active in the Black Paper movement, could claim that 'the forces of the Right in education are on the offensive. The blood is flowing from the other side now'—a strangely violent image from a head teacher of a London comprehensive, albeit one who enthusiastically advocated the use of corporal punishment.[6]

Over time the Black Papers became bolder, their thinking more in line with an array of right-wing think tanks and groups that were emerging in this pre-Thatcherite period. The most prominent of these was the Centre for Policy Studies, set up in 1974 by Margaret Thatcher, Keith Joseph and Alfred Sherman; there was, too, the Education Research Group, Friends of the Education

Voucher Experiment in Representative Regions (co-founded by Marjorie Seldon, mother of Wellington College head, Anthony Seldon), and the Salisbury Group, established in 1977, which went on to produce the *Salisbury Review*, edited by the right-wing philosopher Roger Scruton. The long-established Institute of Economic Affairs also played an important part in moving the education debate towards the idea of the marketisation of schools. But Brian Cox parted company from many of these new-right ideologues. He could not stomach many of the ideas that came from The Centre for Policy Studies and Alfred Sherman, whom he did not like. Cox became 'convinced that schemes for parents to use a voucher to pay for the cost of their children's education at the school of their choice would not work in practice. They would create a new bureaucracy, and the children of poor parents in the inner cities would be left to stagnate in run-down comprehensives.'[7] In 1980 Cox retired from active educational policies, and returned to literature and writing poetry, his first true loves.

But some Black Paper ideas were having a strong impact on the Labour Party of this period. Perhaps the clearest example of this was the intervention of Prime Minister Jim Callaghan in October 1976, in his now famous 'Ruskin Speech' on the condition of state education. Like many premature school-leavers, Callaghan had an exaggerated respect for schools and teachers, but a clear passion for his subject. He consulted widely on his Ruskin speech, including with ministerial colleagues and with civil servants who had been compiling the so-called Yellow Book, a collation of civil-service concerns about schools, methods, managements, and account-ability through the inspectorate system. The furore over William Tyndale, in which it appeared that primary-school children had run amok as a result of misplaced idealism, teacher incompetence or both, lit the touchpaper of concern.

Callaghan's Ruskin speech, in which he called for a core curriculum, reform of the examination system and a limit on education spending, is variously described by educational and political commentators as a monumental contribution—putting Labour back on track in terms of mainstream thinking about the purpose of schools—or an unhelpful rightist intervention. Reading it today, it comes across as rather plain and restrained, decidedly cautious in terms of trespassing on the sanctity of teachers, schools, and learning itself. Callaghan seemed nervous to be even dipping his toe into educational waters: 'There is nothing wrong with non-educationalists, even a prime minister, talking about [education] ... It would be a betrayal of concern ... if I did not draw problems to your attention.' His criticism of progressive freedoms seems equally mildly expressed: 'there is the unease felt by parents and others about the new informal methods of teaching which seem to produce excellent results when they are in well-qualified hands, but are much more dubious when they are not.' Callaghan's speech was seen as an implicit endorsement of a 'discourse of derision'—in Stephen Ball's words—aimed at schools and teachers by the Black Papers, some industrialists and sections of the media, in particular the *Daily Mail*.[8]

Certainly, Callaghan gave voice to the anxieties of business and industry. 'I am concerned on my journeys to find complaints from industry that new recruits from the schools sometimes do not have the basic tools to do the job that is required ... There seems to be a need for more technological bias in science teaching that will lead towards practical applications in industry.' Schools should 'equip children to the best of their ability for a lively, constructive place in society, and also to fit them to do a job of work. Not one or the other but both.'

But if Callaghan's Ruskin speech marked the beginning of the end of the ideal of education for education's sake, it was also the end of a period of relative political non-interference in the system. Education was now considered fair game for politicians with various agendas for change. Since the late 1950s, pressure groups on the right had built up a critique of state control of public services, and were keen to set schools free from excessive local authority control and give parents more choice. Labour, meanwhile, were fatally divided on how to develop comprehensive education—with a more radical rank and file movement, keen to consolidate comprehensive education, facing a cautious, corporatist leadership in the 1970s, and then, back in power from the late 1990s onwards, finding that many of the market arguments of the right had seeped into the New Labour leadership.

Yet all governments of this period were to be marked by the same paradoxes. In their different ways, the governments of Thatcher, Major, Blair and Brown all advocated versions of parental choice and greater school freedom while tightening the control of the daily life of schools from the centre. All would scale back the powers of local government; all would display degrees of ambiguity, ambivalence and downright aggression toward the principle of comprehensive education. None, Gordon Brown excepted, would concede any substantive value in, or achievements to, comprehensive reform. This was to be expected from the Tories, perhaps. But in the case of Blair's premiership, it was not until the middle years of his time in power that the depth of his visceral political dislike for an egalitarian agenda in education, and his determination to seek radical, market-based alternatives, were to emerge.

It took time for Thatcher's government to grind into gear on education policy. Keith Joseph, her first education secretary, was a leading rightist ideologue but surprisingly ineffectual in government. The most significant development of Thatcher's first term in office was the creation of 30,000 government-subsidised places in private schools, the Assisted Places scheme. In theory, assisted places were to enable the ambitious working-class child to escape the state system. In practice, the places largely went to the children of educationally advantaged families in relative financial difficulty.

Joseph investigated the idea of voucher-style systems, but was prevented by Thatcher from further developing the policy. Nevertheless, when asked in the late 1980s (by the academic Stephen Ball) what his greatest contribution to education policy had been, Joseph, head in hands—a mix of hammery and genuine despair— thought for a while and said: 'Bankruptcy'. In other words, he had at least introduced the idea that in a quasi-market system, schools would have to go to the wall. Neat economics, poor politics; the inscription, surely, on Joseph's political tombstone.

In contrast, his far less ideologically driven successor Kenneth Baker did a great deal. Sleek, smart, confident and with 'the hide of a rhinoceros', Baker's 1988 Reform Act was a massive piece of legislative interference, which came in two distinct parts.[9] First things first, the government wanted to break the power of local authorities over school admissions, administration and financing, and set up new government-controlled rivals to the neighbour-hood comprehensive. Under Baker, two new kinds of school were established: Grant-Maintained Schools and City Technology Colleges. CTCs, fiercely opposed by Labour, were forerunners of their later City Academy programme: specialising in one, two or three subjects, they derived part of their costs from private spon-sors, who in return had a controlling say in the ethos and running of the school, and attracted greater funding from government. Local-authority hostility to the idea of a separate layer of state schools in the late 1980s and 90s blocked the developments of some CTCs and in the end only fifteen were established.

Grant-Maintained Schools were also given favourable treat-ment, but remained nonetheless 'maintained'—part of the local authority. Granted extra funds, they could set their own admis-sions policy—a crucial freedom for any school, given the clear link between attainment at entry and attainment at GCSE and A level. Baker also weakened the connection between local authori-ties and schools by giving more schools the power to run their own affairs. Under 'local management of schools', the vast majority of the schools budget was now devolved to heads and governing bodies. 'Open enrolment' reduced local authority control over pupil placements, supposedly giving parents a greater choice at secondary level.

In *The School Report*, his incisive analysis of Tory and Labour reforms of the late 1980s and 90s, *Guardian* journalist Nick Davies charts the shattering effect of open enrolment on two schools in Sheffield in the late 1980s, and the ensuing polarisation of the community. The book now stands as a classic account of how a still fledgling, and in some ways already flailing, comprehensive system was further wrecked by a mix of government policy and economic emergency; how, under pressure from unemployment, cuts, the collapse of the property market, and the movement of migrants into disintegrating inner-city areas, schools in such areas began to reflect the growing economic inequality.

But if the 1988 Act used the concept of freedom and parental choice to enable middle-class and white flight, it also extended the arm of the state into our schools in an unprecedented manner. If Callaghan's Ruskin speech had been an acknowledgement of the vacuum that had grown up in the absence of a national curriculum, the Education Reform Act went further than any politicians had previously dared imagine. Baker's Act prescribed 95 per cent of the school week from Whitehall, with detailed directives on chief subject areas, rates of development and modes of assessment. Eight hundred staff had to be brought in to help administer the reform. According to Jenkins, the Cabinet 'gleefully obeyed Parkinson's law of triviality and spent hours rewriting the mathematics and history curriculums. Ministers who would agree a billion-pound missile design wrangled over when history began, or whether an English adviser was ideologically sound.'[10]

The academic and journalist Ted Wragg was caustic about the new national curriculum and its attention-seeking political master, Ken Baker. 'Keen on publicity, he turned each report [on the curriculum's main subject areas] into a press jamboree: ten subjects, ten photo opportunities.' The first draft of the national curriculum was absurdly complex, with seventeen attainment targets in science and fourteen in maths. The history syllabus for junior-school pupils was overstuffed, and as Wragg joked, 'History at Key Stage 2 covered over 4,000 years, allowing about one and a half minutes per year. The message was simple: avoid teaching the Spanish Armada in the hay-fever season, as someone will sneeze and the class will never know who won.'[11] The National Curriculum for Wales included the same core subjects as in England, but also included Welsh language and the study of the culture and heritage of Wales. The National Curriculum was extended, with some modifications, to Northern Ireland by the 1989 Education Reform (Northern Ireland) Order. The 1988 ERA did not apply to Scotland, which developed its own curriculum framework.

Some noted an uncanny similarity between the 1988 curriculum and that of the syllabus of 1904. Schools were denied any real flexibility or choice. Overnight, teachers became the most controlled—and oppressed—group of professionals in the country. Some of the Act's greatest critics came from the libertarian right, who believed the national curriculum hampered the freedom of schools to respond to market pressures in terms of what their own curriculum could offer.[12]

So the interference went on. John Patten's Education Act of 1993 was even more ambitious in scope. Once more, the aim was to undercut local comprehensives and local authorities through encouraging further 'specialisation' in the system. Two new school types were introduced: technology schools and technology colleges, the latter sponsored by business and directly funded by government—a canny way of increasing the grant-maintained stock overall. A new Funding Agency was to handle revenue to the new schools, and local authorities were banned from setting up competing schools nearby. The only problem was, most schools didn't want to 'opt out'. By the 1997 election, under 20 per cent of children in secondary education were in opted-out schools. In Scotland, not a single school chose to become grant-maintained.

It was Patten who introduced the controversial league tables for GCSE and A levels, and Standard Assessment Tests (SATs.) By 1995, children were being tested at the age of seven, eleven and fourteen, and the supposed academic success of schools could be read off at a glance. These score cards came, of course, without reference to such crucial factors as the social class composition of the school in question, or the fact that comprehensives by definition educate a spread of pupils while grammars and private schools only select the more academically minded. Schools now became like shops, with league tables, a kind of shorthand indicator of desirability, regularly published in upmarket newspapers and weekend supplements; league-table talk came to dominate the anxious chatter of the middle-class state-school parent. League tables also spelled the death of extra-curricular activity in state schools. Heads and teachers now had to concentrate on creeping up the results league, and as Simon Jenkins says, 'sport and music instantly declined and there was a widespread selling of school playing fields. The number of playing fields in England fell from 78,000 to 44,000 over the next ten years.'[13]

In their 1996 survey of some 1,500 schools and colleges in England, Scotland and Wales, Benn and Chitty found that 90 per cent of children were in comprehensive schools. The 'all-in' schools had clearly survived, but there was a resounding and growing contradiction at the heart of education. Ostensibly, governments were supporting the comprehensive principle—but this support was clearly lukewarm. Tory attempts to bring in new forms of selection made it clear that they, in truth, 'had no confidence in an education that did not prejudge an individual's worth or facilitate an escalation of enclaves for the favoured few'.[14]

In retrospect, it is much easier to understand the contradictions of New Labour's first term in office. Despite the passionate rhetoric about education of those May days in 1997, there was never any serious desire or intention to tackle the big picture: the inequality embedded in favoured schools, particularly the remaining grammars, the relatively new CTCs and the private schools. New Labour's aim was, always, to level up, without touching the inequalities written into the structure of education. This was beautifully expressed by the mantra of the moment—'standards, not structures'—which could be recast, in political terms, as Let's Do the Very Best with What We Have and Don't Rock the Boat. David Blunkett's famously mouthed *read my lips, no more selection* had been taken by Labour activists to mean that Labour, once in power, would phase out the grammars; only 164 remained, but these were enough to distort the intake, and blight the chances, of hundreds of other schools. Blunkett's subsequent feeble claim that he had only ever meant no *more* selection—and even this promise was not kept—encapsulates the lack of clarity of the New Labour leadership during this early period in power.

In the event, the decision to get rid of grammars was left to local education authorities, but the ballotting regulations introduced by Labour's 1998 Act were so complex and weighted towards the grammar schools that they were used only once, in Ripon in 2000. Voters included private-school parents whose children were deemed to be in 'feeder' schools for grammars, but excluded many schools and parents whose children were destined for secondary moderns. Unsurprisingly, the result of the vote was overwhelmingly pro-grammar. It has never been tried again. Soon after, the New Labour Government declared itself not interested 'in hunting down the remaining grammars', as if those campaigning for greater fairness in schools were akin to pedagogical fox-hunters, enjoying the suffering of their quarry just for the sake of it.

Still, it would be churlish to suggest that New Labour did not make a difference. It did. State education, like so much of the public estate, had deteriorated during the Tory years; in many areas of the country, schools had fallen into disrepair and demoralisation. The anger and despair that this created fed directly into the strength of support for Labour in 1997. Tony Blair chose to deliver his first speech as prime minister at the run-down Aylesbury Estate in Southwark, South London, where he declared that 'there will be no forgotten people in the Britain I want to build'.

Early New Labour education policy-making was hyperactive. Within months of taking office it had charged primary schools with carrying out 'baseline assessments' of all children, introduced setting, developed the idea of specialist secondary schools each with their own distinct 'identity and expertise', and created a new grade of Advanced Skills Teachers. Voluntary-aided and foundation schools were to be in charge of their own staff and their own premises, and to have new freedoms on admissions. New partnerships between state and independent schools were to be developed. New Labour's first White Paper was warmly welcomed by many. According to the Campaign for the Advancement of State Education (CASE), the proposals seemed designed 'to benefit the many, not just the few'.[15]

So there were successes—many of them. The government may have let the gloomy Chris Woodhead loose on the teaching profession, but Tony Blair and other public figures popped up in glossy ads remembering brilliant teachers from their past, an advertising campaign in early 1998 for the Teacher Training Agency that lifted spirits. The literacy and the numeracy hour may have been overly prescriptive, but no sensible parent recoils at proposals to improve basic standards, and it worked, at least in the beginning. Building Schools for the Future, its reputation later shredded by a partisan, penny-pinching Michael Gove, represented a new energy and dynamism as well as Labour's discomfiting relationship with the private sector. It produced many memorable school buildings that let light into students' learning and lifted teachers' morale. The retiring Labour MP Chris Mullin claimed that he had only to walk around his constituency in Sunderland to see the difference that public investment by a Labour government had made to people's lives. An *Independent* reporter who went back to the Aylesbury estate a few years after Blair's famous post-election speech, found that the number of GCSE passes by residents had leapt from 17 to 40.3 per cent.[16]

In education, Labour was very like its leader: restlessly dynamic, forever unsatisfied. The legislation of the period included the School Standards and Framework Act 1998, Teaching and Higher Education Act 1998, Education Act 2002, Higher Education Act 2004, Education Act 2005, Education and Inspections Act 2006. And it yielded results. In 1997 roughly half of all children left primary school without reaching the expected levels in English and maths. Today, that figure is about 20 per cent. In 1997, some 45 per cent of pupils achieved five good GCSEs. Now, the figure is over 60 per cent—more than three times the proportion that left school with five O levels in the vaunted 'golden age' of the grammars. The school buildings programme may have been costly and over-bureaucratic, but for generations of pupils it provided access to top-class facilities for learning, art, drama and music for the first time ever.

Labour's record on investment was impressive, but many in the teaching profession felt overloaded, and over-controlled by the government. One head teacher claimed that she received so many bits of paper from central government that when she tried to put one term's worth of instructions in a wheelbarrow, she couldn't shift it. Such 'Big Brother'-style lunacy was neatly summed up by Ted Wragg, a keen observer and satirist of education policy under Blair, in which one Tony Zoffis (Tony's office) played a leading role. Wragg claimed that 'Head teachers were being harangued to meet their targets. Governors were whipped into a frenzy to hobble defaulters ... Targets have become a cruel master, not a benign servant, focused on narrow, mechanical objectives, not pupils' right to educational advantage; imposed instead of negotiated and discussed, alienating rather than engaging.'[17]

Blair himself was never sympathetic to comprehensives. In *The Journey* he tells a story of visiting an inner-city school just before the 1997 election and observing a group of students scuffling in the foyer, near to where he was standing and talking. Blair was surprised that the head teacher did not move to quell the aggressive behaviour—'He was, by the way, a nice guy, and committed.'[18] Later the head tried to explain the social context of the school to the Labour leader, including the significant home problems of the children, and the fact that his school was used as a dumping-ground locally for children excluded from other schools. There were many ways that a Labour politician might have interpreted this brief encounter, and the information gleaned from it. But for Blair it merely fortified his resolve that he personally would never send his child to 'a school like this'—the clear implication being, 'to a comprehensive'—and that the Labour party must not be seen to condone this kind of 'failure'. Reading this passage, one can almost see him recoiling in distaste from a bunch of losers—including, in this case, the nice committed head. But if he was clear that he needed to offer escape routes to other parents like him, it was never quite clear what he thought about the rest of the population. Should they wait their turn, until every school in the country had been remade by him, or did they perhaps deserve their scuffling, second-class fate?

To those who knew them then, it was no surprise that the Blairs did not choose local secondary schools for their own children. In 1994, while living in Islington, they preferred to send their eldest son across the city to the London Oratory, a selective, voluntary-aided Catholic school. When Harriet Harman sent her son to St Olave's, one of the country's top grammars, Blair vigorously defended her—much to the annoyance of his chief aide Alastair Campbell, who remained a champion of local schools and an advocate of middle-class involvement in them. The Harman decision caused a tremendous row within the Labour party, but this dispute, and others like it, never changed its leader's mind. Among most of Blair's close associates, there was no criticism of those who chose private or selective education—indeed, there was sometimes a covert sense of congratulation. Instead, it was their critics they derided, briefing against them as political has-beens, woolly-minded liberals who condoned low standards. Peter Hyman, a chief speech-writer for Blair before he left to become a teacher—and latterly, the chief founder of a free school in East London—wrote of how friends and colleagues wrestled with their consciences over the question of private education, only to find that 'quite simply what was on offer was much better'; there was no turning back.[19] None of this helped to create the impression of a reforming administration.

There were some barbed remarks about 'bog-standard' comprehensives—a phrase of Campbell's believed to have originated from Hyman—and 'not touching some schools with a barge-pole'—this from a demoralised Estelle Morris, who subsequently resigned as education secretary. All in all a dangerous air of negativity about local schools prevailed, an inability to acknowledge that many comprehensive schools were diverse, dynamic and flourishing and that there were often substantive, structural reasons when this wasn't the case. Inevitably, the 'bog-standard' doctrine had a detrimental effect on parental confidence. If politicians and their most trusted aides saw no reason to trust, support and therefore build on the inheritance of comprehensives, and indeed preferred selective or even private education for their own children, then why, thought many parents, should we? In education, increasingly, familial self-interest became New Labour's calling card.

Blair's choice of the London Oratory for his own children played its part in making faith schools an increasingly popular avenue of alternative choice for the middle classes. Throughout the 2000s it was clear that many faith schools were becoming middle-class enclaves. This did not make them socially exclusive in the same way as private schools, but it made their comprehensive 'mix' a far more favourable one, attractive to nervous middle-class parents: results could be boosted, league-table positions improved, and the virtuous circle set in motion. Meanwhile, community schools in areas of deprivation, particularly in the inner cities, were struggling to deal with large numbers of children on low incomes, many with poor English and/or behavioural problems linked to difficulties in family or home life. Here, then, a vicious circle was all too often in place, despite the best efforts of heads and teachers.

Admissions policy had become the new battleground. The growth in the number of schools that were their own admissions authorities—meaning they had the power to decide who to take and who to reject—and their use of complex and sometimes unfair practices, clearly distorted school populations. Research by Anne West of the LSE showed that in 'own admissions' schools, just under half were operating some sort of covert-overt selection. The introduction of aptitude tests by David Miliband when he was schools minister, permitting schools to select 10 per cent of pupils, provided another tool for picking and choosing pupils. City Technology Colleges, the forerunners of the academy programme, were virtually free to design their own entry criteria, using 'structured' discussions along with applications; Thomas Telford School, a successful CTC in the West Midlands, invited prospective pupils for assessment to provide a copy of their Year 5 reports. The headmaster, selecting from nine ability bands, took into account 'those applicants most likely to benefit from the education on offer at the School and who have the strongest motivation to succeed'.[20] Many faith schools were using interviews, primary-school references and consideration of the family's 'commitment' to the school ethos and value. In one high-performing London church school brochure, it was explained that primary-school heads were being asked to 'show that the applicant and her family's attitudes, values and expectations are in sympathy with this Church of England school'. Some of these practices, such as interviews between secondary school and parents, were banned under a revised admission code drawn up before the 2006 Education and Inspections Act, and consolidated under Gordon Brown's premiership after 2007.

Blair largely dismissed these arguments. He believed that school success was down to ethos and effort. Grammar schools and private schools did not have an advantage, he claimed, 'because they were selective ... because the parents are middle class, better-off and the facilities are better'. Of course all this made the job of the school 'easier', but in reality these schools were good because they were independent and innovative, and exhibited a strong ethos and leadership.[21]

Blair's conservatism on education was evident in other ways, such as his rejection of the 2004 Tomlinson Report. This proposed a new, integrated structure of qualifications, linking vocational and academic credits, so suited to the modern comprehensive school. Blair was reluctant to ditch A levels, the precious 'gold standard' so prized by the private sector. His greatest interest was in established institutions, and those possessing power and success. Struggling institutions were expected to adopt and ape these qualities, without any reference to context, and were berated if they did not.

The story of one secondary modern in Buckinghamshire during this period neatly illustrates the New Labour paradox on education. The vicissitudes of this 'upper school', as it is known, during New Labour's time in office have been written up by one of its governors, although she has deliberately chosen not to name the school.

Despite its leafy middle-England associations, Buckinghamshire is one of the most deprived of England's counties, where academic selection still divides the school population at the age of eleven. This leaves the county's upper schools—secondary moderns—dealing with high proportions of children from families on low incomes, often with language or behavioural problems as well. Chronically low levels of funding from the local authority during the Thatcher and Major governments had left thirteen of Buckinghamshire's 21 secondary moderns on a deficit budget by the end of the 1990s, while the grammar-school sector enjoyed surpluses of over three quarters of a million pounds. The county's upper schools were not only poor but, in effect, invisible within an authority obsessed with its elite grammars, some of them with their own private-school-style boarding facilities. One grammar even ran its own wine club.

However, from 1999 onward the government began to channel investment to the school, first under the Excellence in Cities (EiC) initiative, which provided £3 million, and then through several school improvement programmes that had a tremendous impact on classroom teaching. In 2006 it was announced that the school was to receive £31 million under the government's Building Schools for the Future programme, after the government had chosen this particular upper school as the county's school 'of greatest need'. The third major state intervention came under the more controversial National Challenge scheme, set up in 2008 to identify schools falling below a certain 'floor target' in terms of GCSE results. Such a 'stigma of failure' caused predictable resentment in a school and a sector whose intake, to quote one of the governors, was 'skewed from the outset' by the continued existence of the eleven-plus.

Writing about the story of this school under New Labour, upper-school governor Katy Simmons clearly sets out the contradictions of government policy. On the one hand, she is critical of the government's failure to tackle the academic selection that has had such a crippling impact, over decades, on this and other upper schools in Buckinghamshire. 'Why, we ask, did they not choose in 1997 to finish the job started by Circular 10/65 and end selection once and for all …? If we imagined our school in a non-selective system, then a number of the major challenges facing us would be resolved. We'd have an ethnically balanced and more socially mixed intake, and we'd have large cohorts of students achieving at a higher level, with no need for intervention via the National Challenge.'

Even so, Simmons believed, unlike the Tory Government before it, New Labour had 'a clear and unwavering' commitment to students from less favoured backgrounds. She felt grateful that 'the neediest young people, such as those at our school, have been the focus of government policy'. In her view New Labour really has made a difference to young people who had, before, been invisible. 'They are, at last, in the picture.'[22] Of course, the same could not be said of the many thousands of children in secondary moderns which did not receive such generous investment.

The New Labour paradox was even more apparent in its controversial academy programme. During the Thatcher and Major years, Labour had fiercely criticised the privatisation of state education. It had opposed City Technology Colleges on the grounds that they made the job of neighbouring schools more difficult, reduced the involvement of schools in communities, and the accountability of those schools to their communities. Yet within three years of taking office, Labour had come up with an almost identical model in the form of city academies, aimed at providing a 'fresh start' for struggling inner-city schools. The city academies project was announced in 2000; the first academy opened in September 2002. For those who had long argued for significant investment and an injection of dynamism into deprived urban areas, academies initially posed something of a dilemma. It was cheering to see government invest vast sums of money in some of our most run-down neighbourhoods, providing well-designed, aesthetically pleasing buildings and state-of-the-art facilities. However, the price of this investment and innovation was a new partnership with the private sector and the church, granting these bodies far-reaching new powers while bypassing local authorities altogether. The freedoms granted through this privatisation had dangerous implications, and the results they achieved in return for their financial and political privileges were, in many cases, highly questionable, as we shall see. What is not in question is that Labour paved the way for the new school revolution.

The early academy programme spawned plentiful jokes about car salesmen and creationists, masking far more serious questions about why private individuals and religious groups necessarily possessed greater skills to run a school than a local authority, and whether they would bring their own discrete agendas to education —which of course they did, in return for a relatively small amount of capital, some of it never actually paid. Question marks also hung over the degree to which the rich and powerful were goaded into sponsorship in return for political honours; these charges, investigated by the police, were eventually dropped, but left a lingering impression of inappropriate collusion, if not corruption, right at the heart of government. In many areas, local authorities were effectively told that if they wanted Building Schools for the Future money, then they had to include a plan for an academy. This 'no academy, no school' ultimatum put a lot of councillors, teachers and parents in a difficult position, particularly where there was a desperate need for new schools and for extensive repairs to the old ones—and a local shortage of school places.

By now, it was clear that New Labour had changed its tune on education. From its early concentration on 'standards not structures', a mission to improve quality in the classroom, the government was once again tearing the system up by the roots. There was growing unease within the labour movement about the implications of the academy programme and the direction that Tony Blair and his closest adviser on education, Andrew Adonis, wanted to take on education. After the 2005 election, it was clear that New Labour intended to push ahead with major privatisation of state schools and to further diminish local authority control and influence. In fact, local authorities had not directly run schools for a long time; their role was increasingly to organise the planning of school places, oversee fair admissions, and distribute the national education budget according to local demand, particularly in relation to the growing number of children deemed to have special needs. The 2005 Education White Paper, proposing a major expansion of the academy programme, was a step too far for many MPs, 58 of whom set up an alternative White Paper group. Widespread unease at the political implications and effectiveness of the scheme was echoed by the finding of a Select Committee in early 2006 that 'no causal link has been demonstrated between external partners and the success of a school, or between the independence of a school from local authority control and its success.'[23]

At a packed meeting in Committee Room 14, in early January 2006, to launch a pamphlet that Fiona Millar and I co-authored in defence of comprehensive education, Neil Kinnock, the former Labour leader, finally broke publicly with the direction of the Labour Government on state education—although he pledged himself to a 'merciful rescue' rather than a 'malicious rebellion'. Former Education Secretary Estelle Morris spoke for many when she expressed her deep unease at 'the direction of travel' of the Labour Government.

The dissident MPs in the Alternative White Paper group won some important concessions from the government on fair admissions and preservation of the role of the local authority. Even so, the Education and Inspections Act of 2006 only passed into law with the support of the Conservatives. Two years later, Andrew Adonis, the real architect of Labour's schools policy, was moved to a post at transport, a sign of his leader's recognition of the limits of his waning power on public service reform. Meanwhile, Blair's feelings of impatience and exhaustion about the political opposition that he faced over his schools policy were best summed up by a single half sentence—more of an exclamation, really—in his recent autobiography: 'But what a fight it all was'.[24]

III
THE WAY WE LEARN NOW

Chapter Four

The Politics of Selection

A grey Wednesday morning off the Fulham Road, West London, and I am on my way to meet a group of primary-school mothers, long-time campaigners in their home borough of Hammersmith and Fulham for a good, mixed, community school—a secondary equivalent to the primary schooling that they have so appreciated for their children, and which led them to form the Parental Alliance for Secondary Schools (PASS). Their strategy was ingenious and hands-on: to get involved with several local secondary schools by approaching them as a 'free advertising agency' to the primary community they were part of. The mothers became governors at Hurlingham and Chelsea school, Fulham Cross school, Henry Compton school, Phoenix School and William Morris Sixth Form Academy—all schools with rapidly rising results, good or outstanding Ofsted reports and strong and dynamic leaders. They hoped that with support, hard work, and building on their inside knowledge, the schools could attract a greater mix of local parents.

Now it's crunch time for these campaigners as parents, as their children come up for secondary transfer. The process has aroused painfully mixed feelings. Their close involvement with a number of local schools has profoundly impressed and changed them: they speak with respect and admiration of the excellent heads, exceptionally committed staff and impressive students they have met and worked with, in the kind of schools that many middle-class people dismiss out of hand. One mother laments, 'There's so much ignorance among people, even my friends, the ones who go private. I mean, the way they talk about these schools and these children. We start having arguments and I just can't bear what they say, the ignorance. I have to get up and leave the table. But that's exactly why social cohesion is so important. To break down that ignorance.'

But the school they longed to help create and where they dreamed of sending their own children, the secondary school with a genuine social mix, has still not materialised. In wealthy Hammersmith and Fulham, according to 2008 figures, over a quarter of parents use private education, and over half of parents who choose state schools educate their children outside borough boundaries. There are three oversubscribed CofE single-sex faith schools for which, in the wry words of one mother around the table, 'you have to have been baptised at three months'. In the north of the borough, the renowned Phoenix school draws almost all of its intake from the nearby White City estate.

This leaves a series of community schools and newly established academies, with varying results and reputations. 'I went round one,' says one of the mothers, of a single-sex boys comprehensive, one of her nearest schools. 'The kids were polite, there was great artwork on the wall, the head was nice. What these staff do is phenomenal.' But her anxious demeanour tells another story as she explains that the school has a 'terrible local reputation'—a child from the school was recently murdered in an inter-school brawl at Victoria Station—and she is frightened of how her two boys would fare in such an environment. Another mother, a Christian, talks of a single-sex school in the south of the borough. It got an outstanding Ofsted report, but its intake is 80 per cent Muslim. What about Hurlingham and Chelsea, I ask? Results continue to rise year by year: the head teacher, Phil Cross, has brought about astonishing changes in behaviour, atmosphere and aspiration at the school. And yet the middle classes still aren't going there. Its reputation of five-plus years ago continues to stick. As one mother says, 'It's as if there's an unshakeable class-driven agenda swirling around and we can't beat it.'

These might seem the kind of parents that London's chief adviser for schools, David Woods, was referring to when he talked about families who, 'while perfectly prepared to buy into state primary education, have an innate prejudice against their local state secondary school. Despite what you hear from the chattering classes—by which I mean the dinner parties of Islington—London's state secondary schools are doing very well. Almost a quarter have been judged outstanding. There are parents who, given a very good state school on their doorstep, would not send their children there because they have an innate prejudice against it. Why don't they go in and spend a day there? Parents have a perfect right to make their own decisions, but I think sometimes it is done on the basis of prejudice.'

The PASS group do not fit this stereotype. Woods's complaint was against parents with too little knowledge, not too much. These PASS parents fear not the schools—the heads, the staff, or the quality of the work—but something different, the vicious circle of modern inner-city secondary schools: unbalanced intakes, perceived collective low aspirations and rough reputations. While each is left wrestling with an individual decision concerning their own children's future, they have discovered over time how the so-called choice agonies of the modern parent connect, directly, and at every level, to local and national politics: from the silence that surrounds a highly divisive private sector, to the selective admissions of faith schools or the machinations of a local council, too often more interested in privatisation than in meeting the needs of the local community.

Like thousands of families around the country, these mothers have come up against the byzantine, bewildering realities of our school system. Parents in England today are supposedly offered increasing diversity and choice. In fact, many face a 'dizzyingly steep hierarchy of institutions'—to use Professor Tim Brighouse's memorable phrase—in which schools consistently reflect and reinforce existing social divisions. In many ways, not much has changed since R. H. Tawney wrote, in 1931, that the 'hereditary curse upon English education is its organization upon lines of social class'.[1]

How does our school system really work? Both Scotland, which has 374 secondary schools and 2,128 primaries, and Wales, with 223 secondary schools and 1,462 primaries, have a comprehensive system. Northern Ireland, with 219 secondary schools and 886 primaries, is in the prolonged and painful throes of phasing out selection. England has a multi-tiered schooling system offering a vast and confusing array of official school types. Among England's 3,333 secondary schools and 16,971 primary schools we find community, foundation, trust, voluntary-aided, and voluntary controlled institutions; add to these the state-funded 'independents', directly funded by central government, the academies, City Technology Colleges, and soon, the free schools.[2] By the end of Labour's term of office, there were 203 academies. The new 'conversion academies' have brought that number up to 600 within a year, with hundreds and possibly thousands more, including many primaries, predicted to convert over the next few years.

Politicians like to pretend that parents choose schools; most education experts would agree that, on the whole, schools choose pupils. Despite being officially phased out over forty-five years ago, selection still defines and moulds our education system. Every piece of legislation over the past twenty-five years has resulted in more, rather than less, selection, covert or overt, including the Academies Act of 2010. Academic selection has been compounded by social selection, and, increasingly, selection on grounds of faith. The eleven-plus may have been abolished in most parts of the country but schools still find multiple ways to filter applicants, manage their intake and develop niche identities. Not for nothing has *intake*— the word that most troubled the PASS parents—become one of the most significant terms in the educational lexicon.

So how does the pyramid of provision take shape? At the top, private schools select firstly by parental wealth and then by entrance tests of varying rigour, thus creaming off up to 7 per cent of the country's most affluent children; the figure is much higher in certain areas, such as wealthy city boroughs. The country's remaining 164 grammars retain use of the eleven-plus. Selection still operates in 36 of the 152 English local authorities; 15 operate a fully selective system, and 21 have varying numbers of grammar schools.

Like a stone thrown into a pool, academic selection has a significant ripple effect. Thousands of children are rejected by grammar schools every year, an experience that can leave a lifelong mark on their self-confidence. The 'creaming off' of the most accomplished pupils by grammar schools has a knock-on effect on surrounding schools; it has been estimated that 500 schools are affected in this way. Then, in selective areas, some other schools still partially select on grounds of ability.

And while the number of grammars has remained steady over the past few decades, the number of children educated at grammar schools increased by almost 30,000 between 1997 and 2007, and the overall percentage of pupils in selective schools grew from 4.2 to 4.7 per cent during this same period—rising to 4.9 per cent in 2009.[3] In Northern Ireland, falling pupil rolls have meant that grammar schools, while defying government demands that they become non-selective, have filled up their places with pupils from a wide range of ability, making them in effect all-ability intakes, causing some to question why they need to remain selective at all.[4] Yet Northern Ireland's grammar schools continue to test ten- and eleven-year-olds in a process that many other school leaders have called an 'annual charade'. In May 2011, the Catholic Principals Association, which claims to represent the majority of Catholic primary and secondary schools, criticised grammar schools for continuing to select their pupils; it said they should not 'pick and choose' students, but embrace a genuinely inclusive system.[5]

In general, grammars have increasingly become the preserve of the better-off, with intensive tutoring for the eleven-plus. According to an article in the *Observer*, 'competition is now so fierce that children often need to score in excess of 90% in entrance exams to have any chance of winning a place. In the most extreme cases, 20 children or more are battling for each place—and increasingly, private tuition is seen as the difference between a pass and a fail.'[6] There is now a thriving tuition industry in parts of the country where grammars still exist. Parents are prepared to spend thousands of pounds on private tutoring, and primary-age children spend hours each day going over practice questions and exam papers. One newspaper feature on the private coaching industry opened with the journalist accompanying a Year 6 child to her lesson, beginning at five a.m. It has been reported that Buckinghamshire local authority has not yet published an educational psychologist's report it commissioned into the impact of coaching, because it fears challenge to selection on the grounds that unless every child has access to the same private tuition, it is impossible to judge the test results fairly.

There is now clear and consistent evidence that grammar schools educate very few children from poor homes. According to the most recent figures, only 0.6 per cent of pupils known to be eligible for and claiming free school meals, and only 2.3 per cent of children of black ethnicity, were attending grammar schools in Year 7 in 2010.[7] In a considered speech in 2007, David Willetts (then Tory front-bench spokesman on education and employment) bravely broke with his party's consensus view that grammars promote social mobility, concluding that

> the evidence is overwhelming. Children from poorer families are more likely than average to end up at their local school if it is very bad, and less likely to end up there if it is very good ... research shows poor children are half as likely to go to good academic schools as other children ... giving schools powers over their own admissions has not spread opportunity either. We have to do better ... *We must break free from the belief that academic selection is any longer the way to transform the life chances of bright poor kids* [my italics]. This is a widespread belief, but we just have to recognise that there is overwhelming evidence that such academic selection entrenches advantage, it does not spread it.[8]

Willetts's speech remains a seminal moment in the political history of UK education. When David Cameron publicly defended

Willetts, the resultant storm became known as Cameron's 'Clause Four' moment.

Of course, the vast majority of children in selective areas are educated in secondary moderns. Despite the outstanding work that many of these schools do, a fair number qualified for the last government's National Challenge programme, which aimed to lift the results of low-performing schools; others have been converted into academies, in an attempt to give them a new identity and a fresh start. But, of course, all this structural tinkering completely failed to address the fundamental problem, which is that they are part of an institutionally divided system.

Becky Mathews, a veteran parent campaigner against the eleven-plus in Kent, has lobbied successive prime ministers on this issue and states the problem succinctly.

> If you are a child in Kent, you will be labelled by a test at ten years old, you will be educated in a school exclusively populated by middle-class prosperous children, or you will be educated in a school populated by children who have failed, probably with a disproportionate number of Special Educational Needs students and emotional and behavioural difficulties, with little or no sixth form and second-rate facilities. These outcomes are largely determined by social class.[9]

Beyond the overtly selective schools, different methods are used to 'top up' pupil numbers with motivated and high-achieving pupils. Any school with a specialism can select 10 per cent of their schools by aptitude; experts agree that the difference between aptitude and ability is almost impossible to identify. However, if a school can attract a key percentage of high-attaining, ambitious students, it can make the difference between success and stasis, or worse. Other schools use opaque admissions procedures to 'cream-skim' pupils and maximise league table results. Among the biggest offenders are some voluntary-aided (church) schools which often use absurdly complex admission criteria, and favour parents who can undertake regular activities to support the church.

Ensuring fair admissions, however, is rather like solving an endlessly recurring series of minor crimes; it takes persistence and a fair degree of inside knowledge to work out whether a school is sticking to the letter or the spirit of its admissions policies. While researching this book, I asked parents, teachers and other school leaders to pass on common admissions tricks they had observed. These included: branding the school in a way that can actively discourage certain kinds of families from applying (the West London Free School's trumpeting of Latin as a core subject would be a good example of this); filling up 'lower-ability' bands with siblings of students whom you have to admit anyway, which means you can gather a fresh crop of 'higher-ability' students from a wider pool; selectively picking the right sort of family and pupil from the waiting list; bringing in talented students in the years above Year 7 (often including transfers from private schools: so-called sector shifters); selectively promoting the school in certain areas by means of leafleting; prioritising attendance at one particular church; and holding banding tests on school premises, perhaps on a Saturday morning—which inevitably attracts the more motivated families—rather than holding the tests in local primary schools, which would inevitably include all children eligible for a school place. Some schools practise 'ghosting', where parents of troublesome children are quietly persuaded to leave.

All schools where the governing body is the admissions authority, which includes voluntary-aided, foundation, and now academies and free schools, are given the right to draw their own catchment area, enabling them, should they wish, to include more affluent areas and exclude residential pockets of deprivation. The PASS group were very critical of the way that the new Hammersmith Academy in their area had drawn its proposed catchment area around all the smart middle-class wards that surround it, as if deliberately excluding the local poor. One mother said, 'Their Open evenings were held at the highly desirable St Paul's girls school and the Lyric Theatre—it was clear who they were hoping to attract.'

*　　*　　*

The overall effect of this cumulative selection is twofold. It forces the label of 'comprehensive' on many schools that are, to all intents and purposes, secondary moderns, and impedes the development of honest public discussion about how to achieve a more equal system. In human terms, the main losers in this highly segregated pyramid are poor pupils. Barnardo's, the children's charity, point to a Sutton Trust report that shows that Britain's top-performing secondary schools take on average only 5 per cent of pupils entitled to free school meals, while half of all children on free school meals are concentrated in just a quarter of our schools. Barnardo's also found 'clear evidence' that schools which control their own admissions, such as faith schools, are more socially selective than those that do not. Further, 'middle-class parents tend to be strongly engaged in getting the best results from the admissions process— even to the extent of moving house', while disadvantaged parents are less likely to exercise their right to choose and more likely to simply opt for their local school.[10] So often, when politicians or commentators talk about a 'failing' school, they are referring to a school that caters for the poorest children in the community.

Taking high numbers of children on free school meals or from disrupted, occasionally disruptive, family backgrounds does not have to mean failure, but it requires tremendous focussed effort, and sustained funding, to create the conditions in which learning becomes possible. Lilian Baylis Technology School in Kennington, South London, became famous in 2003 when Tory politician Oliver Letwin, a local resident, said he would 'rather beg in the streets' than send his child there. Soon after Letwin's unhelpful intervention, a new, lively young educator, Gary Phillips, took over as head and results began to climb. Ofsted now judges the school to be 'good with outstanding features', and yet it is, inevitably, shaped by the social, economic and ethnic divisions of the inner city that surrounds it—where, according to Ofsted, many of the children live in 'challenging circumstances that include frequent interrupted periods of schooling'. Lilian Baylis students are some of the poorest in the country. In 2010, 74 per cent of the students were on free school meals, compared to around 14.5 per cent nationally. Over 85 per cent of its pupils were from minority ethnic groups, and over 50 per cent had a first language believed not to be English, compared to 11.4 per cent nationally; 42.5 per cent had Special Educational Needs—the figure is 21.1 per cent nationally. Eight per cent of students were statemented, that is, equipped with an official local authority declaration of special needs, ranging from attention deficit disorder to depression. The number of children nationally with a statement is only 2.5 per cent.

Lilian Baylis is thriving under the dynamic leadership of Gary Phillips. But in general, schools with such a high percentage of children with often intractable problems in their home lives have difficulty attracting, and retaining, the best teachers; they have greater discipline problems and tend to put far greater emphasis on vocational studies, confirming class stereotypes and diminishing poor children's access to a genuinely broad and balanced curriculum. Conversely, schools with lower proportions of poor children and/or a high-attaining intake find it easy to attract good teachers, discipline is less of an issue, and the school is in a good position to raise its results and create that most prized phenomenon: a positive ethos.

All of this adds up to poorer results for poorer children. While over half of the nation's students get five 'good' GCSEs, including maths and English, only 27 per cent of young people on free school meals do. Results from the 2009 Programme for International Student Assessment (PISA) showed that in the UK, the gap between the reading abilities of our quickest and slowest learners is wider than average. Most of the differences in results between schools is explained by differences in the socio-economic background of students in these schools; in short, we operate a kind of educational apartheid. Among OECD countries, only Luxembourg has a bigger gap. Clearly, our overall performance is pulled down by the degree of segregation and inequality we have in our school system.

These subtle forms of selection and exclusion inevitably shape patterns of university access. Michelle Obama's visit to Oxford in spring 2011, with a group of girls from the Elizabeth Garrett

Anderson school in Islington, during which she urged each of them to aspire to a top university, may have inspired many; but it also created the false impression that any clever child from an inner-city school could make it to an elite university if only she—or he—had enough determination. Fewer poor children go to university, and the more prestigious the university, the fewer poor children you will find there. Teenagers from the 20 per cent most advantaged homes in England are seven times more likely to get a place at the most selective universities than those from the poorest 40 per cent. The gulf has widened over the last fifteen years, when the richest were six times more likely to get a place in the top third of universities, despite Oxford, Cambridge and other leading institutions spending, on average, £45 million each year on improving access.

And this is often not for lack of exam achievement. According to the Office for Fair Access, 4,000 pupils decide not to apply for top universities despite achieving high enough grades. Thousands of others are disadvantaged because their schools do not offer the subjects that elite universities want, such as modern foreign languages or single sciences, the review says.[11] Universities have, until very recently, kept to themselves which A-level subjects they prefer or reject, further disadvantaging those not 'in the know'.

Polly Toynbee is right. 'Oxbridge admissions are the inevitable end result of the nation's growing social rigidity, not the cause.'[12] Roughly 40 per cent of Oxbridge students come from private schools. The breakdown of household income for 2009–10 shows that nearly 73 per cent of Oxford's intake in that year were students from households with an income above £50,000. The proportion of university entrants going to Oxbridge from the top-performing thirty independent schools is nearly twice that of the top-performing thirty grammar schools, despite having very similar average A-level scores.[13]

But with universities like Oxford and Cambridge under political and financial pressure to make more offers to students from poorer backgrounds, the pendulum looks set to swing back and forth on this issue. There was a mini media maelstrom in late 2010 when it was revealed that twenty-one Oxford colleges took no black students at all. Six months later, the university announced with barely disguised glee that it was on course to have its highest numbers of state school entrants ever, with state school pupils receiving 58.5 per cent of offers, after record numbers of applications from them. David Cameron did not help matters by mistakenly claiming that only one black student was admitted to Oxford in 2009, based on figures concerning a lone 'black Caribbean'. In fact there were twenty-seven black undergraduates at Oxford in 2009—hardly a cause for pride.[14] There was widespread disbelief when it was revealed in spring 2011 that the Coalition was exploring the possibility of allowing extra places for UK undergraduates who could pay their tuition fees up front, particularly when ministers then spoke of how such a move could be achieved in a 'socially progressive' manner.[15]

The issue of selection goes to the heart of two vitally important issues in contemporary society. The first is relatively straightforward: how much do we want children of different religious backgrounds to be educated separately? The creation of separate schools for separate faiths has been confirmed by the free school programme, which amounts to a virtual open-ended offer to religious groups to attempt to secure state funding for their own schools. The British Humanist Association has spoken out against the risks of permanently entrenching religious segregation in the school system. The new religious academies will be able to discriminate against children and staff on religious grounds, excluding those of the 'wrong' religion or none. In the current climate it is unlikely that faith schools will ever become more inclusive, and they could expose children to extreme religious views, including creationism.

But selection is also at the heart of the crucial link between schools and social class. For decades, the most common line of attack against comprehensive education has been that it has contributed to the slowing down of social mobility. By abolishing grammars, talented children from less well-off backgrounds were never given the chance to get a good education and so compete against the privately educated.

The debate was reignited by a 2005 Sutton Trust report, which argued that 'children born to poor families are now less likely to break free of their background and fulfil their potential than they were in the past.' Comparing two boys born in 1958 who left school in the 1970s (tracked in the National Child Development Survey), one of whose parents earned twice as much as the other, they found that by their early thirties, the richer boy earned on average 17.5 per cent more than his poorer friend. For two boys born in 1970, who left school in the 1980s (tracked by the 1970 British Cohort study), the advantage of the richer son leapt to 25 per cent. The study also showed that while Britain has mobility levels similar to the United States, it rates well below Canada, Germany and the Nordic countries, although the US seems to have fared somewhat better, despite having similar rising levels of inequality. It also found that the relationship between family income and children's higher education attainment had grown stronger between cohorts completing their education in the 1970s and those doing so in the late 1990s, and that 'the expansion in higher education in Britain has benefited those from richer backgrounds far more than poorer young people.'[16]

Commentators jumped on these 'findings' with relish. 'Long live the grammar schools', was the *Observer* headline. The *Sunday Times* argued that 'the abolition of most grammar schools kicked away the ladder for children from poorer backgrounds', while Tim Luckhurst in the *Times* suggested that 'only a blend of ideological zeal and intellectual dishonesty could now defend the comprehensive system.'[17] These sorts of argument seeped, unchallenged, into the mainstream, where they have lingered like an unpleasant smell; a typical report by the *Wall Street Journal Europe*, on a speech by Ed Miliband in early 2011, was introduced in the following way: 'Britain has dreadful social mobility problems, and the situation is getting worse. Education is at the heart of the problem.'[18]

However, few reported on the wider findings of the LSE–Sutton report, or on subsequent academic challenges to its methodology.

There was no mention of the fact that the countries with the *highest* levels of social mobility, the Nordic countries and Canada, all have well-established systems of comprehensive education. Little mention was made of the report authors' own admission that education was not, nor could it be, the main engine of social change; major upheavals in the economy and intensifying inequalities in society in general were just as likely to have contributed to lower levels of mobility. Whereas in the 1950s, most of the UK population were in what would be defined as working-class occupations, by the 1970s most people were working in service and other white-collar sectors. Most of the shift 'upwards' would have happened within the time frame of the earlier cohorts, rather than of those born in 1970, who faced the subsequent decline in economic opportunity and the entrenchment and widening of inequalities. In other words, a working-class boy born in 1958 might have been able to ascend to a managerial or supervisory post within a manufacturing context, whereas a boy born in 1970 would have entered a workforce where educational qualifications were more highly prized.

The report focussed on the changing economic and professional fortunes of fathers and sons. But of course, from the 1970s onwards, the daughters of the middle class were beginning to enter higher education and employment. By the 1990s women had begun to enter the job market in large numbers and to occupy service positions which previously would have been restricted to men, or that might once have given working-class men opportunities that were now granted to educated women.

The original survey also fixed on the *birth* dates of the two cohorts. But a child born in 1958 was obviously not educated in 1958. He or she would not enter secondary school until 1969; by this time, large sections of the country were operating a comprehensive system. The report also pointed out that the educational and employment opportunities of a third and later cohort, born in the 1990s, are proving 'more mixed'. Here the economic/mobility picture is a rosier one, which, again, rather detracts from the idea of comprehensive-school failure.

It is interesting to reread the Sutton Trust report and see what they recommended in terms of government action. Restore the grammars? Dissolve the comprehensives? Not exactly. 'Policies to raise intergenerational mobility also need to focus on raising children's attainment through targeted services ... such as early years education, improved schools for poor communities and steps to promote participation in post-compulsory education [such as] Sure Start ... and the Educational Maintenance Allowance.'[19] Both of these programmes have been cut back since May 2010. The report also concluded that 'the results provided consistent evidence of a significant causal impact of family income on educational attainment.'

Yet the same old storyline about the tragic decline of the grammars marches on, as in the recent television documentary by a *Sunday Times* editor, Andrew Neil's *Posh and Posher: Why Public School Boys Still Run Britain*. The promising title suggested that the programme might take a critical look at the privately educated elite. Instead we watched a rather mournful Neil wandering around the corridors of power, searching for talented poor kids like himself who would have had no chance of the glittering success they now enjoyed if they had been born into today's world. There was an odd, short sequence unfavourably contrasting the sixth form of Neil's old school Paisley Grammar, now a comprehensive, with the current sixth form of Westminster public school, but giving us very little hard data on how the former compares with the latter in terms of A-level success or university admissions. And no mention was made of the number of senior political figures today, such as William Hague or Ed Miliband, who were educated at comprehensives.

It would probably have made no difference to Andrew Neil— but a month after his film was broadcast, a major survey on social mobility was published, analysing data from the National Child Development Survey, which tracks all children born in Britain in a particular week in 1958. Some of these children were among the first comprehensive-school pupils, during the transition away from a selective system. Unlike previous researchers, Vikki Boliver and

Adam Swift not only compared the social mobility of children who attended comprehensives with those from grammar schools, but also included secondary modern schools in their analysis. They looked at children from all social backgrounds, rather than just those from working-class or low-income families, and they compared children of similar measured ability at age eleven.

The study looked at the children's subsequent progress in terms of income and class, and found that overall the selective schools gave no advantage in social mobility. Going to a grammar school rather than a comprehensive did not make children from poorer backgrounds more likely to succeed. Lead author Dr Vikki Boliver explained: 'Whereas much media discussion focuses exclusively on grammar-school pupils, with many bemoaning the introduction of the comprehensive school as depriving academically able children of a crucial ladder of opportunity, our analysis provides a more rounded approach.' Dr Adam Swift added, 'We must compare school systems, not merely individual types of school within them. Looking at the full picture rather than at grammar schools alone, we find little to support the idea that comprehensive schools had a negative effect on their pupils' mobility chances.'[20]

Anti-comprehensive campaigners have traditionally justified selection on the grounds that grammars, which select on ability, are fairer than 'selection by postcode', which means that a child born in a poorer neighbourhood is likely to go to a poorer school, whatever their ability. It is a fair point, and one often raised in Scotland, where catchment areas and effective residential segregation overdetermine school choice and have created, in the view of some, a three-tier system: the independent sector, the aspirational comprehensive sector located in wealthier areas, and the struggling comprehensive sector located in deprived areas. The problem here, as in England, is not so much 'poor schools' but the corrosive, and cyclical, effect of poverty and poverty of aspiration, problems that need concentrated political solutions and resources, some of which I discuss in the final chapter.

But if we seriously ask how to break free of this ingrained connection between selection and segregation, the answer is not more academic or social selection. Despite the existence of serious social segregation, Scotland still has higher levels of attainment and participation by working-class youngsters, who 'consistently outperformed their English peers'.[21] The international evidence is equally clear: whether it's Finland or South Korea or the province of Alberta in Canada, genuinely non-selective education systems routinely top the world league tables. The best school systems are the most equitable, in other words students do well *regardless* of their socio-economic background. Conversely, schools that select students based on ability at an early age show the greatest difference in performance according to a child's socio-economic background.

In some ways, we are at a potentially fruitful political moment. High-performing voluntary-aided faith schools and some of the new academies are paying a backhanded tribute to the comprehensive principle: they recognise the importance of a genuine academic, and social, mix to the success of many schools. Most politicians, including many on the traditional right, now accept that genuinely comprehensive schools are not only desirable on grounds of natural justice, as well as political expediency, but also have been seen to work, whenever the right conditions are in place.

Surely the next step should be to initiate a widespread debate on how we might consolidate this excellence on a broader basis. What conditions would have to be in place for that to happen? How might it work, area by area? How could we overcome the problems posed by yawning social and economic divides in our big cities and towns? These are the real questions that face us, yet nowhere are they honestly addressed—certainly not in mainstream political debate, where politicians and other leaders would rather tiptoe carefully around difficult truths and hard choices.

There are exceptions. When the Bishop of Oxford, John Pritchard, chair of the Church of England's Board of Education, frankly suggested that church schools should return to their original mission to educate all the community and so take only 10 per cent of Anglicans within every school, he faced a hail of criticism.[22] Comprehensive campaigners have put forward some very positive ideas on how to phase out selection with minimum disruption to the education of all children.[23] These have yet to be taken up by any of the mainstream parties.

In the meantime there has been a long, rolling debate within the comprehensive movement about how to resolve the difficulties posed by a non-selective system in a deeply unequal society—not to mention a society shaped by consumer power, where people feel it is their right, if not their duty, to exercise choice over every aspect of their lives. (There would clearly be a great deal less anxiety among parents, and vastly improved schools, if choice were a less prominent aspect of our education system.) It is important to keep the link between schooling and local neighbourhoods, particularly for families that may need to draw on additional services, from early years care, to parenting advice and support, to homework clubs after school, and so on. At the same time, cementing this link between school and neighbourhood can risk trapping children in environments with depressed expectations. Some schools can reinforce isolationism and cultural poverty. A Teach First graduate, sent to a school on the outskirts of a major city which served only the surrounding estate, told me how he found pupils who were 'culturally and economically isolated ... it felt as if the school belonged to the estate and others would never pass through it.' When he took his class on a trip to the centre of the city, 'some of the pupils had never been on a train before'. The writer Lynsey Hanley, who grew up on an estate on the edge of Birmingham and went to a school that essentially served the estate, has called the effect on her and others as 'the Wall in the Head'. Used to being considered a geek at her local school, it was not until she went to sixth-form college that she began to experience the clash of identities and opinions and range of classmates that her circumscribed school experience had denied her.[24]

But if the word most often used by campaigners for fair admissions is 'balance', closer scrutiny of this concept again exposes some real problems. What do we really mean by, or want from, a 'balanced' intake? We know it when we see it, but do we know how to achieve it, and how it can be secured in every school? Obviously, the idea of 'balance' refers either to the social composition of pupils within a school or to the distribution of children by so-called ability, a quite different measure. For some parents, the former is as important as the latter, which explains the popularity of some schools where exam results are relatively poor but the social mix is good: in other words, parents often seek a favourable peer group as much as they seek a good school, recognising, or at least fearing, the effect of poverty on their own children's expectations and effort.

Theoretically, there are good arguments for having both kinds of balance. Children from all backgrounds gain knowledge and understanding of the wider world in which they live, through daily contact with those who are different from themselves. Having a 'critical mass' of children whose parents care about education and are involved in their children's learning helps a school to develop an ethos of aspiration and achievement for all. Similar arguments apply to having a mix of attainment in the school. High-attaining and highly motivated students raise the game of the rest; schools do not have to struggle with such large numbers of pupils who find learning difficult.

But can schools really aim to have a social balance? Filling a school is not like throwing a party, although listening to some admissions tutors at private schools, their deliberations did remind one of a party hostess trying to set up the most interesting mix possible. But private schools can accept or reject without having to account to anyone. State schools have an obligation to all children, not just the most attractive or intelligent or quirky.

It would be virtually impossible to engineer a good social blend in every school, even if such a thing were considered desirable. It makes greater sense to try for a mix of attainment, through banded entry to schools. Researchers, teachers and heads all confirm that such a mix is one of the most crucial elements in a successful school. Without a significant proportion of high achievers, its overall academic standards are likely to be depressed. However, in terms of arranging entry, this inevitably presupposes a judgement on each child's intellectual ability which risks reproducing, if in diluted form, the problems of the eleven-plus. It may be that this is an interim price worth paying; there is certainly nothing to stop schools operating mixed-ability teaching once their intake is agreed.[25]

Ultimately, such decisions need to be made on a local basis with collaboration between all schools in a given area, and the restoration of admission forums which could thrash out the complex details of local admissions and exclusions. It might be agreed, for instance, that every school in a given area should take roughly the same percentage of children on free school meals and that no school takes less than its fair share of 'difficult to teach' children. Occasionally, schemes like random allocation—also known as a school lottery—could be considered, to ensure a fair spread of pupils in every type of school. That scheme was introduced in Brighton in 2007, and while some feel it has been very successful, others say that the area in which a family lives is still very important for winning a school place. The Coalition Government's decision to abolish the existing school admissions forums was a retrograde step. So, too, is the decision to downgrade the power of the national school adjudicator.

Complex and convoluted as these deliberations might appear, they would certainly be no more difficult to sort out than the issue of school funding, which must also balance practicality with fairness. The current government is in the process of consulting on a new formula for budget distribution to schools. This assumes a general agreement that some areas, schools and pupils require more resources and greater help if they are to flourish. Why not presume on the same common sense regarding admissions, so that we can now take forward the important principle of non-selective education?

Chapter Five

Going Private

In the playground, a man resembling a US secret service agent, dressed in neat fitted jacket and wearing dark sunglasses, oversees playground duty as a mass of London teenagers, dressed in the school's trademark red-edged grey blazers, spend a chilly break in the autumn sunshine. From the outside, the low-lying blue and yellow building designed by the celebrated Richard Rogers partnership fulfils the architect's aim to fit discreetly into the surrounding urban landscape. Inside, the high atriums, impressive auditorium and light-filled classrooms make the building feel both softer and more dramatic.

Welcome to Mossbourne Community Academy, one of the country's most successful 'independent state schools', lavishly praised, and regularly visited, by politicians of all parties. Tony Blair heaps praise on the school in his autobiography *The Journey*, and when Arne Duncan, Barack Obama's education secretary, came to London last year on a flying visit, Michael Gove took him straight to Mossbourne, as this country's most shining example of the kind of privatised school that the Coalition would like to develop, in homage to America's US charter school movement.

I visited the school a few weeks before Arne Duncan made his much publicised stopover. As one of the country's most celebrated head teachers, Sir Michael Wilshaw is clearly used to visitors. He takes me briskly through key moments in his own career, each one neatly illustrating his personal disillusionment with elements of the 'old' local authority regime and his enthusiasm for the new privatised model, a zeal that has made him such a valuable asset to government ministers over the years. He tells me of a moment when as deputy head of a Catholic boys' school in Newham, he was unable to recruit the support of apathetic staff, and realised 'you're on your own ... you grow several skins.' The day that schools got their own budgets, under local management of schools, introduced in the late 1980s, is cited as another significant turning point. It meant he could promote people who were 'on side'. Interestingly, when he was still at Newham, Wilshaw invited Diane Abbott, the Labour MP who famously sent her own son to City of London private school, to come and see what he had done there, particularly in relation to the education of black boys. Abbott, who later had her doubts about academies, was nevertheless deeply impressed by the air of 'calm and order' Wilshaw created.

Ofsted reports on Mossbourne are consistently positive, praising the school's good discipline and culture of high aspirations and expectations. The teaching is rated good, often outstanding, and the school itself merits an 'exceptional' rating within the category of outstanding. Its exam success is stunning, for a school at the heart of one of the most deprived communities in the country. In 2010, 83 per cent of Mossbourne students achieved five A*–C grades, including English and maths, putting it in the top 1 per cent of secondary schools nationally, according to value-added measures. In the same year the school received ten offers from Cambridge, and fifty-five from Russell Group universities. On the school website Wilshaw declares: 'We expect a majority of our young people in the Sixth Form to enter Oxbridge and the Russell Group of universities. Nothing short of this will satisfy us.'

For Wilshaw, 'the previous failures of comprehensives was nothing to do with the kids, but the wrong structures and systems.' The key is high expectations, tighter structures, setting by subject ('mixed-ability teaching requires really experienced teachers'), not employing staff who are 'always looking at the clock' but instead the kind of teacher prepared to be a 'surrogate parent to lots of the kids', which includes providing meals to kids in the evening, home–school contracts and unstinting pastoral care. His approach—with the exception, perhaps, of his high expectations of staff in terms of time, and a certain 'can-do' attitude—is common in many inner-city comprehensives. Wilshaw is very much a Superhead. A few weeks after I meet him, he is quoted in the *TES* comparing school leaders like himself to lone heroes in a Clint Eastwood western.

> A head teacher is all about being the lone warrior, fighting for righteousness, fighting the good fight, as powerful as any chief executive. I'm not that bothered about distributed leadership; I would never use it; I don't think Clint would either. We need head teachers with ego. You see heads who don't use 'I' and use 'we' instead, but they should.[1]

Mossbourne was one of the earliest city academies introduced under New Labour, and opened in 2004. Wilshaw talks with evident personal and professional fondness of the school's original sponsor, Sir Clive Bourne, a businessman and philanthropist who named the school after his own father, Moss. Bourne used to visit the school weekly, even when he was very ill, right up until his death in 2007. One can easily imagine the two men strolling the corridors together, enjoying the sights and sounds of what they had built together. The school sponsor is now UPS parcels, part of Bourne's business empire.

Wilshaw would argue that city academy status, with all its supposed freedoms, is the key to Mossbourne's success. In fact, many of Mossbourne's achievements can be put down to three key elements, none of which are intrinsically bound up with privatisation. Firstly, it puts huge emphasis on testing, getting students exam-ready at all times—with clearly successful outcomes. Secondly, it has a tough discipline code that is evident to even a casual visitor. Uniform policy is strict; it is not unusual to see teachers chiding pupils for minor infractions of the code. A video on the school's website claims that such strict discipline helps children to better express themselves academically and artistically, and yet former staff and some children speak of a chilly atmosphere, and make not entirely jokey references to the 'prison camp'. Wilshaw is unapologetic, as he believes constant vigilance is needed in an area warped by gang culture, just seconds from a road dubbed 'murder mile' because of its multiple gangland shootings.

But the third and perhaps most important feature of the school's success is its genuinely comprehensive intake. Wilshaw is vehemently opposed to academic selection. He thinks grammar schools were a 'disaster'. But for the comprehensive model to work there has to be a genuine spread of students. Mossbourne operates a carefully banded entry system. The presence of higher-achieving students helps raise achievement for all. Wilshaw makes great play of Mossbourne being a Hackney school, taking from Hackney primary schools and radically improving the work of underperforming students. But it is that key concentration of higher-attaining students that makes all the difference.

Supporters of academies and privatisation like to tell a simple story: 'bad' local authority school closed down to make way for dazzlingly effective private academy. But the real story is not so simple. Hackney Downs, the local authority school that was on the same site but closed down several years before Mossbourne was built, had been seriously underfunded for a long period before its closure, its intake largely made up of very low achievers and children with special needs. In January 1995, 77 per cent of Hackney Downs pupils were eligible for free schools meals. The figure for Mossbourne in its opening year, 2004, was about half that; a high figure by national standards, but not in the Hackney context.[2]

As we have seen, private sponsorship was at the heart of Labour's academy project. The idea was to bring supposedly 'independent' energy and enterprise to the ailing parts of our school system, particularly in run-down inner-city areas neglected by government in the 1980s and early 90s. Some academy heads were glad to be shot of what they saw as incompetent, compromising local authorities; others were keen to work within a local neighbourhood context, to act in partnership, not to lord it over less well-resourced schools.[3]

Perhaps the ultimate irony of the academies was the small amount of money that private sponsors brought to the table. The academy programme was, in fact, a highly managed and supported kind of privatisation, in which central government handed over control of schools to enthusiastic industrialists or church bodies in exchange for relatively small amounts of capital, and in some cases—when the sponsorship money was not forthcoming—none at all. The programme also proved to be much more expensive than it was first thought. Initially, academies were projected to cost £10 million each, but the first twelve cost approximately £23 million each, and one, the Bexley Business academy, eventually cost just over £35 million.[4] Free schools are shaping up to be similarly expensive.

The political talk was all of innovation and freedom. The reality was, and continues to be, a significant decrease in local democratic control that might yet prove to be the privatisers' undoing. Conditions are determined by a separate funding agreement—known as the model funding agreement—between central government and individual schools, that ensures certain freedoms. Academies are not required to abide by national pay and conditions for teachers and support staff. Although some academies sign up to national agreements, others choose to negotiate their own pay and conditions, including higher pay for longer hours. Parental rights are also significantly diminished, with governing bodies largely appointed and controlled by the sponsor. Academies are their own admission authorities, granted the same freedoms as foundation schools and voluntary-aided schools to set their own admissions arrangements. Parents also have fewer avenues of complaint against school decisions, although schools are currently required to abide by the national admissions code. Academies have a greater say on the curriculum, the right to set a longer—or shorter—school day, freedom from local authority financial arrangements, school organisation proposals, and local authority intervention. Should the school not be satisfactory, the secretary of state has to intervene. The local authority has no power to increase, or decrease, the size of an academy or to propose its closure.

Academies also have a greater freedom to exclude troublesome children. Evidence published by the Local Schools Network in March 2011 showed that, on average, non-academy state secondary schools permanently exclude 1.7 students out of every 1,000 each year, whereas academies exclude 3.1 out of every 1,000—that is, 82 per cent more students. Some exclude far more. New Line Learning Academy in Kent permanently excluded 25 students in 2008. Other academies with high levels of permanent exclusion included Grace Academy in Solihull with 14, Harris Academy in Croydon with 15, and St Matthew Academy in Lewisham with 13. In general, academies exclude at twice the rate of maintained schools. This additional right can help a school to keep order, but it also means that another school and another set of teachers are always picking up the pieces.

There is a lie at the heart of the 'freedom from bureaucracy' narrative that has justified so much privatisation. Baroness Eaton, chair of the Local Government Association, is waspish about the role of the 'other' state in this process:

> Although much of the recent education debate has focused on 'freeing schools from local authority control' the real story is that as council control has steadily diminished, interference from the centre has massively increased. *In the last decade no fewer than 1,000 separate pieces of legislation affecting schools have been passed.* … head teachers and governors of maintained schools face an overwhelming burden of central regulation, with new governors expected to digest almost 5,000 pages of central guidance.[5]

Opponents of local democracy like to point to the history of local education authorities in places like Islington and Hackney, Walsall and Bradford, whose functions and responsibilities in relation to schools were taken over by private companies or learning trusts, although not always with any greater success.[6] Claims by the CBI among others that outsourced authorities outperformed the public sector have proved, on examination, to be flawed.[7] Little attention is paid to, let alone praise heaped on, the achievements of highly successful authorities from Hampshire to Tower Hamlets, which have developed and sustained first-rate and highly innovative schools, often in challenging circumstances. Imagine what they could have done with similar levels of investment to Mossbourne or some of the other academies.

The truth is, local authorities do—or have done up to now—an essential job. They plan for school demand, according to population developments; co-ordinate teacher training and professional development as well as manage pupil admissions and support services, and alternative provision for excluded children—although these powers were threatened under the 2011 Education Bill. Part of their job is to balance the interests of the whole population against powerful interest groups, a vital task in terms of education but not always a popular one, as became clear in the Kirklees free school campaign—one of the earliest and most well-known campaigns, publicly supported by David Cameron during the run-up to the election.

On the surface it looked like the crusade of local parents, frustrated by an uncaring bureaucratic council, but the real story was much more complex. The BBG Parents' Alliance wanted to convert a closing middle school into a 900-place secondary school, serving their cluster of villages: Birkenshaw, Birstall, East Bierley and Gomersall. With Serco, a private education provider, the parents put together a plan for the new school; but before the 2010 election, the plan was rejected by Kirklees Council, which refused to sell the group the site. But why? After extensive consultation, the council had drawn up an alternative plan for schooling in the local area, which involved closing down the middle school and sending children in the BBG cluster of villages to two comprehensives, a few miles away. A report commissioned by Ed Balls, then education secretary, from Professor David Woods, the National Challenge adviser, reveals how carefully Kirklees Council consulted and deliberated on its local school strategy in order to come up with a viable, area-wide plan involving several other schools. Were the Kirklees parents' plans for a 900-place trust school to go ahead, surplus places would be created in these other schools, putting their viability at risk. Woods declared himself 'impressed by the passion and determination of the parent group who are championing a relatively small school for their own very specific community', but made it clear that 'the proposals would have a negative impact on other schools in the area.'[8] Local heads, at both primary and secondary level, were against it. One head of an existing comprehensive told Woods she was disturbed that 'the concerns of one lobby group should be set against an extensive consultation process and the views of the majority of children and families.' Kirklees council was clear: the aim of its reorganisation was to end the 'parallel lives' lived by communities within Kirklees. Woods stressed that council plans would 'create schools which are more diverse in terms of ethnicity and socio-economic background [and] will help them tackle religious, social, racial and cultural division and meet the statutory duties to promote community cohesion and well-being.'

Take away the democratic elements of school planning and you are left with, on the one hand, a kind of widespread anarchy, where anyone with special determination, good contacts and influence, or a particular plan can push ahead, and, on the other, a series of mini-fiefdoms, controlled by powerful interests, who are permitted to run schools as they see fit. For all their flaws, local councillors, and many school governors, are elected. They can be removed, re-elected, or challenged at any time.

In 2007, I got a glimpse of how the privatised future would work when I investigated a competition, then taking place within the Tory local authority of Westminster, for a takeover of Pimlico school. Once an iconic comprehensive, it had suffered a familiar story for many schools in the last decade or so: staffing problems, underfunding, excessively harsh judgements from Ofsted and, in this case, a Tory local authority keen to get the school off its hands. Parents and staff were angry at the plans to turn the school into an academy. Only 4 per cent of those polled wanted this. This made no difference to Westminster Council, which put the school out to prospective bidders with the promise of millions of pounds in funding to effect a rebuild and total makeover. At first, the word was that Westminster (private) School would take it over. In the end, a charitable trust run by Tory donor John Nash, non-executive partner of Sovereign Capital and director of Futures— which already ran one London private school—won out in negotiations that many local critics believed to be unfair and insufficiently transparent.

I spoke at a meeting organised by Pimlico parents, desperate to retain their community school and its many fine traditions, not least an impressive music programme. But the writing was already on the wall; the parents were themselves divided on the way forward, and facing a formidable opponent. A struggling comprehensive school, proud of its diversity, is no match for a determined private organisation backed by a politically partial local authority, keen to offload all of its schools into private hands.

When I interviewed John Nash, at that time the potential sponsor of the new Pimlico, he talked about his 'passion for the underprivileged young' and his 'highly aspirational vision'.[9] He affirmed the key principles of the new school revolution: high expectations, if within a certain narrow framework, and strong emphasis on discipline. 'We will bring in role models from a similar background. There will also be strong emphasis on literacy and numeracy and a concentration on behaviour management. No one can learn if the school is not relatively calm.' He evoked the closeness of Pimlico to Westminster barracks and his ambition to set up an 'an army and police cadet programme'. Mair Garside, chair of governors of Pimlico from 2005-07, echoed my unease. 'He talks in depressing and patronising ways about wanting to help "deprived" children. It just doesn't sound like a comprehensive school.' Too late; Pimlico went private, at taxpayers' expense.

Pimlico appears to be run on very similar lines to Mossbourne. The last Ofsted report judged it 'outstanding', while parents and teachers within the school describe a regime of strict discipline and a harsh exclusion policy, that has permanently rid the school of persistent troublemakers. The school also has generous—even luxurious—resources. In the words of one Pimlico insider,

> there has been an extraordinary, a huge amount of money spent on this school, although none of us know where it came from. It's very, very hard to get information on the school, even when you work inside it. But there is always plenty of money for equipment, trips out, and there has been a doubling of senior management and a lot of ancillary support for those who need it, although we have been told recently that there will soon be cutbacks. There's a real pressure here to get your lessons rated good to outstanding—and not much tolerance if you don't manage it. The staff are quite isolated and work long hours. As for the students, there's definitely been a clampdown on creativity.

In December 2010, John Nash confirmed his place at the high table of the new educational establishment when he was invited to be one of four new non-executive members of the Department of Education board, in the company of Anthony Salz, executive vice-chairman of Rothschild, and Theodore Agnew, non-executive director of the Jubilee Managing Agency.

For the new school privatisers, efficiency is the new accountability. Whatever works: whatever it takes. Tony Blair was unequivocal. 'Today, of course, the results are clear: academies are improving three times faster than other schools.'[10] Actually, the evidence is much more ambiguous. By the end of New Labour's third term, it was clear that so-called independence did not have the magic effect of curing school failure that Blair et al. claimed. A report from the Centre for Economic Performance found that overall, academy results at GCSE rose by between 9.6 and 14.1 percentage points—but these improvements look less impressive when set against other poorly performing, matched state schools that did not become academies, where standards rose by about the same amount. 'Overall, these changes in GCSE performance in academies relative to matched schools are statistically indistinguishable from one another. The same pattern emerges if all state schools in the academy's local authority are used as the comparator group.'[11] Studies by Price Waterhouse Coopers have come to similar conclusions. A special Sutton Trust report on academies found that where results have significantly improved in academies, this might be down to a change in intake, although, as the Trust notes, it is remarkably difficult to get definitive evidence on the intake of these 'independent state' schools.[12]

There are serious questions about the genuine quality of results in academies, and the degree to which they use vocational equivalents to boost league table results. A study of 102 academies in the summer of 2010 found that 34 per cent had not a single pupil passing the English Baccalaureate; 43 per cent had only 1.5 per cent pass, and only 10 per cent had 10 per cent or more. In other words, only one in ten academies managed to get even one in ten of its pupils up to this new 'standard'.[13] A similar analysis published in the *TES* revealed that of the sixteen academies controlled, altogether, by Harris, Ark and Haberdashers' Aske's—three of the chains that Michael Gove claims to admire most—where GCSEs were sat last year, only three saw more than 6 per cent of its pupils achieve the E-Bacc. In three of the academies, no pupils at all met Mr Gove's standards. According to the *TES*, 'Figures show that other major academy chains also fared badly on the E-Bacc. Large discrepancies between E-Bacc scores and other, looser, GCSE benchmarks suggest widespread use of "equivalent" qualifications, dubbed "pseudo-vocational" by critics.'[14]

This heavy emphasis on the vocational was evident to me when I went to visit one of the new Manchester academies. Perched on the edge of a motorway, Manchester Enterprise Academy feels slightly marooned. There is a touch of the aircraft hangar about this white box of a building, doubly appropriate (or unfortunate) given that the school's chief sponsor is Manchester Airport. High-ceilinged, airy, with large expanses of bright block colour, this pleasant building is reminiscent in many ways of Mossbourne. The facilities are impressive, largely dispensing with corridors and square classrooms in favour of expansive atriums and open spaces. Classrooms are fitted with state-of-the-art equipment, including workshops for motor mechanics and hair and beauty studios. The school day starts at 7.30 a.m. with supervised breakfasts, free before 8.30 a.m.; there is a study club from 7.30 a.m. and also after school, from 3.20 to 5 p.m. The school is segregated by year groups rather than by subject; glass-walled staff offices ensure there are few parts of the building where children can't be overseen. Class sizes are small, fifteen to twenty on average, and the students seem busy and well supervised by the efficient staff.

The pupil population is overwhelmingly white and poor. I am introduced, by the deputy head, to two girls from the younger end of the school; we have a brief conversation about their favourite subject—English—and how both girls want to be lawyers. Do they know any lawyers? The girls shake their heads, too shy to talk much. Unemployment is high in Wythenshawe; of the girls' parents, only one has a job: a mother who works part-time. Later, the deputy head tells me that the average reading age of MEA parents is a frighteningly low nine years old.

What's quickly obvious about MEA is that this is, in effect, a beautifully refurbished, well-resourced and supported secondary modern, its educational goals shaped by corporate imperatives, its curriculum limited by the presumed nature of its intake, although there is no reason why this should be so. On the day that we visit, Year 9 students are working on a leisure and tourism project. In the sixth form the only language available is Spanish, business levels One and Two. MEA feels a world away even from a community school in the inner city, with its mix of families and wide-ranging offer of subject and extra-curricular activities.

The involvement of sponsors reinforces this image of a learning experience shaped by sponsor offers and sponsor demands: a captive future workforce. This is made abundantly clear on the website of the new sixth form, describing courses on offer in 2011–12 which amount to a list of sponsors—from Manchester Airport to Michael John Hairdressing—who clearly work closely with sixth-form pupils, offering work experience and placements. The pledge to students is clear. Referring to a set of qualifications currently being developed in partnership with the lead sponsor,

Manchester Airport, students are told: 'There is a possibility that this could lead to permanent future employment upon successful completion. Students are, therefore, encouraged to think about the "package" of qualifications on offer to ensure the widest window of opportunity awaits them when they leave us.'

But academies are only the tip of the iceberg in terms of the privatisation of state education. Stephen Ball of the Institute of Education, author of *Education Plc*, describes it as 'a ratchet process. Each Education Act has opened up something new— every circular has offered a new opportunity.' There have been 35 such moments since 1988—each one letting the private sector into state education. And the more private companies have moved in to the education market, the more the tendency is to consolidate. During the 1990s, there were 120 different companies involved in the inspection of schools. By 2003, that had dwindled to seven national contracts. And now there are only three—based in the three big regions. 'You can now hire companies that future-proof your school in a 15- or 30-day consultancy which a school buys in for a few thousands pounds. Or you can get the kind of package offered by Edison Schools UK which offers you a performance management system.'

'Privatisation' does not quite do justice to what Stephen Ball calls 'the enterprising' of the state itself; 'state-subsidised privati- sation' might be a better term for the way the relationship between private capital and central government has developed over the past decade and a half. For Ball,

> the selling of their retail services by the education businesses is linked to the New Labour project of 'transformation' through the re-modelling of schools, colleges and universities, the instilling of new management capacities and the arts of performance manage- ment, and the insertion of narratives of enterprise. This is not a simple story of economic determinism and the triumph of business interests. There is a complex inter-relation here between compa- nies and state.[15]

Politicians, of any political stripe, seem remarkably coy about the fast-growing role of the private sector in education. They prefer to talk in abstractions, rather than of profit. Perhaps they sense the instinctive unease of the average British citizen at the prospect of the language of business invading our classrooms, along the lines of a recent CBI publication entitled 'Fulfilling Potential: the business role in education'. Reading it, one can trace a direct line from James Callaghan's 1976 Ruskin speech, on the relationship between education and employability, to the first sentence of this publication, which proudly proclaims: 'Business is a major stakeholder in education'. Here, over thirty years later, is an extraordinary sense of presumption concerning the right of private enterprise to interfere at every level in our education system. Business has not merely a legitimate concern for schools and the job they do; schools and the job they do are now an integral part of business itself. The entire document is saturated with the familiar, deadening language and acronyms of the market: a lesson is not a lesson but an 'education input', creating a better school system becomes a question of 'system, scale and replicability', and good ideas put into action by inventive people become 'outcome-focused commissioning arrangements, rather than input-driven procurements'. Such arrangements will, of course, 'improve return on investment'.[16]

According to some estimates, the education market is worth over £100 billion.[17] Continuous outsourcing since the Thatcherite period means that business now largely does the job that was once done, in-house, by local authorities; no job is too large or too small not to attract a potential profit, be it photocopying, accountancy, building design, or continuous professional development.

A typical company working in this area is Amey, which markets itself as a leading public services provider. Amey employs more than 11,000 staff and works in more than 200 locations in the UK, in both the public and private sectors: aviation, central government, defence, local government, rail and strategic highways. Its website trumpets a range of education-related services including ten major education partnerships, and contracts for services ranging from school improvement and special educational needs to the delivery and management of new schools, encompassing cleaning, catering, janitorial, security and building and grounds maintenance. Its catering arm delivers healthy school meals. One of its biggest contracts is with Renfrewshire Council, 'as part of their overall educational commitment to provide secondary, primary and nursery education to over 7,000 children in ten brand-new schools'. Under a contract agreed in 2005, the company delivered four new schools—one primary and three secondary schools, and then a further five primary schools and one secondary. The company was also awarded the contract to provide Facilities Management to all schools within the council, incorporating the provision of cleaning, janitorial, catering, buildings maintenance, security, and grounds maintenance services. Catering for the schools is now being marketed to the pupils through a brand called 'Reload' which links up to local suppliers and uses fresh, local produce, ensures school meals are healthy and limits chips to once a week. So successful has Reload been that it is now being used by catering teams in schools in Northampton and Speke in Liverpool.

The company website makes no reference to Amey's ill-fated early involvement with the city academy programme. The company was the original sponsor of Unity City Academy in Middlesbrough in 2002, putting up the requisite £2 million which the government matched with no less than £25 million. Since opening in 2002, Unity struggled with poor results, staff and discipline issues. In 2005 the staff voted to strike over proposed job cuts and plans to make new teachers work early mornings, evenings and weekends. Ofsted inspectors in 2006 found that pupils made exceptionally poor progress between the ages of eleven and fourteen, with English and science results 'among the lowest in England'. In its first two years, it was criticised for expelling large numbers of disruptive pupils.[18]

Children from poor backgrounds scored particularly badly, and overall only 6 per cent of teenagers got at least five C grades at GCSE in subjects including English and maths. Inspectors were also critical of the academy's unusual buildings, designed with a series of open balconies, modelled, rather incredibly, on a Tuscan mountain village. 'The nature of the building, while impressive at first sight, means that some students do not feel safe or secure. The layout of corridors is confusing, and high, open balconies and stairwells are daunting.' Bullying was also 'a concern' for some pupils.[19]

By 2008, only 12 per cent of pupils were getting five good GCSEs, including English and maths, and press reports had it that the company was planning to pull out. Amey itself put an unconvincingly positive spin on their decision to withdraw, telling the *Daily Telegraph*: 'We have now seen four years of continuous improvements at the Academy. This is a fantastic achievement, and is a great testament to the hard work and commitment of UCA staff. We are now working with the Department for Children, Schools and Families to identify the best way forward.'[20] That way forward proved to be a rapid move towards the door marked Exit.

Pearson, owners of the *Financial Times* and the Penguin Group, is another fast-growing global brand in education. Its website quotes Alexander Pope, a Gove favourite: 'A little learning is a dangerous thing'. Luckily, it is also a vastly profitable one. Pearson Education is the rapidly expanding 'learning arm' of this multinational employer of 37,000 people based in more than sixty countries. According to Chief Executive Marjorie Scardino: 'Around a decade ago, we set out to make this a learning company. We can't stop at a little; there is so much more to do. Tens of millions of students still don't even have a chance to go to school.' Pearson provides educational materials, technologies, assessment and related services to teachers and students of all ages. In 2010 Pearson sold its 61 per cent stake in Interactive Data, a rival provider of financial information to Reuters and Bloomberg, and pledged to invest the $2 billion thus raised in education. In late April 2011, it announced that it had purchased Schoolnet, a company that analyses data from US educational institutions and uses it to improve the teaching of individual students. It also bought up educational businesses in Brazil and India; education now accounts for 74 per cent of its revenues and 81 per cent of its profits.[21] Pearson Education has contracts with five academies for textbooks, and for providing pupil assessments, teacher training and software to track pupils' academic progress and disciplinary records. It has also expressed a clear interest in helping to run the new free schools and academies—the latest boom area for business.

Probably the biggest trend in the edu-market is the growth of 'chains', organisations running groups of schools, often nation-wide, with sufficient resources to rival a local authority—a development that many believe will soon dominate the education landscape. Among the best-known names in this field are ARK, the Academies Enterprise Trust, E-ACT, the Harris Federation, the Oasis Trust, the Priory Federation, the United Learning Trust, and GEMS. Then there are the profit-making providers such as Cognita, the largest private operator of schools in the UK. Formed in 2004 by Chris Woodhead together with Englefield Capital LLP (renamed Bregal Capital LLP in 2010), Cognita spe-cialises in moderately priced private education. Its international schools division was created in October 2006. It currently has fifty-two schools (including nurseries, prep schools, primary and secondary schools), most of them in the UK, but with a growing profile in Europe and South-East Asia. It employs 3,500 teaching staff and delivers education to over 15,800 pupils.

In April 2011 Cognita came under fire from parents at one of its most successful schools, the Southbank International School in London. They accused Cognita of turning the London school into a 'money-making machine'. A letter from some disgruntled parents claimed that the company had 'no serious interest in max-imising the educational experience of ... children if it impacts on their bottom line'. Apparently, Cognita made £3 million in profit from the school in 2010, with 'almost 20% operating profits', had 'provided no added value to the school since they became owners' three years ago, and had 'cynically underpaid staff' before an inter-vention from parents last year. The letter circulated by the parent group adds: 'The reason for this aggressive milking of the school is to pay interest on debt and maximise profits for a sale of Cognita likely via an IPO in the stock market. They paid £22 million for the school, which had no real assets since the school buildings were all leased. In order to pay back this purchase debt, their strategy has been to aggressively raise fees and minimise investment in teachers and facilities.' The allegations came at an awkward time for the Coalition Government, which many believe is softening up public opinion in order to let profit-making companies come into the school market. Like almost every other company in this field, Cognita has expressed enthusiasm about working with emerging free school projects, but unless—or until—profit-making bodies are allowed into the free school market, it would have to set up a charitable wing to manage any such project.

One of the newcomers to the UK schools market, although not yet profit-making, is Kunskapsskolan (The Knowledge School), Sweden's 'largest secondary-education provider'. Founded in 1999 and operating thirty schools, the company now sponsors the Learning Schools Trust which has three academies, in Twickenham, Hampton and Ipswich; the company also provides development, management services and a special educational programme, based on its personalised learning approach, to other schools.

Kunskapsskolan is certainly different. Visitors to its schools in Sweden have commented that 'many pupils seem to be mostly hanging around'. They describe a relaxed atmosphere, devoid of the traditional rows of desks and chairs. Instead a large university-style lecture theatre acts as a hub, surrounded by smaller rooms where pupils work. In one room, a pair of students might be collaborating on a science project while a third works quietly on an essay in the corner. The Kunskapsskolan template offers a genuinely personalised education where pupils decide how best to tackle assignments, and are trusted to work on projects at home. Regular meetings with a personal tutor, who monitors their progress throughout their school career, keeps them on track. Students keep personal log books and are given individual targets to which they are accountable. According to

Anders Hultin, a Kunskapsskolan co-founder now heading its UK operation, 'Teachers are very important, but they are not the first priority of our schools. We don't say to teachers that if you are doing a good job then we are satisfied. It is about whether pupils are meeting their individual goals.'

ARK—Absolute Return for Kids—is probably the best known of the charitable chains. Sir Michael Wilshaw is one of its main advisers. ARK describes itself as an international 'philanthropic co-operative' children's charity, running education projects in southern Africa, India and Eastern Europe. At the time of writing, it runs eight academies on US charter school lines, and hopes to expand further. ARK's founders are both hedgefund chiefs: socialite billionaire Arpad Busson, of EIM, and Paul Marshall of Marshall Wace, one of the biggest hedge funds in the City. Marshall, estimated to be worth £100 million, is also described as an adviser to Nick Clegg.

According to someone who has worked closely with the organisation, ARK 'brings the defining, inevitably personal vision of its founders direct to the classroom'. Marshall said recently:

> As a committed Church of England Christian, I believe we are all made in God's image, that we all have gifts and that education is the key to realising our potential. My view is that state school provision failed at least two generations of disadvantaged children, but that Andrew Adonis [the former Labour schools minister] has set in train an exciting revolution through the academy programme that can make a difference.

ARK's mission is typical of the high-performing academies like Mossbourne. According to Marshall, 'if you set high expectations, robust discipline and focus relentlessly on literacy and numeracy, poor children can achieve as well as prosperous ones.' Marshall describes his group as having 'the most successful results in the country'. He also makes clear that he wants to expand. In ten years' time, he says, he wants to be running a chain of twenty secondaries and thirty primaries, all for less privileged kids. 'We will only do schools that help disadvantaged children.'[22]

School chains like ARK stress the importance of core subjects. 'A strong command of English and mathematics is a vital foundation for the whole curriculum. We prioritise depth before breadth, so that all pupils secure firm foundations in these core subjects as early as possible.' Marshall is also a leading member of a new tranche of school impresarios who bring business methods—and language—to solve social problems, via the likes of Teach First, KPMG (who run the Every Child a Chance scheme), the Private Equity Foundation or the Sutton Trust. Again, as an edu-industry insider observed, 'These groups—and individuals—are dedicated to finding the deserving, bright poor. Many of them were themselves self-made, so they believe children should be taught to be enterprising, and to make the system work for them.'

Some charitable trusts have proved a little less high-minded. E-ACT, established by Lord Bhatia's British Edutrust Foundation and formerly known as Edutrust, runs a chain of eleven academies, has four more in development and recently announced plans for major expansion. It, too, has shown interest in the expanding free school market. The home page of its website declares, 'we are consulting parents on plans to set up free schools'.

The Association of Teachers and Lecturers publication, 'England's Schools: Not open for business', describes how Lord Bhatia was forced to step down from the board in March 2009 after a government review found E-ACT had failed to comply with 'financial management requirements' and had 'inappropriate governance arrangements'. Most of the £70,000 misspend related to excess rent paid to the Ethnic Minority Foundation, of which Bhatia is co-founder and chair. E-ACT also failed to effectively address conflicts of interest, showed poor record-keeping and paid for items not 'properly chargeable to it'. After the review, Bhatia and BEF no longer had sponsorship control over the running of E-ACT academies, but BEF still raised funds on their behalf.

In April 2010, E-ACT whistleblowers revealed how the company's directors had claimed thousands of pounds of public money for luxury hotel rooms and long-distance taxi journeys; they also used chauffeur-driven limousines to visit academies around the country. The director general, Sir Bruce Liddington, was reputedly paid £265,000 a year, almost certainly the highest salary of any education executive in Britain. He claimed £1,436 on deluxe hotel suites for two nights for himself and a colleague. Another senior director was accused of repeatedly claiming £250 to take a taxi from Lincolnshire to his home in South Wales. As the ATL document points out, 'Almost all of E-ACT's funding came from Labour Government grants worth approximately £250 million.'

From the outset, the Coalition and its allies have looked to Sweden and America for inspiration and example. Early public discussion concentrated on the free school model in Sweden, but government enthusiasm for this became somewhat muted when no less a figure than the former head of Sweden's school inspectors claimed that free schools had not, in fact, improved Sweden's school results. The *Independent* reported on a study from the Centre for Economic Performance, by Sandra McNally and Helena Holmlund, which raised doubts about the model. 'The Tories have misrepresented the case for free schools by only quoting the good part of some very mixed evidence from the US and Sweden,' said McNally. 'There are serious issues around this. It might raise standards but I am concerned about social mobility. Will the pupil premium for disadvantaged children be large enough to attract people to want to run schools in poor areas? If not, non-free schools will have to pick up all the social problems, and they will also struggle to get teachers because they won't be able to pay as much as other schools.'[23]

A recent summary of all the available evidence on Swedish free schools suggests that they have had a moderately positive impact on academic performance at the end of ninth grade (the end of lower secondary school, ages fifteen to sixteen). But the greatest beneficiaries are children from highly educated families; the impact on children from families that are not already well educated, and immigrants, is close to zero. Further, the advantages that children educated in free schools have accrued by age sixteen do not translate into greater educational success in later life. Although there is some (weak) evidence that pupils in areas with many free schools are more likely to take an academic track in high school, they score no better in high school exit tests at the age of eighteen to nineteen. They are also no more likely to participate in higher education than those who were schooled in areas without free schools. A number of researchers have explored a variety of explanations for this, but conclude that the educational advantages of school competition are simply too small to persist into any long-term gains for young people.[24]

A more vivid picture of the impact of free schools was recently painted by ex-government minister Lena Sommestad, of Sweden's Social Democrat party. In Sweden, she said, free schools can employ unqualified staff, and they 'are set up to do just this'—a direct result, she hints, of government unhappiness with the framework for teachers' pay.

> Small schools that are not economically viable within the framework of national pay and conditions will get start-up costs, and public buildings and land, and then will sink or swim as a cottage industry for people who don't want their children to mix with children who aren't just like them. It licences parental choice on the basis of race, faith and particularly class, though no doubt the founders of all Free Schools will deny this until they have their hands on the money.

Before free schools were introduced, she says, it didn't matter what school you went to. They were all broadly similar and would achieve roughly the same results, and Sweden came top of many international league tables. But once the idea of choice was introduced, on the premise that this would increase effectiveness, the opposite happened. According to Sommestad,

> Many years on and there are now dramatic differences in the quality of the education offered in different schools, overall results are down, and Sweden's international ranking has been falling since 2003. The introduction of 'freedom' into our education system has meant that those with the financial resources to move into areas which have schools considered good, do so. Those without the

resources to move are left with the schools no one else wants. We are now seeing segregation in our schools, along lines of social class.[25]

More recently, attention has turned to the United States, with much praise lavished on the charter school prototype and in particular the Knowledge is Power Programme (KIPP). Paul Marshall of ARK talks openly of his admiration of the KIPP, claiming that 'we model ourselves on the American KIPP schools that have 80 per cent on free school meals and send 80 per cent to university'. Rachel Wolf of the New Schools Network has favourably compared charter schools to traditional public (state) schools, saying that whilst children in many ordinary public schools in America have absolutely 'no aspirations', the children in charter schools 'are convinced, absolutely convinced that they are going to college. It's amazing ... that for me is what it is all about. Why should children in deprived areas not have the same sort of choices that children from wealthier families have?' In America, political writers of all persuasions have been dazzled by the achievements of the charter school movement. The documentary film *Waiting for Superman*, made by Davis Guggenheim (director of the hugely successful environmental hit, *An Inconvenient Truth*), unashamedly proselytises for the new schools. *Waiting for Superman* received huge acclaim but also stringent criticism, both in the US and the UK, when it was released in 2010.[26]

Charter schools are privately run state schools, whose funds are often significantly bolstered by philanthropic and private sources. There are now around 5,000 charter schools in the States, educating well over a million and a half children, and 99 KIPP schools that educate 27,000 children. They have attracted powerful support from wealthy and influential people in the United States. Given the hostility to the teaching unions that characterises the modern charter school movement, it is fascinating to learn that the charter school experiment was begun by a leading member of the teachers' union, seeking ways to re-engage the disaffected and impoverished students whom he, and other teaching colleagues, felt were lost in large, impersonal neighbourhood schools. Albert Shanker was the president of the American Federation of Teachers from the mid 1970s to 1997. He had the idea in 1988 that a group of public-school teachers would ask their colleagues for permission to create a small school that would focus on the neediest students, those who had dropped out or were otherwise failed by their education. He wanted these schools to collaborate with public schools and help motivate disengaged students.

Five years later, Shanker had turned against the charter school idea after realising that for-profit organisations saw it as a chance to make money, and he began to warn against the politics of panaceas and privatisation. By the time Shanker wrote his final *New York Times* column shortly before his death in 1997, he appeared to be even more concerned at how what had been intended as a progressive initiative, to improve the public school system, could be turning into the means to destroy it. One of the key figures in the charter school movement in America, Michelle Ree—prominently featured in *Waiting for Superman*—gained her teaching experience working for Education Alternatives Incorporated, one of the earliest for-profit organisations. Today, charter schools are not seen as collaborators with American public schools but as direct rivals; the same situation is emerging here in the UK.

Charter schools are routinely presented as more successful than comparable public schools. Certainly, some individual schools do produce dazzling results, not always for the most obvious reasons. But overall, charter schools do not seem to have been such a success story. The biggest non-partisan analysis on how charter schools have worked in sixteen states across America, undertaken by Stanford University in 2009, presents an uneven picture. On average, charter schools perform no better than their state-run counterparts. Seventeen per cent of charter schools reported academic gains significantly above those of traditional public schools; 46 per cent showed no difference; 37 per cent were significantly worse. Black and Hispanic children, in particular, perform badly in comparison to their state-school counterparts.[27]

A study from Western Michigan University which looked at

60 KIPP schools, all across the US, found a number of worrying features Firstly, the high drop-out rate. About 15 per cent of students 'disappear' each year, and between Grades 6 and 8, KIPP participation dropped by an astonishing 30 per cent. The study also pointed out that while KIPP enrols large numbers of ethnic-minority and low-income students, it takes very few English language learners or children with disabilities. (Overall, KIPP schools take 11.5 per cent of English language learners, compared to 19.2 per cent in public schools, and 5.9 per cent of children with disabilities, compared to 12.1 per cent in public schools.) In the words of one commentator, KIPP's success, as many have long believed, is down to picking 'low-hanging fruit', the exceptionally motivated low-income students, who do very well if they stay the course. Just as traditional private schools siphon off the motivated wealthy, the new charter schools siphon off the motivated poor. One might expect the new free schools and 'conversion' academies to do something similar.

Secondly, the high attrition rates are probably a key explanation for KIPP's success in raising test scores. According to one *Washington Post* report, 'When KIPP tried to take over a regular public school—where the students are not self-selected, but are assigned to the school; and where students not only leave, but large numbers of students enter—KIPP abandoned the field after just two years. KIPP long ago realized that what we charge regular public schools with doing is far more difficult than what KIPP seeks to do.'[28]

Thirdly, KIPP schools, like charter schools, often receive far greater funding. According to the Western Michigan study, KIPP schools receive over $6,600 more per year per pupil than their mainstream counterparts. The study also revealed the extent to which private contributions top up state funding, something the schools, and the scheme itself, do not always care to mention. The Western Michigan research found that while none of the KIPP districts reported any private revenues in the national school district finance dataset, a separate analysis of these districts' tax forms for 2008 revealed substantial private contributions. Per-pupil contributions for the eleven KIPP districts that the researchers looked at came to over $5,500, much more than the $1000 to $1,500 additional per-pupil revenue KIPP estimates as necessary for their programme. In a couple of districts, schools received more than $10,000 per pupil in private revenues. When these were added to the (already inflated) public revenues, KIPP schools received, on average, nearly $18,500 per pupil in 2007–8.[29]

The problem is not that these semi-independent schools spend generous sums on the education of poor children, but that they claim superiority, in approach and method, to a state system that is educating far more challenging pupils on far less money, and then they suggest—as politicians and right-wing policymakers are increasingly arguing in the UK—that revenue is irrelevant to school performance and results.

Waiting for Superman focusses on the Harlem Children's Zone, run by Geoffrey Canada, another figure much praised in the US and the UK. Canada does not just run two charter schools in New York; he also operates a cradle-to-college support system of social and medical services, which ensures that any family or medical problems that threaten to disrupt a student's learning are taken care of by the school and associated services. The amount of money going into the Harlem Children's Zone is phenomenal, and almost certainly could not be replicated on a national scale; the organisation has assets of more than $200 million, and Canada's board is packed with wealthy trustees. Canada himself is paid $400,000 dollars a year. It is absurd for *Waiting for Superman* director Davis Guggenheim to compare what the HCZ is doing to the work of other New York City public schools, while affirming, once again, that money is not an issue in the education debate. Another school featured in *Waiting for Superman* was the SEED charter boarding school in Washington, which has high rates of graduation and college acceptance. SEED spends $35,000 dollars per student, while comparable public schools receive one third of that amount.

Even so, the schools in the HCZ do not always get spectacular results. In 2010 state tests, 60 per cent of the fourth-grade students in one of the charter schools were not proficient in reading; nor were 50 per cent in another. *Waiting for Superman* omits to mention that Geoffrey Canada expunged 'an entire first class of middle-school students when they didn't get good enough test scores to satisfy his board of trustees'. This sad event was documented by Paul Tough in his equally eulogistic account of Canada's Harlem Children's Zone, *Whatever It Takes* (2009).[30]

Charter and KIPP schools also raise important questions about the kind of schooling culture we are creating in the name of test success. KIPP advocates, and their supporters over here, point to the importance of a rigorous school culture, sometimes called the 'no excuses' approach. The school day is long, students have to sign draconian contracts promising to fulfill all the require-ments demanded of them, and the atmosphere is authoritarian. According to my LSN colleague Francis Gilbert, who investi-gated KIPP schools when the then Tory opposition first showed enthusiasm for the model,

> the evidence provided by inspectors suggests that pupils' experi-ences are mixed. KIPP schools are often authoritarian, demanding high levels of obedience, which is frequently manifested in the form of chants, songs, ritualised greetings and public humiliations. Much classroom time is conducted in silence, with pupils being shamed for the smallest of mistakes; in one account, a student was publicly reprimanded for missing out one full-stop in a piece of work. It appears that pupils are micro-managed to a prohibitive extent. One inspector reported: 'At 9.35am, the school leader says "KIPP one" and students respond, "Be one." She gives students seven seconds to put their morning work in their folder, close their folders, place their pencils on the side and put their name tags on.'

Josh Zoia, the founding principal of KIPP Academy Lynn in Boston, told Gilbert:

> At some point, everyone at my school has thought about quitting. It's tough here. Kids get up at 5.30am, start school at 7.30am and finish at 5pm or 6pm, and then have two or three hours of home-work. Then they go to bed. If I sat the kids down and asked them

who has ever wanted to quit, every single kid's hand would go up. The staff's, too!

As a consequence, teacher turnover is high.[31]

Is this a model that we in the UK seriously want to follow? In a competitive, choice-driven system, the predominant way to judge the success of schools, teachers and students seems to be by raw data. Concentration on quantity—high test scores—pushes out any consideration of quality. I have watched this dependence on data grow throughout my lifetime, from when I was at school to now, as a parent. The climate now verges on the obsessive concerning results, while there seems less concern with quality than ever before. Tests and exam results matter more and more, as the defining, but ultimately unreliable, guide to what constitutes an education. They matter to the anxious parent, who increasingly sees good grades as the passport to a brighter future. They matter to the child, who finds herself within a strait-jacket of peer comparison from nursery to sixth form. And they increasingly matter to schools, caught in a league-table war of attrition; the primaries hostage to their Key Stage 2 SATs, the secondaries to their GCSEs and A levels.

The results culture has intensified in tandem with the choice culture. To use Warwick Mansell's useful phrase, we have moved into a phase of 'hyper-accountability' whose effects can be seen everywhere: the obsessive press attention on results days every August; schools working relentlessly to drive up their A–C measures, working hard on the C borders or the 'key marginals' as they are rather amusingly known; the totting up of A stars; the long shelves of glossy revision books and bundles of practice papers in A4-size brown envelopes; the after-school tutoring; the new E-Bacc measure, driving virtually every hard-working school back to the bottom of the class.

And last but not least, the dreaded 'teaching to the test', the soulless reduction of subject knowledge to formulas and specifications, assessment criteria and acronyms. VCOP: vocabulary, connectives, openers and punctuation. When I was shown round Mossbourne, I noticed bits of card dangling from the ceiling in some of the classrooms, emphasising key pointers in subjects, clearly helpful to exam success. Michael Wilshaw demonstrated an impressive, if slightly alarming, knowledge of students' 'levels'. When we entered a classroom he would randomly choose a child, and say: 'So and So, you came to this school with level 3 English. What are you hoping to get in your key stage 3 tests?' 'Level Six, sir.' 'That's right. Level Six. Don't forget to use ambitious vocabulary. Good boy.'

Some parts of the UK have refused to follow this constricting model. Ten years ago, Wales chose to dump the whole testing/league-tables paraphernalia and to concentrate on learning instead. Results have risen in Wales, but not as fast as results in England; critics blame this on the country's comprehensive framework and the decision to reject testing. Wales has come in for some punishing criticism from the new education evangelists. But Leighton Andrews, the minister for education, is bullish in his support for comprehensives, and the deeper structural reasons for Wales's slow improvement. Wales, he says, spends about a thousand pounds less per pupil per year than England, and overall, Wales is a poorer country. He acknowledges that

> we need to do more. Welsh Labour wants to raise standards in our schools. We will introduce a national system for the grading of schools that will be operated by local authorities across Wales. All schools will be graded annually. We will introduce a national reading test which will be consistent across Wales, and will be designed to ensure that far fewer pupils are falling behind their designated reading age.[32]

At the same time, Andrews robustly defends the decision not to test their schoolchildren to educational death, and not to muck around with school structures. He comments wryly: 'We are perfectly happy to watch England be used as a laboratory experiment in education.'

*　　*　　*

The results conundrum brings us back to schools like Mossbourne and my old school Holland Park, nowadays another much vaunted example of the high-performance, tough-love culture. When writer Michele Hanson, once a music teacher there, went to visit the school, she noticed how staff must always 'be on their toes. They must "Check, monitor, assess, challenge student progress/performance by rigorous application of current results against predicted data". And "Middle Leaders: are you role-modelling teaching techniques ... and developing the skills of your team by monitoring and coaching best practice?"'[33]

The language may be deadly, but these developments have provoked a lot of discussion among parents and educators. Are these places appalling, soulless exam factories or are they common-sense, durable versions of the comprehensive vision for troubled modern times: tightly run ships focussing on exam success, particularly for those students whom it has eluded up to now? School leaders in the maintained sector generously acknowledge that it is possible to learn something from the Mossbourne model, such as the close attention paid to individual progress; excellent pastoral care and rigorous data monitoring, while retaining a more informal pedagogy, direct lines of accountability and a generally warmer atmosphere. This is the direction to go in. But it is not the official version. Given the current direction of English schooling, the strange marriage of privatisation and hyper-accountability, with all its pressures and restrictions, looks as though it is here to stay.

Chapter Six

The New School Ties

Approaching Wellington College by its grand, sweeping drive-way, one could be forgiven for thinking one had stumbled upon a vanished world. Set in four hundred acres of Berkshire countryside, the school, an imposing collection of roccoco-style buildings, has all the elegant grandeur of a vast, sprawling, stately home. Beyond the gorgeous pomp-and-circumstance facade, visitors move between facilities that could easily grace a five-star hotel—a large restaurant, an elegant conference suite, an outdoor pool, the latest sports and art facilities—and the restored remnants of the school's ancient past, including its elegant chapel and boarding houses, with their narrow staircases and dark hallways.

Designed as a monument to the Duke of Wellington, military hero and arch-opponent of parliamentary reform, Wellington College inevitably retains many of its links to the vanished world of empire and elites: the public schools of old, forensically dissected by writers such as Robert Graves, George Orwell and Graham Greene. So confident was Graham Greene of the demise of the English public school that in 1934 he announced: 'whatever the political changes in this country during the next few years, one thing surely is almost certain: the class distinctions will not remain unaltered and the public school, as it exists today, will disappear.'[1] The conservative educationalist Brian Cox once thought much the same. 'When in the early 1950s I was a young man I believed that British State education would get better and better, and that private schools would gradually wither away.'[2]

Eighty years after Greene's confident prediction and fifty years on from the idealistic hopes expressed by the young Cox, the system has not vanished at all; rather, it has been ingeniously reborn. If the English establishment's supreme talent is to adapt itself with understated charm to social upheaval and changing mores, while holding fast to a splendid array of privileges, Wellington and its thirteenth Master, Anthony Seldon, are perfect exemplars of both arts: leading players in a sector that has transformed itself in remarkable ways over the last decade. Today's private schools are very different places from their predecessors; shaped by modernity, the market and consumer demand, nowadays they pose more as engaged and diverse democrats than as superior, stern pedagogues. But never for one moment do they forget their unchanging purpose: to provide paying customers with an elite education.

A visit to Wellington puts the resources argument in relation to education firmly at the centre of the stage. Anyone who seriously argues that the state can do just as well for its children in, say, a suite of abandoned offices or a converted cinema (two examples of the regulation-light suggestion for school expansion trawled in a special consultation paper on schools development in October 2010), should spend a day at Wellington. With annual fees approaching £30,000, a year at the school costs more than the entire average UK salary of £25,000. The students here—currently just under a thousand—enjoy not only small classes but an astonishing array of sporting and extra-curricular opportunities. The school has sixteen rugby pitches, two floodlit astroturf pitches, a state-of-the-art sports hall, twenty-two hard tennis courts, twelve cricket pitches, an athletics track, two lacrosse pitches and six netball courts, a shooting range, a nationally acclaimed nine-hole golf course, six art studios, its own section on the Saatchi website (Wellington@Saatchi), its own theatre, that puts on at least one school production a term, open to the public, its own TV crew— filming Wellington set-piece occasions—a professional recording studio for aspiring musicians, and a number of concert venues.

Meeting Seldon in his large and elegant study, I am aware, suddenly, of an interesting intergenerational element to the school wars. Judging from his courteous but faintly weary air throughout our conversation, I suspect that he is, too. Seldon's parents were active members of the educational radical right. His father, Arthur, was a founder of the Institute of Economic Affairs in 1957, the right-wing think tank which laid the basis of so much of Margaret Thatcher's philosophy in government; his mother Marjorie was an early advocate of vouchers in education. Seldon dedicates his pamphlet on 'factory schooling' to her. Did Arthur and Marjorie Seldon at any point come across, clash with or curse those of their opponents such as my own parents, Tony and Caroline Benn, who were socialists and energetic advocates of the comprehensive ideal from the 1960s onwards? No explicit reference is made to these differing heritages during our exchanges, yet the entire conversation—that touches, inevitably, on the central question of the ways in which parents shape their children's values as well as life chances—feels suffused with the ghosts of battles past.

Under Seldon's astute stewardship, Wellington has risen from being a middling academic performer to join the first rank of public schools; it is also admired as innovative. There's no talk here of five A*–Cs; that's piffling stuff for the plebs. The college website records *only* the percentage of higher grades. In 2010, 93.2 per cent of its A levels were awarded at A* to B grade; at GCSE, students achieved 63 per cent A* to A grades. But even these measures are rather old hat. The school is proud of its International Baccalaureate and Middle Years Programme, an IB-style programme for younger years. In fact, during conversations with Wellington academic staff it becomes clear that they no longer consider A levels and GCSEs fit for purpose.

Later, I am shown an airy classroom dominated by an oval table, part of a school experiment in pioneering the Harkness approach, in which the teacher guides learning rather than lecturing to students. Wellington also emphasises what Seldon calls 'roundedness', or what the press liked to call 'happiness lessons' when first introduced, to much media fanfare, in 2006. Students are taught 'well-being' as part of the development of 'multiple intelligences', learning about the importance of deferred gratification, physical good health, empathy and flourishing and so on—although given the school's general sumptuousness, one suspects little gratification need *be* deferred here, nor flourishing become an overly onerous task.

This emotional education, Seldon has said in the past, helps the students to 'become themselves. What is a school if it isn't helping people find what they want to do? I don't just mean careers. I mean teaching how to sing, dance, paint, act, write poetry, play tennis, play the guitar. We'd be a better, more harmonious society if people had these interests developed when they were young. But they don't.'³ He reiterates this point to me in person, claiming that emphasis 'on more than the academic—on roundedness—has great appeal to Wellington parents, but of course we're all under great pressure to produce results,' he adds somewhat mournfully. 'It chokes the quality of what goes on in schools.'

Running a top school isn't enough for Seldon, a man of remarkable industry: the biographer of John Major and Tony Blair, and author of over thirty works of history and politics. Under his headship, Wellington has turned into a kind of rolling literary festival, conference centre and forum for contemporary— small-'c'—conservative political debate. On the day we visit, the school is hosting a conference of 'sixth-form leaders' from across the state and private sector; a group of seemingly overawed girls from a West London comprehensive mingle uncertainly with the self-assured representatives of England's premier public schools. Every summer, the school plays host to the the *Sunday Times* Festival of Education, drawing together many of the top players in politics and education.

When Eton College was founded in 1440 by Henry VI, it was to teach '70 poor and needy scholars' from Windsor. As Simon Jenkins comments caustically, 'To this end it was lavished with holy relics, pilgrimage rights and the freedom to pardon sins … Today Eton has almost 1,300 boys and if any are truly "poor and needy" it is because their parents must find fees of £26,490 a year. Its holy relics are its old boys, and the pardon it sells is privilege.'[4]

According to the Fleming Committee on public schools and the general educational system of 1944, the first recorded use of the term 'public school' appears in a document of 1180, probably referring to non-monastic establishments. By the late nineteenth century, it was taken to mean a school with a governing body run by a non-profit-making institution, as opposed to a school with a private proprietor. By the late 1960s, this distinction had lost its relevance as more schools were compelled to become non-profitable in order to gain tax benefits, and 'public school' came to denote membership of particular associations—in particular the prestigious Headmasters' Conference (HMC), which originated in 1869. (As of 1996 it goes by the snappy name of the Headmasters' and Headmistresses' Conference. Technically, it is the heads who are members, not the schools.) Scotland, incidentally, has never lost its clarity on this issue: north of the border, all fee-paying schools are known as private schools. In England meanwhile, the public/private schools have energetically rebranded themselves in recent times as 'independent' schools.

Over the last hundred years, a remarkably uniform 5–8 per cent of the school-age population have been enrolled in private schools of greatly variable quality. As the *TES* noted in its millennium edition, private education in 1900 was dominated by just 64 boys' schools, educating about 20,000 pupils, and a smaller number of girls' schools. By the 1930s, there were thousands of private schools, of varying sizes, educating approximately 300,000 pupils: 7 per cent of pupils in England and Wales by 1938. After World War II, this proportion declined, until 1979. It then rose again, as a result of demographic change and the introduction of the assisted places scheme in the 1980 Education Act and again in the 2000s. In the UK in 2011, the private sector has about 2,600 schools, educating 628,000 children.

The 1869 Endowed Schools Act proposed a three-tier stratification of the private sector: the boarding schools, largely teaching a classical curriculum and providing access to universities; the day schools, teaching Latin and Greek with a leaving age of sixteen; and the day schools teaching a little Latin to prepare students for employment at age fourteen. Then, as today, Latin played its symbolic part in denoting class status. Only the common study of Latin would allow for the possibility of social mobility, via scholarships, for exceptionally bright children. According to historian Gillian Sutherland, 'a central feature of that demand [of the middle and upper classes for formal schooling] was its increasingly sharp social differentiation ... those who wanted their sons to become gentlemen seemed at least as much interested in the capacity of the school to provide a degree of social segregation, as in any curriculum content.'[5]

For much of the twentieth century, the line between state and private schools was rather more blurred than it is today, especially given the lack of a truly national state system before World War II. Under a percentage grant system introduced in 1918, private schools had to admit a certain proportion of state elementary pupils free of charge—usually 25 per cent. In 1926, these schools were given the option of choosing between local and central government. Those which opted for the latter became direct grant schools, which were finally abolished by Labour in 1975. (At that time, direct grant schools were given the choice of entering the maintained sector or becoming fully independent, and about a third became state schools.) Meanwhile, those schools which stuck with local authority funding in 1926 were fully integrated into the state system (as grammars) under the tripartite arrangements of 1944.

The private-school system has come under serious threat at several points over the last century. Towards the end of World War I, London's education committee called for greater registration and inspection, an incursion resisted by the private sector. By the late 1930s the public schools were subject to intense criticism. In *Goodbye to All That*, Robert Graves excoriated 'the fundamental evil' of 'what passed as the public school spirit'. Sir Cyril Norwood, who had identified several public schools under financial threat at that time (including Harrow and Marlborough) wrote in the *Spectator* of the 'growing hostility to public schools', and rashly claimed: 'It is hard to resist the argument that a state which draws its leaders in overwhelming proportion from a class so limited as this is not a democracy but a pluto-democracy ... it is impossible to hope that the classes of this country will ever be united in spirit unless their members cease to be educated in two separate systems of schools, one of which is counted as definitely superior to the other.'[6]

Private schools were at their most vulnerable toward the end of World War II. The radical upheaval of the war led many to argue that such schools were anachronistic; they should be abolished and brought within the state system. Winston Churchill and Rab Butler, the key architects of the 1944 Act, believed that the private schools were so weak that they would inevitably be incorporated into the new universal state system. Rab Butler, in charge of plans for education reform, avoided tackling the problem head-on, choosing instead to set up yet another committee to consider the matter. There was no pressure from the Labour benches on this question either. Astonishingly, not a single Labour MP supported an amendment to the 1944 Act which would have required all parents to send their children to a local authority school—just one sign of Labour's deference toward the public schools.

By the time the Fleming Committee set up by Butler finally reported back, in 1947, the public schools had rallied and were in a stronger position to bat off state intervention regarding their privileges. A small window of reforming opportunity had closed—much to the frustration of The National Association of Schoolmasters, forerunner of NASUWT (National Association of Schoolmasters and Union of Women Teachers), who described the lack of action as a 'retrograde step ... the time is opportune for all private schools to be eliminated. It is futile to attempt to relate our educational system to democracy while the great public schools, with their satellite preparatory schools, the admission to which is by birth and privilege, are to be permitted to retain their privileges.'[7]

There were the usual English-style attempts at compromise, with vague proposals for local authorities to subsidise 25 per cent of public-school places for the less well-off; but with 'public-school headmasters making only a token effort in this direction, and local education authorities increasingly reluctant to favour a particularly bright child', the idea never took off.[8] Thus, said Rab Butler, 'the first-class carriage had been shunted onto an immense siding.' A rare political opportunity to unify the country's education system had been lost.

Private education rallied post-war, thanks to an increase in the birthrate and renewed economic momentum. Private schools shifted their emphasis away from games and the classics, towards a more scientifically-oriented education. But the real boost came from middle-class families whose children had failed the eleven-plus, and who were determined that they should not as a result be shunted into a secondary modern. Ironically then, the post-war Labour Government ended up invigorating the public school system rather than scrapping it, and admission rose by some 20 per cent.

By 1965, Tony Crosland was in charge of education policy in Harold Wilson's government. A decade earlier, Crosland had written that the British system of elite private schools 'is much the most flagrant inequality of opportunity, as it is a cause of class inequality generally, in our educational system; and I have never been able to understand why socialists have been obsessed with the question of the grammar schools, and so indifferent to the much more glaring injustice of the independent schools.' There were, however, stark divisions within the party on this issue. In 1943, the National Executive Committee of the Labour Party had demanded 'acceptance of the broad democratic principle that all children of school age shall be required to attend schools provided by the State'; Labour's policy document of 1972, *Programme for Britain*, would later declare that 'our aim is to abolish fee-paying schools'. Others, however—including Crosland himself—stuck to the common view that restricting people from paying for education would be immoral. In addition, abolition or assimilation would be expensive, and difficult to justify in the face of more pressing educational costs. (As for the public, 67 per cent of respondents to a 1968 survey said the government should leave fee-paying public schools 'as they are'.)

Once again, the problem was put out to committee. The Public Schools Commission reported twice: in 1968 and 1970. It proposed to remove the tax advantages of private schools, but its main recommendation was for the implementation of a peculiar scheme providing assisted places for difficult children, which failed to please anyone—least of all the report's authors—and was flatly ignored. When, as secretary of state for education and science, in 1970, Margaret Thatcher was asked in the Commons what action she intended to take on the reports, she replied succinctly: 'None, sir.'

The next year Thatcher told pupils at Bloxham School: 'Please never apologise for independence. It is worth stimulating and nurturing for its own sake. You do not have to justify it. It is those who wish to finish it who have to justify their case.' Direct grant schools had been abolished by the Labour Government in 1975, but one of the first acts of the incoming Tory Government in 1979 was to create the Assisted Places scheme—state funding for the education of able children from lower-income homes in the private sector. In fact, the majority of children who won assisted places came from well-off homes with already 'educationally advantaged' parents. At the same time, the scheme reinforced the idea that comprehensive state education was unable to offer all children an adequate education, bolstered the private sector considerably and increased the percentage of pupils staying in private schools after the age of sixteen. Seventy million pounds of public money was spent on the Assisted Place scheme in the first seven years alone. One of the first acts of the incoming Labour Government of 1997 was to abolish it. In the decades since, a cross-party consensus has emerged that, far from being a thorn in the side of state education, private schools should lead the way in shaping the development of the public sector, sprinkling its poor, benighted state-school-siblings with some of its glittering DNA.

*   *   *

When I spoke to the primary-school mothers in Hammersmith and Fulham, they seemed surprised at their own anger at private education. As one mother exclaimed, 'Close down the private schools. Take away that choice'—and then looked shocked that she had said it. I hear that argument a great deal, and most often, interestingly, from parents who use private education. They are in pole position to understand how it divides society and perpetuates inequality, even when they are personally in thrall to its advantages. Such conversations remain rather hole-in-corner, however, reflecting a peculiar silence in our culture—not about the educational merits and occasional eccentricities of private schools, but about what they do to, and mean for, our society, and the kinds of people they produce and do not produce. Could that silence be in part attributed to the fact that most of the elite in this country, including the most powerful editors, broadcasters and commentators, who largely dictate the terms in which state education is discussed, educate their own children privately? Some choose to denigrate state schools, often to justify their own personal choices; others are embarrassed and prefer to say nothing at all.

According to *Guardian* columnist George Monbiot, himself privately educated, 'The system is protected by silence. Because private schools have been so effective in moulding a child's character, an attack on the school becomes an attack on all those who have passed through it. Its most abject victims become its fiercest defenders. How many times have I heard emotionally-stunted people proclaim "it never did me any harm"? A ruling class in a persistent state of repression is a very dangerous thing.'[9]

But silence, on either side of the divide, does our society no favours. The political and moral argument may have moved beyond angry calls for abolition, but that should not prevent us from dissecting, and discussing, the full impact of private education on our society.

Let's state the obvious. Private schools perpetuate segregation and inequality, divide neighbourhoods, friends and even families and, year after year, rob the state system of the most affluent and often high-achieving pupils. Most private-school fees are well beyond the ordinary British family. According to a recent ISC census, the average annual fee in 2010 was £10,100 for day pupils and £24,000 for boarders. Some charge even more. Private-school fees have risen almost three times faster than average income over the past two decades: fees increased by 83 per cent, after inflation, between 1992 and 2008, while the average income for a family with children rose by only 30 per cent in the same period.[10]

Seldon himself has frequently used the term 'apartheid' to describe the reality of the private/state divide, and claims it is 'one of the great sadnesses' of the system. He is clear that 'independent schools perpetuate inequality in Britain, and we would be blind to the truth if we did not recognise this'. However, he seems to think that this is not a difference of power or status so much as an experiential chasm. When I ask him how he justifies the education of an elite few, away from the majority, he responds: 'We all live in a world which is our own world, and our own bubble, and children who grow up in a Rochdale comprehensive live in that bubble. What good schooling should be about is trying to open people out, to want to celebrate and to know about and to connect with and to experience very different ways of living their lives.'

As for the argument that bursaries provide a route to educational excellence for the poor, I shall not quarrel with his assessment—expressed elsewhere—that these arrangements merely take the 'brightest and best out of state schools' and feather the nests of the private schools, while allowing them to claim they are doing something 'worthy and high-minded'.[11]

The private sector has its labyrinthine hierarchies, its own pyramids of prestige, from the grand old boarding-based public schools—Eton, Rugby, Harrow, Charterhouse—to the metropolitan day schools like St Paul's, Highgate, or Glasgow Academy, down through the smaller preparatory schools in the shires, to the cheaper private schools like the Bolitho School in Cornwall or Moor Allerton preparatory school in Manchester, part of the international school chain GEMS. Anthony Seldon used to teach at St Dunstan's, in Catford, 'where it was common for cabbies to be sending their children—they all wanted to know about the school. And both [the parents] would work [in order to afford it], so that had a very different kind of profile, but in today's terms the fees there would only be about £12,000, so that's considerably less than a school like this where you're paying for boarding. Boarding is a huge factor, hugely expensive.'

Over the years, private schools have increasingly developed academic strategies that help them—and their pupils—pull ahead of the state sector with relative ease. Many offer the IGCSE (International GCSE, not offered in state schools until 2010), the International Baccalaureate and the Middle Years Programme. In 2009, Manchester Grammar School announced that it would be dropping traditional GCSEs altogether. High Master Christopher Ray said they 'may well provide a very good answer for very many boys and girls, but not for our boys'.[12] Around the same time, the Independent Schools Council announced that the number of pupils taking IGCSEs in the fee-paying sector had jumped from 15,000 to 40,000. Sixth-form students in private schools receive significant help with preparation for university entrance, including preparation for the growing number of admission tests involved, and interview coaching for Oxbridge and Cambridge. For all these reasons, private schools can confidently assert that they offer a stronger guarantee of both good results and a place at an elite university than the vast majority of state schools. Private-school students are fifty-five times more likely to win a place at Oxbridge, and twenty-two times more likely to go to a top-ranked university, than students at state schools who qualify for free school meals.[13] Overall, the proportion of university entrants going to Oxbridge from the top-performing thirty private schools was nearly twice that of the top-performing thirty grammar schools—despite having very similar average A-level scores.

The academic and material benefits of private schooling are continually emphasised by journalists and writers, while the schools themselves enjoy virtually wholesale freedom from press intrusion and negative comment.[14] The public are encouraged to admire and aspire rather than to question, and certainly not to criticise. Pieces with headlines such as 'The awful truth: to get ahead you need a private education' constantly confirm the long-term advantages of a fee-paying education. Four in ten (42 per cent) of the UK's most prestigious scientists and scholars, over a third (35 per cent) of MPs elected in the 2010 General Election, and one in six postgraduates are privately educated; while a study from the Centre for the Economics of Education found that the education and earnings differentials between children educated in the state and independent sectors have widened.[15]

Yet for all this supposed success, there has been a deliberate attempt by the private sector in recent years to transform its public image, as discussed in an interesting report commissioned by the Independent Schools Council. The report found that the 'public-school' narrative of unearned and self-perpetuating privilege poses particular problems for the sector. In fact, 'public-school' has been a mildly abusive epithet. 'It is embodied in the character created by the comedian Harry Enfield and known as Tim Nice-but-Dim: a white male of limited intelligence but large bank balance, whose public-school accent and networks give him undeserved access to elite positions denied to more talented individuals educated in the state sector.' But this has changed in recent years, as 'fee-paying schools have been successful in creating a competing narrative— the 'independent school' narrative. This stresses high academic standards, good discipline, motivated staff, operational efficiency, high levels of extra-curricular activities and so on. It also counters the accusation of self-perpetuating privilege by highlighting the number of first-generation parents entering the sector, and the numbers of parents coming from low-income areas.[16]

In many ways the new, more relaxed image, with its illusion of greater egalitarianism, is much more dangerous than the old stereotypes of boaters and bullying. One can see it reflected on the websites of many metropolitan private schools, which present themselves rather like upmarket comprehensives: increasingly co-educational, ethnically diverse, welcoming children from all backgrounds, while never forgetting to sell themselves on both traditional academic results and wider life-skills. One girls' school talks of 'preparing the girls for a future in which the pace of technological, professional and practical change will become faster and more challenging.' A successful product of a modern private school will confidently employ the language of both high and low culture: Shameless and Sparta, Bach and the Black-Eyed Peas; it is fluency in both languages that counts.

David Cameron and Nick Clegg typify the more relaxed, informal style of the new establishment, light years away from the stiffness and strangulated tones of post-war grandees like ex-Etonian Alec Douglas Home. While a landowning aristocratic elite has faded, a new bourgeois elite has risen. According to writer Simon Head, Cameron and Clegg are most definitely children of the city, not the shires. 'Global London has often been part of their world from the beginning ... They are streetwise, free of the sneer of cold command, less conspicuous than their forebears, but more formidable.'[17]

A few years ago, my friend and fellow campaigner, Fiona Millar, went to address the John Locke Society at Westminster school about the state/private school divide. At the end of her talk, a young man stood up in the front row and asked why the divide mattered, since, as he put it, 'Surely the country needs people to sweep the streets?' Speaking at a debate at the Cambridge Union several months later, Millar encountered a rather more sensitive student from another school, who told her that 'the gulf between the London private school and a neighbouring comprehensive was so great that the students were instructed to use separate tube stations for their journeys each day.'

In both these encounters, what is revealed is the gap between what we could call brochure—or website—culture, and real life: the discrepancy between what is put on show and the daily values that guide and bind an institution. George Monbiot makes the same point, with heartfelt eloquence:

> I went through this system myself, and I know I will spend the rest of my life fighting its effects. But one of the useful skills it has given me is an ability to recognise it in others. I can spot another early boarder at 200 metres: you can see and smell the damage

dripping from them like sweat. The Conservative cabinets were stuffed with them: even in John Major's 'classless' government, sixteen of the twenty male members of the 1993 cabinet had been to public school; twelve of them had boarded. Privately-educated people dominate politics, the civil service, the judiciary, the armed forces, the City, the media, the arts, academia, the most prestigious professions ... the Charity Commission. They recognise each other, fear the unshaped people of the state system, and, often without being aware that they are doing it, pass on their privileges to people like themselves.[18]

Monbiot is unusual in his willingness to denounce his educational background. On the whole, our culture lacks modern equivalents of Orwell or Graves; writers or commentators prepared to turn a critical eye on the values of the institutions that shaped them. Instead, we must be satisfied by occasional sightings of eccentricity or crass ignorance. Who didn't wince at Jacob Rees-Mogg, ex-Etonian and new MP, when he appeared on Andrew Neil's TV documentary *Posh and posher*, braying, without an ounce of self consciousness, 'I am a man of the people ... *vox populi, vox dei*'? Just as telling, perhaps, was the privately educated girl from South London, caught on camera by Channel 4's Cutting Edge programme, saying 'I don't give a shit what state school kids do— they can go and die for all I care.'[19]

Such attitudes have consequences for those on both sides of the state/private divide. A teacher in a leading private school told me that he was sometimes shocked at his pupils' ignorance about the way most people live. But life can be difficult, in another way, for those who have finally to step out of the gilded cage. One woman now in her early forties, educated at a top London private school, where she became head girl, described it as follows:

> I discovered a shocking truth [after leaving school]. I didn't have the first idea about my place in society, and I still don't. I remember seeing *The Shawshank Redemption* and my heart freezing in the cosy cinema at the scene where the old man who had spent most of his life in prison is released, and promptly hangs himself in his halfway house because he doesn't know how to live outside the

walls of the institution. The visceral sense of not knowing how to cope away from what became my norm has been acute in me for over twenty years now, and it's not easy to live with.

At a recent school reunion, she found her feelings shared. 'Within an hour of sitting down to lunch, we were, universally, questioning the sense of superiority, the levels of unrealistic and unhelpful expectation and the lack of social grip which had accompanied our private education. It gave us so much, and left us with so little.'[20]

The Independent Schools Council firmly believes, however, that the private sector 'benefits from the "confidence narrative"— the widespread acceptance of the sector's unique ability [*sic*] to turn out confident and socially adept young people. Occasionally, however, these confident young products of the independent sector can be resented as overbearing or arrogant.' When, just before the 2010 election, David Cameron assured us he had no difficulty empathising with ordinary people, fellow ex-Etonian Alex Derber hit out at such a 'risible' claim, repudiating the idea that a school

> where pupils went fox-hunting on bicycles, did scuba-diving for PE and bullied each other in Latin produced individuals in touch with the lives of most of the nation. This raises the question of whether I and other Old Etonians are similarly incapable of such understanding. I think we are. While the school's pupil intake is more broad-based now than forty years ago, and while many may care deeply about those less well-off, most alumni lack an adequate frame of reference to really understand lives radically different to their own.[21]

Over the years, private schools have been encouraged to become more involved with the state system. Much of this was at the urging of the last Labour Government, who set up an independent/state school partnership group within a year of taking office, later developing some ambitious 'twinning' schemes between the sectors. In a speech to private-school leaders in 2008, Labour minister Lord Adonis—formerly Andrew Adonis—suggested that state schools could learn from the 'educational DNA' of the private system, a remark that caused intense irritation within the state sector. One blogger actively engaged in campaigning against the establishment of the Midhurst Academy, a school sponsored by Winchester private school, wrote: 'A more damning insult to the professionalism of those who have [devoted] all their efforts to working in a public service for the benefit of their communities could barely be imagined!'[22] Others expressed distrust at the motives of the private schools, which might be concerned less with equality than with preserving the tax breaks relating to charitable status.

Under Adonis, Labour actively encouraged a number of private schools to sponsor academies, partner failing schools, and help failing private schools to convert to academies. Dulwich College in South London took on The Isle of Sheppey Academy; The Skinners' School sponsors The Skinners' Kent Academy, both in Tunbridge Wells; Wellington College sponsors the Wellington Academy in Wiltshire, opened in 2009 but officially opened in spring 2011, with a brand-new building. Twelve other private schools have opted to become co-sponsors and thirteen have become 'educational partners'. United Learning Trust, whose sister charity, United Church Schools Trust, runs ten fee-charging schools, has recruited two educational co-sponsors from the independent sector, Marlborough College and Winchester College, for two of its seventeen academies.

Under the scheme, Labour exempted private schools from the standard £2 million contribution, requested (but not always received) from corporate sponsors. A rather unctuous letter signed by ten of the heads involved with the academy programme, including Graham Able, Master of Dulwich College, and Anthony Seldon, opined that 'in our case, "sponsorship" involves academic and administrative leadership and governance ... We do not think we have all the answers, but we do feel that the success within our sector suggests that we have something to offer in helping the establishment and development of the academies.'[23]

The day before I visited Wellington College, Seldon and his staff had played host to the staff at the Wellington Academy. They were delighted at the way the day had gone, and full of future plans. The academy link had been another Seldon idea. When the scheme was first mooted, Seldon persuaded a private donor to contribute £2 million towards the project, and the (then) Department for Children, Schools and Families matched the college with the struggling Castledown School, fifty miles away. 'It is the best thing I have done in my professional life, the thing I am proudest of,' says Seldon. Still in its infancy, Wellington Academy looks very like most successful non-selective community schools, with rising results, good sports, art and other extra-curricular activities and a programme of constant innovation. An interim Ofsted report found the school to be 'outstanding', and awarded it the highest Contextual Value-Added results in the country—a measurement that the Coalition Government has now abandoned, on the apparent grounds that it is demeaning to children from lower-income families. When Adonis opened the new building in spring 2011, including a special boarding wing, there was much excited local coverage, particularly of the glamorous 32 million-pound-building, bringing 'world-class standards and scale' and a renewed sense of confidence to the local community. Head Andy Schofield expressed delight and gratitude to Wellington College for 'extending the Wellington family'.

Andrew Adonis has admitted to disappointment that more private schools have not taken a larger role in the academies programme. But others have different objections. No-one could quarrel with the impact that world-class facilities, and concentrated support, can have on the education of lower-income children. But private-school sponsorship of struggling state schools raises important questions about ethos, accountability, governance and long-term sustainability. The governing body of Wellington Academy, apart from one parent-governor, is largely made up of business people, politicians including the local Tory MP, current and former members of Wellington College staff, and army personnel—the academy is near a military garrison and draws from a high proportion of military families. Anthony Seldon sits on the governing body, naturally. The school's patron is the Duke of York.

One of Seldon's many publications is called *Partnership not Paternalism* but—for all the school and Seldon's authentic enthusiasm—there seems to me an enduring risk of both patronage and self-congratulation in the entire enterprise. It is inevitable, perhaps, when the powerful and well resourced decide to rescue the less fortunate, however benign their intentions. Such schemes bring to mind that famous Clement Attlee quote about how 'charity is always apt to be accompanied by a certain complacency and condescension on the part of the benefactor; and by an expectation of gratitude from the recipient, which cuts at the root of all true friendliness.' Students from Wellington College are brought over to the academy for visits and to give talks; as one student said of her reception at the Academy, 'I could not believe how quickly they took down everything I said.' There are regular lectures from military men and Tory MPs, wheeled in to share their views on the Big Society.

And do such schemes always work? Many of the high-profile academies of the New Labour era have already run into serious trouble. So, it seems, have the new private-school partnerships. At the Isle of Sheppey academy, sponsored by Dulwich college, truancy figures are now the fifth highest in the UK.[24] As many sceptics of the programme observed, private schools have no more experience of the challenges and possibilities of state schools than do private companies, precisely *because* their DNA is so radically different.

Interestingly, one of the few public figures to point out potential problems with the institutional merging of the two sectors is the reliably irascible Chris Woodhead, former Chief Inspector of Schools who called it

> patronising nonsense. Does anyone seriously believe that teachers from top HMC schools can solve the multitude of challenges faced by teachers in sink comprehensive schools? The answer appears to be yes, some people do. Well, as someone who, unlike Mr Shepherd [of the Independent Schools Council], has spent considerable time in both kinds of school, I can only say that they are living in cloud cuckoo land.[25]

Woodhead also believes that the more use state-school pupils make of private-school facilities, and the more time private-school teachers spend preparing resources for or working in state schools, the greater the danger that pupils in private schools will suffer. Seldon, incidentally, is always very careful to point out that his fee-paying students lose nothing by his school's charitable venture.

Private-school heads are always pontificating about state schools; the reverse would be unthinkable. Seldon is a prolific commentator on the troubles of his poor educational relation. In *An End to Factory Schools*, he argues that 'Reluctant students are processed through a system closely controlled and monitored by the state. The new world does not need container-loads of young men and women whose knowledge is narrowly academic and subject-specific which they can regurgitate in splendid isolation in exams.' (He might want to re-emphasise this point to Michael Gove should they come to debate the curriculum review, and many of the rigid cultures of the new schools, at one of Wellington's future education conferences.) He also suggests that state schools should take tips from the private sector on discipline, by introducing American-style 'honour codes' setting out the behaviour acceptable on school property, and introducing a private-school-style 'house system'.[26] When I put this idea, and a few others, to one of the most experienced state-school heads in the country, a strange expression spread across his features—not quite a grimace, nor yet a smile. I suspect he shares Woodhead's view about the naivety of private-school leaders: Seldon has never held a single post in the state system, although not for want of trying, as he is keen to point out.

Seldon couches his criticism of state schools in the manner of a sorrowful or disappointed parent. Not all private-sector luminaries are so careful. In June 2008, former rear admiral Chris Parry, the newly appointed head of the ISC, resigned after a series of ill-judged attacks on state schools. Parry first courted controversy by telling MPs on the Commons Select Committee for Children, Schools and Families that not only was there a 'sectarian divide' between state and private schools but that he found it 'very offensive' that he could not find suitable provision in the state sector for his children, describing the schools in his area as 'very poor'. He also claimed that lecturers were 'bullying' trainee teachers not to apply for jobs in private schools. In a later newspaper interview, he complained that some children in state schools were unteachable and their parents were ignorant.

The blustering remarks by Parry, who was forced out of his post at the ISC, were clearly completely out of step with the new 'caring and sharing' tone largely employed today in the higher reaches of government and private schools, although other private-sector leaders have attacked the state system in stringent terms. In October 2010, a report by the HMC 'damned the state sector for producing teachers who have formulaic teaching methods and are uncomfortable teaching off-piste'. State-trained teachers coming into the private sector were reluctant to 'embrace new freedoms', and often unwilling or 'less keen' to lead extra-curricular activities at the weekend. But according to John Bangs, visiting professor at London University's Institute of Education: 'There is a nostalgia for a magic past, like in *The Dead Poets' Society* or *The History Boys*, when teachers were free to go off-piste, but those sort of teachers were the exceptions to prove the rule and there was great inequality of teaching. We now have a system where standards for most are high across the board.'[27]

Does private education have a genuinely charitable function? Not according to Simon Jenkins, who acidly observes that

> what [Eton] does, along with 2,500 other private schools in Britain, is respond to a demand from parents eager to buy social status and a good education for their children, uncontaminated by contact with those who use the state sector. An exclusive education is not a public benefit—if anything, the opposite. It is far from the dictionary's 'voluntary granting of selfless help to those in need'. Many schools [exist] to help rich parents compete for university places with those in need. As for tax relief, it is anything but voluntary. Under charity law it is a compulsory donation to these schools from the taxpayer.[28]

Since the 2006 Charities Act, the private sector has been under pressure to prove it provides 'public benefit', and the Charity Commission has set out new rules; public benefits must be easily identifiable, widely available, and not exclude the poor. But as removing charitable status is a complex legal process (and always politically sensitive), private schools have been required by the Charity Commission to illustrate their public benefits either through providing bursaries (amounting to from 5 to 15 per cent of fee income), sharing teachers or opening up facilities. In 2009, the Charity Commission examined the efforts of five private schools to meet these requirements. Two failed the test, and had to give back a percentage of their fee income in the form of bursaries. The ISC reacted angrily to the judgment.

There is something almost surreal about private schools having to prove that their benefits are 'widely available' and 'do not exclude the poor', when they so clearly do. Does the extension of bursaries or the sharing of facilities and teachers really plug the gap? There are question marks over bursaries; although means-tested, they are made available to parents on £40,000 or below, which is hardly the poverty line. On the whole, they don't cover the full costs of schooling and don't take account of further costs, both of which act to exclude the genuinely poor. And, of course, they siphon off able children from state schools. There is no information about how many children on free school meals get bursaries to private schools; the ISC only gives information about postcodes, and yet there can, of course, be wealthy pockets within postcodes that are deemed to be disadvantaged overall. The whole scheme is ripe, in Fiona Millar's words, for 'colonisation by the children of credit-crunched, middle-class parents ... as the assisted places were.'

The Independent Schools Council would now like to return to the pre-2006 position, with schools not required to prove public benefit at all. At the time of writing, the ISC is planning to challenge the guidance of the Charity Commission, which they would like to see repealed on the grounds that private schools already educate a 'sufficiently wide' section of the public to a very high standard, while not explicitly barring entry to anyone else. A cynic might retort that the high, sometimes cripplingly high, fees implicitly exclude a large number of pupils, and that this freedom of entry is on a par with the welcome that Harrods or the Island of Mustique extend to your average UK family.

Some campaigners for a fairer distribution of resources within our school system argue for the abolition of the tax break altogether, on the grounds that it is morally untenable, particularly in the current economic circumstances. David Miliband surprised many by recently coming out in favour of scrapping charitable status for private schools outright. Given the Coalition's swingeing spending cuts, he said, 'taking money from the poorest children—by scrapping the child trust fund, even from kids in care—while continuing to subsidise private schools to the tune of £100 million a year is just wrong. That's half a billion pounds over the lifetime of a parliament. We should be looking at savings like that, rather than cutting jobs and hospitals.'[29]

IV
WHAT NEXT?

Chapter Seven

The Shape of Things to Come?

Anne West, one of the country's leading experts on school admissions, is sitting behind her neatly ordered desk in her sunny office at the London School of Economics, getting to grips with the possible shape of the schools landscape in England in the twenty-first century. West is a formidably precise woman; she rightly shies away from making any definitive predictions. 'It's difficult. We don't really know how it's going to work out. There's certainly going to be major, massive fragmentation, with a lot of very different [school] providers and [a lot of] schools converting to academies.' She's not sure that the free schools 'are going to be such a big thing, but there will certainly be problems for parents getting places [in some schools], with many more schools becoming their own admission authorities.' According to West, the biggest problems will come in 'the big conurbations—where you might get a toxic mix of cuts, and [the new] academies and weak local authorities.'

Changes to admissions policies will make it much more difficult, says West, to know who schools are taking in: 'There will be no way of knowing what they are *meant* to be doing and what they are actually doing.' Even in research, she says, it's hard 'to get a grip on the admissions issue. Schools say they do something, but do they really do it?' And who's going to check, she wonders? With academies directly accountable to central government, are parents really going to complain to Michael Gove or his successor about failing to get a place? If they do, they may not get an answer. Within a fortnight of my meeting with West there are already accusations of a 'shambolic' Department of Education, unable to keep up with a backlog of thousands of unanswered letters.[1]

West's own research has played a leading part in revealing the degree of social segregation in our existing system. Will the new schools revolution make the situation worse? 'It's a tricky one. All-ability academies probably won't lead to more, but some free schools and some "converter" academies with a religious character might become attractive for children of higher ability.' I met West around the time of intense public debate over whether Church of England schools should reserve only 10 per cent of places for children from Anglican churchgoing families—because, in the words of the Bishop of Oxford, 'our primary function and our privilege is to serve the wider community.' According to West, 'if voluntary-aided school governing bodies take on board this guidance, the composition of CofE voluntary-aided secondary schools with a religious character could change markedly, and segregation could also reduce quite markedly.' Within weeks of Pritchard's revolutionary suggestion, the Church of England had issued a statement saying that it would not impose a 10 per cent limit on places reserved for children from churchgoing families. Instead, that new guidance would remind schools of the 'original intention' of the Church to 'provide free schools for the poor'.

West doesn't see the future schools landscape harking back to the simple division between grammars and secondary moderns. 'The picture will be much more fragmented than that.' It is clear, however, that certain types of schools are moving inexorably towards pseudo-grammar status; others are bedding down as de facto secondary moderns. This won't be the only divide, but it will be an important one of the future. Let's call it soft-focus selection. How will it work? According to one governor of an outstanding school in the north-west, that has converted to academy status,

> I would like to see [the school] become innovative, but I think it
> will become more traditional, cut off. It will focus on academic

subjects and become a rather traditional, status-obsessed school. If it forms a federation with local primary schools, which also looks likely, hysteria will be pushed down the schools chain, with parents obsessed with getting in the right primary school in order to access the secondary.

Twyford, in West London, is a successful voluntary-aided comprehensive, currently much praised by Coalition ministers. Applicants to the school, in classic church-school manner, have to prove 'their commitment to their faith with evidence of attendance at a place of worship going back to the age of six'. Alice Hudson, head of Twyford, acknowledges that her school takes a larger than average proportion of children who, in the past, would have gone to grammar schools. 'Schools that make it evident they care about academic achievement attract more able students.' Twyford casts its net far beyond its local area, and relatively few of its pupils qualify for free school meals.[2]

Tom Packer, head teacher of the new West London Free School, puts a similar point of view. He told the *Independent*: 'It might be that that kind of curriculum [devised for the WLFS] is not appropriate for all children—but it is a curriculum that will enable them to think for themselves,' he says. 'It is not just about results and packing children in for easier subjects so the school gets more A star to C grades for the league tables.'[3] Add to these institutions the increasing numbers of faltering grammar and private schools which hope to shelter under the free-school umbrella, some continuing to academically select.[4]

It is not hard to imagine, then, the confusing, multi-tiered shape of an emerging local market economy of schools: a market whose general characteristics I and others were predicting back in 2006, when New Labour pressed ahead with its city academy and trust school plans. Clear differences were already emerging then between the more academic schools and the vocational academies, their results artificially swelled by vocational qualifications but not—at least according to Alison's Wolf's 2011 report on vocational education—providing real children with useful skills or real jobs.[5]

We will continue to see the hardening of old polarities. With light-touch regulation of admission policies and few means of redress against school decisions, the more successful of the 'converter' academies and a few of the burgeoning free schools, popular in sophisticated but divided inner-city areas, will continue to attract better-off families and consolidate their position as the academic magnets of their area. Such schools will certainly take a smattering of children from low-income families; they would otherwise be both shamed and shown up, but these may well be higher-attaining children. Current indications that a revised schools admissions code will 'permit' schools to prioritise children on free school meals might facilitate this, like a cut-price version of the old Assisted Places scheme. At the same time another, more paternal type of free school will emerge, along the lines of charter schools in the United States, aiming to attract highly motivated families, particularly within the ethnic minority community.

We will certainly see a growth of secondary modern/vocational provision, serving less advantaged areas and pupil populations. There will be three kinds of school here: the new university technical colleges—currently being established by former Tory education minister Lord Baker, who has said he wants to see 100 of them up and running by 2015 and 300 by 2020; a large tranche of community schools—starved of funds by the decimation of local authority budgets and the leakage of some middle-class families to the new schools network; and possibly the majority of city academies set up under Labour, many of which have already concentrated on vocational qualifications. Schools like Manchester Enterprise Academy (see previous chapter) present the most attractive face of the revamped secondary-modern-style school: bright, brisk, beautifully equipped, but largely geared to the world of work. Even the buildings won't look so bright in ten years' time.

We might see the emergence of a new form of selection and the old tripartite division; let's call it the fourteen-plus. It is widely recognised that dividing children at eleven is not only too arbitrary and brutal but massively unpopular, not least for the majority deemed to be academic failures. But there may be far fewer public objections to an informal or unofficial separation of children along the lines of their apparent 'interests' and 'talents' emerging in mid-adolescence, with some persuaded towards a more vocational path and others directed to the pseudo-grammars. Once again we will revert to the old pattern in English education, in which all are encouraged to know their place.

The creeping privatisation of primary education might mean that the process now begins much earlier. Primary-age children could well be guided to one kind of secondary or another by discussions between heads and teachers and parents: a conversational form of the old eleven-plus, selection—or direction—by word of mouth. With the establishment of more and more federations and school chains, certain primaries will become known as feeders for particular secondary schools and the battle of school choice will begin in earnest at nursery. Get on the wrong conveyor belt, and you could lose your child a chance of winning a place at one of the most prized schools in the area.

Among the early models for Coalition educational plans were the Swedish free school system and the American charter school programme. As we have already seen, the evidence on rising results in these schools is mixed at best. But what about the social impact of these new models? How might that translate to our situation?

Sweden and the US start out from very different points. Sweden is a more equal and stable society, which had far higher school quality before the introduction of free schools in the early 1990s. A strong state helped to control social segregation and promote social equality. The free schools policy has increased social and ethnic segregation, particularly in deprived areas. According to education researcher Suzanne Wibourg, 'if the neoliberal reforms increased inequality of achievement in Sweden, a country with a universal welfare state and a relatively high level of social equality, then other countries could risk an even greater increase in inequality from implementing similar kinds of independent schools.'[6]

She's right. The effect in the US, where levels of inequality and lack of state support for poorer households are nearer to our own model, is alarming. As in Sweden, the evidence on results is equivocal. While some charter schools do really well, on balance these new schools do not outperform regular public (state) schools. But the evidence on their social impact is staggeringly clear. In fifteen states, 70 per cent of black students in charter schools are attending hyper-segregated schools, where 90 per cent of the students are from an ethnic-minority background. In four of those states, 90 per cent of black students attend such schools. Instead of offering parents a real path out of poverty and racial segregation, charter schools seem to intensify the ethnic separation that already plagues traditional public schools. And there is little that state or federal direct action can do to change this, despite several reports by those concerned at the civil-rights implications.'[7]

The free schools present a more direct danger of segregation. Just as Northern Ireland is moving towards desegregation of its schools, we are moving in the other direction. Northern Ireland has a highly segregated education system, with 95 per cent of pupils attending either a maintained Catholic school or a controlled school (mostly Protestant); but the integrated schooling movement is busy breaking down the barriers. Here, however, we look set to establish many more religious schools. Of the first eight free schools approved, one is a Jewish school, one a Hindu school and one a Church of England school. Muslim and Sikh groups have expressed an interest in setting up their own state-funded schools—including one in Oldham, where the local authority has worked hard to encourage integration, not segregation.

There are already worrying levels of ethnic segregation in our schools. In Buckinghamshire, a county that maintains the eleven-plus, selection intensifies division, with the vast majority of children in upper schools (secondary moderns) classed as non-white. This means, says one school governor, that they are 'educated separately from their white peers ... Parents don't want it to be like this. Governors don't want it. How has this happened? This contributes nothing to the social cohesion of our town.'[8]

In London's Waltham Forest, there are currently ten plans to set up free schools, seven of which would be faith-oriented. These include the Emmanuel Christian Centre, a church whose website features the strapline 'Loving God passionately'; the Noor Ul Islam Trust, linked to a mosque, aiming to 'offer an inclusive Islamic environment where children are encouraged to have high aspirations for academic achievement', and Forest Light Education Plus, a company run on Christian principles. Local teachers' unions believe there are plans for five other schools, including two linked to Islam, one Roman Catholic and one to be set up by a group of science teachers. It is not hard to imagine the chaos and fragmentation that would ensue if even half of these schools got going.

Sharon Wright was a governor of a Church of England primary, but resigned after she felt the school was promoting admissions policies that excluded the poor.

> I resigned at Easter, with a radical new anti-faith-schools perspective born of the journey. I'd never seen anyone rubbing their hands in glee at the chance to pull unchristian dirty tricks behind closed governor doors, but the truth was somehow worse. Wasn't it blindingly obvious how unfair and socially divisive it was to be allowed to reserve priority places for your own churchgoers? And weren't troubled children the most in need of Christian love? Now, I think having a system of state-funded faith schools is actually immoral. We should surely object to how it legitimises discrimination, segregates our children, often fails to embrace the vulnerable with compassion and empowers tiny religious quangos to rule over publicly funded education. I have this fear that in 30 years' time, we will have built up a generation that is not at ease with itself and that has been brought up in a very divisive way. We will rue the day we divided the children.[9]

New school chains are constantly emerging, and it seems likely that the education landscape of the future will be dominated by a few powerful providers. In late March 2011, E-ACT announced plans to open a 'super-chain' of up to 250 schools, making it by far the biggest schools' group in the country, dwarfing the vast majority of local authorities.[10] According to Sir Bruce Liddington,

E-ACT's director general, the group will have a mix of schools within the chain: 50 'traditional' academies to replace under-performing schools, 200 'converter' academies and 50 primary schools. For Liddington, the plans demonstrate the continuation of our 'core purpose to replace underachieving schools in disadvantaged parts of the country … it is then to move into academy converters with schools that are by no means failing, but are not outstanding.' He added that E-ACT was 'really very keen' on free schools, which would allow the chain to respond to what parents want, and was also keen on establishing chains of primaries— cashing in on the fact that as school funding tightens, primary schools are going to need to congregate in order to survive. 'I'm hugely excited about the opportunity for flexibility, and we intend to take advantage of that.'[11] Successful chains, drawing on philanthropic contributions, could easily 'add value' to their brand, boost the competitive edge of their schools and disadvantage ordinary state schools even further. One teacher working as part of a successful chain told me of the extraordinary resources that her school was able to draw on in terms of equipment, support staff and school trips, although staff were deliberately kept in the dark as to the source of the funds, as they were about most elements of the school's financial arrangements.

Interestingly, the Coalition Government seems nervous of the implications of growth on this scale. In a May 2011 letter to members of the Labour education team—directly addressing their fears about expanding chains—Nick Gibb, minister of state for schools, declared:

We are keen to encourage chains of Academies because, like the last Government, we see the advantages to schools and their pupils of collaboration and partnership working. We are not being prescriptive about the size of chains, but we do not envisage them replicating or replacing local authorities, and we want governance arrangements to be sensible and workable. To answer your specific question, it seems unlikely that a single multi-Academy Trust of 250 schools would be able to collaborate well or be governed effectively by a single body.

The website of Innovative Schools, an emerging chain, gives a flavour of this expanding market, even if the educational content feels as yet a little fuzzy. IS currently plans to establish a chain of twenty to thirty non-selective maintained academies in England. They will have 'buzz, energy and vitality ... consult with all [their] stakeholders and employ truly excellent and inspirational teachers.'[12] There is very little hard information about their aims or ethos, other than that IS hopes to be part of a 'group of schools sharing a common purpose', including church schools, GEMS the private operator, and the independent chain, the Girls' Day School Trust.

Surprising providers may emerge. The Co-operative movement has yielded to the inevitable, it seems, and its schools are now opting to be academies, to the disappointment of some. However, a distinctive, socially-minded breed of Co-op trust schools—faithful to ideas of active learning and stakeholder and community engagement—has expanded rapidly, from just 30 in late 209 to 108 in November 2010, big enough for the group to consider itself a 'schools network'. The Co-op move presents real questions to supporters of comprehensive education. At a major conference on Radical Education and the Common School, held in London in March 2011, some participants were tentatively suggesting that practitioners, parents and others passionately concerned with preserving a genuinely creative educational vision should pilot new schools or school groups that would directly contest the dominant corporate model—and provide a flame of hope for the future. It was not the first, nor will it be the last, conversation of its kind in the current climate.

Parents in the future will certainly have 'choice' if the new school revolution stays the course. In fact, they will be dazed and dazzled by it. Secondary transfer will be like Christmas shopping: get out the brochures, scan the websites, pick up hints and tips from more experienced bargain hunters. They could well find themselves, like a mother I met recently, armed with several large spreadsheet-style pieces of paper, buoyed by Ofsted reports and notes of school visits, ready to spend hours working through the various admission criteria of the schools she was interested in: faith schools, foundation schools, free schools, city academies, the new academies, comprehensives (an increasingly meaningless term in such a fractured landscape), and colleges. Parents will in effect be told by government: take your pick. Except, of course, they can't. Some parents, as always, will be disadvantaged by lack of knowledge and confidence; they will not begin to know how, or where, to look. On the supply side, schools will be looking for the pupils that suit their so-called ethos or image, and it won't be too hard to see what kind of child will be made welcome at a school concentrating on Latin and classical music, or, conversely, offering beautifully equipped studios for hair and beauty courses. Almost every school will be a specialist in something or other; some will be highly selective, others partially selective, while others supposedly remain open to all.

But within this landscape of branded diversity, certain trends will be discernible. The fast pace of technology, and the temptation for private providers to cut costs, will increase standardised, centralised learning methods. It will not be unusual in the future for one talented lecturer to record a standard lesson on a key section of the syllabus, a lesson that will then be screened in all the other schools in the chain. Learning will be increasingly online and more software-based, with negative implications for the poor, given the existing digital divide. More than a million schoolchildren in the UK still have no computer at home, while a further two million can't get access to a computer at home.[13]

On the other hand, there will a return to more traditional methods. The new curriculum, currently being considered for existing maintained schools, will certainly return to traditional methods, and is likely to involve memorising the capitals of obscure countries, the English kings and queens and the periodic table. As Stephen Ball says, 'not exactly a curriculum for the twenty-first century or a pedagogy that recognises the recent focus in schools on student learning'.[14] Gove's over-hasty introduction of the English Baccalaureate threw down a challenge to hundreds of schools that must now scale back teaching of religious education and music, timetabling more lessons in core academic subjects that will improve their placing in the league tables, whether it suits their students or not.

More and more schools will develop the tough discipline and 'no excuses' culture of the charter school model, where students are berated if they turn up late or have a hair out of place. One university-based teacher trainer was recently approached by a former student who had left one of the academies. 'She was appalled by the school ... the staff talked about the parents having no order, no morality, that it was the school which had to give these children "moral leadership". She couldn't stand it, she had to move on.'

Harsh discipline and private-school-style uniforms will certainly play a part in many schools within the maintained sector, and in some of the bigger chains. In answer to a recent FOI request for information on the measurable impact of school uniform on results, Mossbourne Academy and ARK's Burlington Danes academy were singled out by the government as 'just two examples of excellent schools where the wearing of neat, clean uniforms is an integral part of the schools' behaviour and discipline policies'.[15] At the Evelyn Grace academy in Lambeth, run by ARK, each child must sign a home-school agreement which runs to seven pages, and includes such clauses as 'I will arrive on time, prepared for learning and in perfect school uniform' and 'I will hand in my mobile phone every morning or lose it for a fortnight'. However, Ofsted only gave the school a 'satisfactory' in a report in early 2011, partly on the grounds that the children were too tightly governed and given implausible targets.[16]

What will happen when some of the new schools—the 'converter' academies and the free schools—run into financial trouble, as they almost certainly will? A little-publicised report from the powerful House of Commons Public Accounts Committee in early 2011 warned of 'increased risks to value for money and proper use of public money', and that 'governance risks will increase as the number of academies grows'. The Department of Education is already struggling to monitor and administer the rising numbers of academies. How will they manage when numbers further climb, as they hope they will? Five per cent of academies were predicted to have an accumulated deficit by the end of 2009–2010, and the Young People's Learning Agency (the body once charged with overseeing academies, abolished under plans in the 2011 Education Bill) foresaw that over a quarter could well require 'additional financial or managerial support to secure their longer-term financial health'.[17]

This prediction was soon borne out by the news, a few months later, that the YPLA had spent almost £7 million in 2010 bailing out troubled academies. Richard Rose Central Academy in Carlisle needed a cash injection of nearly £5 million to survive. Manchester Enterprise Academy, discussed in Chapter 5, was one of four other schools to receive a significant cash handout from government.

One can easily imagine the next step: government giving permission to private companies to make a profit—largely, to get schools off the taxpayer's back. At present, scarcely any state schools are run for profit, although it hasn't stopped some of the non-profit providers from paying their leaders handsome private-sector-style salaries. But for-profit providers are hovering around the UK market. Edison Learning, founded in 2002, have three divisions in the UK—Partner Schools, School Management Services and Expert Services—and claim to be working with 'over 80 primary, secondary and special schools' in a 'holistic three-year transformational programme'. In 2007 they took over the management of Salisbury School in Enfield as part of a three-year programme, under a contract which included payment for reaching agreed targets. The latest Ofsted report (January 2009) rates the school, now called Turin Grove, as just 'satisfactory' (Grade 3 of 4). Already the company is moving away from the ambition to run schools outright. How much does this reflect the fate of its American parent, which backed away from profit-making in the public sector? According to a report in the *Nation* magazine:

In the early 1990s media entrepreneur Chris Whittle became the darling of the free-market, antigovernment right by promising that private, for-profit businesses could manage schools better than public boards of education. His Edison Schools, he claimed, would grow into a corporate giant by educating children better and more cheaply than public schools. Teachers' unions were initially skeptical, then increasingly critical as the results came in. But Whittle attracted both enthusiastic investors and support from politicians like Republican Governors George Bush, Tom Ridge and William Weld. After Edison went public in 1999, its stock price doubled in two years.

But by 2002, Edison was on the ropes. Its stock had crashed from $37 to as little as 14 cents. Whittle had long since abandoned his original, controversial goal of building a network of private, for-profit schools, but even the strategy of contracting to privately manage public and charter schools proved flawed. Plagued by local opposition and severely criticized for its educational performance, Edison was hemorrhaging money ($354 million in twelve years), and had lost one-fourth of its contracts.[18]

The company was only saved thanks to a $182 million buyout in 2003, which took it into private ownership.

The Swedish example is no more reassuring. According to an interview with ex-minister Lena Sommestad in May 2011, the spread of profit-making free schools changed the free school scene from a 'few nice ... schools such as Montessori schools' into one dominated by 'venture capital companies [which] have made quite big profits, which they don't reinvest back into the school or even spend in Sweden—they put the money offshore, into tax havens.' She also said the project had attracted some 'dubious people'. Some companies had promised to deliver vocational training to their pupils, but failed to do so. According to Sommestad, the public mood was turning against free schools.[19]

Expert watchers of the school scene in the UK think it won't be long before companies will be permitted to make a profit from the lucrative market-state. Promises by politicians not to do so lose credibility in the light of the tuition fees U-turn. Peter Wilby, former editor of the *New Statesman* and *Independent on Sunday* and highly experienced observer of the education scene, told a recent conference in London: 'Private companies are desperate to get into education, it's a massive area of expansion.' He recalls the beginnings of the Institute of Economic Affairs, the right-wing pressure group that has played a pioneering role in current policy.

> Long ago, the people running it were regarded as crackpots from the fringes of the political universe. Yet ... that was where it all began. By making allies, developing ideas, publishing pamphlets, holding conferences, putting on a lot of convivial lunches, the IEA eventually brought about Thatcherism and indeed, its political child, Blairism. It believed not only in the privatisation of water, telephones, gas and electricity—and it's hard now to remember that these services were ever run by the state—but also in the privatisation of education and health ... think how close we now are to it.[20]

Wilby believes that with other potential markets, such as energy or transport, now saturated, it makes economic sense for the government to permit capitalist expansion into education.

> Along with social care and health, it's obviously a growth area. There are clearly many companies desperate to get in, and the government under pressure will lift the ban on profit-making companies. Already you are getting leaders in some of the papers urging this development. These leader-writers themselves might be being given a nod and a wink on this one. You can see how easy it would be to squeeze a profit out of it. Edison for instance has its own curriculum already... big chains will practice economies of scale and centralisation. Computerisation will enable standardised lessons, delivered down the chain. Just as you once had distinctive pedagogies and styles of school associated with different local authorities—Leicestershire, West Yorkshire or the ILEA ... now you will have chains of academies—the Tesco academy chain, hypothetically speaking—each with their own distinctive brand.[21]

Stephen Ball also thinks that the 'p' word is inevitable. 'As we see more private providers, so there will be more amalgamation and more opportunity to cut costs. Some of the Swedish schools, for instance, use fewer trained teachers. It's cheaper. So, within a school, you will move from a situation now where you have twenty Learning Support Assistants to having 120 Learning Support Assistants. The balance between teachers and learning assistants will shift.'

He adds: 'And, of course, we will see schools close ... when they start to make a loss. There is no discussion of this issue and the potential of disruption to children's education, the costs of such failure. The state, of course, will have to underwrite this failure.' A few weeks after I met Ball, parents at the South Bank International School, run by Cognita, a provider of independent schools, rose up against a company they saw as 'milking profits' from the school, to the detriment of educational quality.[22]

And yet, right-wing think tanks are now openly urging the government to move in this direction. A report from the Adam Smith Institute argued that the 'disappointing' development of free schools up to now was partly the result of government caution, and reluctance to follow through the logic of their market revolution in schools. 'Proprietorial schools have delivered outstanding results where they have been allowed to operate. The government should unlock this potential in order to meet growing demand in the coming years, with a view to introducing a steadily greater degree of choice for parents and increasing competition among schools.' These schools should be allowed to charge fees at the lower end of the school, and to fill spare capacity with children from low-income families.[23]

For the moment, then, all these highly significant and game-changing developments give rise to a string of simple questions, for our democracy as well as our education system. We could begin with: can our schools be run like shops? What happens when they become half empty, and nobody wants to send their children there? What happens when companies collapse or charitable trusts seize up? At what point do we, the public, and parents, get to debate the educational vision that is shaping the school lives and possible future of thousands of children? If we dislike or fear elements of that vision, how can we intervene? Is there any meaningful, active role for parents in these schools? What does it mean—or matter—if none of these philanthropists, entrepreneurial capitalists or church leaders keen to move in on the emerging school markets send their own children to state schools? How does a school's purpose, meaning and role in the community change when it is, in effect, the property of a benign billionaire?

On every level, public education will become less accountable. Local school accountability is likely to be of less concern to hedge fund billionaires, who have glittering galas to arrange, or superheads who have disadvantaged children to pull out of the chaotic urban slums of the twenty-first century. Nigel Gann, a governor who resigned at the hasty conversion of his school to academy status, puts it bluntly: 'The way things are going, your school staff will be busy choosing between Capita, Cognita, Tribal and Southwest One to provide their support services. If you have a concern that the school isn't dealing with, don't go to the county council—it won't have any powers.'

The loss of local authority involvement is literally incalculable. Centralised planning of school places; important powers of scrutiny over which schools are taking what pupils; expertise and guidance on a range of important school issues, from special needs provision to the appointment of head teachers—these collaborative elements will wither away if the local school landscape becomes shaped by naked competition, rather than managed collaboration. The big school chains will increasingly have their own systems of support and guidance, but they will surely be kept in-house—or sold to other interested buyers.

What this will mean in practice is that a wide range of services and schools that do not pay their own way will be threatened with extinction. To give just one example: in Cornwall half of the primary schools are certified as small, and have fewer than 120 students. Up to sixty such schools in Devon and Cornwall are currently being subsidised by grants from local government, under a scheme known as small schools budget protection. But if some of the stronger schools in the two counties decide to pull out from the local authority, money like this will no longer be available—and who knows what will happen to the other schools. Will they have to close? That would be ironic, under a government that came to power promising to make education more human-scale.

Local authorities will inevitably be left with poorer children, migrant children, and the less consciously ambitious or educationally knowledgeable families. They will become 'a voice for the voiceless', to use Andy Burnham's eloquent phrase; guardians of the poor in an ever more economically divided landscape. They need to act quickly if they are to reinvent their role, and to bring communities together in new forms, to respond creatively to the ominous mix of public service reform and slashed budgets. In Camden in North London, the Council has started a consultation with all the borough's parents, schools and governors to find out what sort of education system they want to see in the future, how resources might be divided in a time of scarcity, how to deal with emerging free schools, and what to do about issues like faith admissions. They have asked Sir Mike Tomlinson, author of a groundbreaking report on 14–19 education (rejected by the Labour Government), if he will take evidence from all members of the community over a six-month period and make recommendations.[24]

It's an unstable landscape, as landscapes moulded by private rather than public interests usually are. As I write, in summer 2011, more and more parents, teachers and governors are standing up and speaking out about the direction of state education. A few individual teachers have complained publicly about the closed and controlling cultures in some of the new academies. But it is hard to do. A teacher at one of the new academies told me, 'Who are we going to appeal to—the governors? They are all friends and family of the sponsor. There seems to be no teacher representative and no parent on our governing body or not that I know of. And of course we have no right of appeal to the local authority, because we are not part of the local authority any more. The entire system is open to abuse.'

Dissatisfaction is spreading. A poll in April 2011, conducted by the National Foundation for Educational Research, found two-thirds of teachers deeply uneasy at the changes introduced by the coalition, with many believing that free schools will lead to greater social segregation. Fifty-nine per cent agree that already privileged pupils are the most likely to benefit from their schools being given academy status. More than half the teachers asked thought that the pupil premium needed to increase significantly to have a real impact; only 27 per cent thought that academy freedoms would improve pupil achievement. Even supporters of the government, like Sir Peter Lampl, head of the Sutton Trust, thought these findings 'very serious'.[25]

The Anti Academies Alliance records campaigns against the new conversions in over forty-five separate areas in the country, from Brent to Broxstowe, Northumberland to Tamworth.[26] In Louth in Lincolnshire, a group of primary-school parents set up a *Save Our School* campaign after learning of a letter sent to all primary heads in the county from not-for-profit body CfBT—which has been running outsourced school improvement services in the county for over a decade—suggesting that they opt out of primary-school control and become academies. The parent group is outraged at the secrecy surrounding a proposal with such major, long-term implications. According to Louth parent Charlotte Hopkinson, 'What is being proposed for primary schools is just terrifying ... Everything is hidden. You get the impression the attitude is: "we are not going to tell you till we have made our decision".'[27]

Protest will surely grow if draconian management, soulless pedagogy and concentration on the profit motive becomes the norm. It has already happened in the US, where the charter schools are beginning to lose public support, even among conservatives. And who knows how long the pupils themselves will march in line past their kindly sponsors, before demanding something richer and more rewarding from their life in school? How long before there is a counter-revolution, spreading up from the new privatised classrooms of the twenty-first century, demanding a return to first principles on the purpose and methods of our children's education?

Chapter Eight

'Go Public': A New School Model for a New Century

We have reached an important turning point. Our state education system is fast fragmenting, and without full and proper public debate. The government currently boasts that two schools a day are converting to academy status, leaving the local, collaborative family of schools to go it alone, becoming accountable only to a handful of ministers and civil servants in Whitehall. Within a few years, at this rate, several hundreds more will have cut loose from local authority control. If, as now seems likely, thousands of church schools join the rush to academy status (guaranteeing them continued privileges in admissions and landholdings), the game might well be up. Will we—parents, citizens, taxpayers— stand by as one of our most vital public services passes into hands of venture capitalists, hedge fund managers and a growing array of faith groups?

Should this continue, the consequences will undoubtedly be profound. Schools are intricate operations, feats of endurance as well as exercises in fulfilment; they are not suited to the passing whims of the kind, curious or determined rich. And when the 'new schools' fail, as some undoubtedly will, the old state will have to pick up the pieces; the danger is, of course, that there will no longer be any credible infrastructure or fund of meaningful expertise, particularly at the local level, on which to draw.

But there is an alternative vision of state education, one formed by the proven strengths of the comprehensive inheritance, as well as by lessons learned from the missteps of past years; one that employs a more genuine model of parental choice, and a broader vision of what education is for. It is a vision to unify, rather than divide us. And, now that we are being urged to consider the innovations of other countries, we, too, can take valuable tips from abroad.

Let's start with some first principles, touchstones for a more practical discussion of what might be done or how we might, one day, shape a different direction for our education system. As our schools become more and more like the fast-food industry—delivering a standardised, mechanised service—we need to remind ourselves of the profound importance of education for education's sake, rather than education mainly as a means of economic and professional advancement. Recent history offers many examples of the transformative effect of this broader conception of learning, even within objectively difficult circumstances. One is the pioneering approach of head teacher Alex Bloom in St George's in the East, in the post-war East End, who refused to regard the teenagers in his charge as unworthy of, or unable to appreciate, the highest forms of culture. Bloom also reckoned that young people could, and should, regularly question their teachers and their methods. The radical Brazilian educator and author Paulo Freire provides another inspiration. Freire stressed the importance of dialogue in good teaching, believing that too much education was like 'banking', in that the educator merely makes 'deposits' in the students rather than actively engaging with them. It's an apt metaphor for the post-crash world.

Richard Pring, the distinguished philosopher of education and champion of the common school, has identified three questions which should shape the education of young people: 'What is it that makes us human?', 'How did we become so?' and 'How might we become more so?' Answers to such questions inevitably require the exploration of both science and the arts, literature and history, social sciences and anthropology, linguistics and history, philosophy and theology. That exploration implies discussion and argument, disciplined by the evidence to be found in these different fields; it also involves empowering students to explore the context of their own lives. Education must 'respect and find a place for their voices and their experience ... it reaches deep into the very souls of the young people themselves. And such is the very purpose of the arts and the humanities at their best.'[1]

We could learn a great deal from the original free-school philosophy of the twentieth century, with its emphasis on collaboration, experimentation and independence of thought. For example, a child who is set to building, with others, a bridge over a small stream, will, over the course of that intricate, important task, encounter many discrete subject areas: geology, biology, mathematics, physics, design/aesthetics, history, literature and so on. The more deeply a child is involved in the process of making something beautiful or useful, the more the child is likely to retain, and be able to apply, the knowledge acquired during the course of the task. There is far too little of this kind of learning in our schools. Lack of resources, unwieldy class sizes, but also narrowness of outlook, prevent this kind of engagement.

A. S. Neill, the Scottish writer, rebel and founder of Summerhill, the most famous of the free schools, was a pioneering educator whose ideas make refreshing reading in today's climate. He believed that the aim of life was to find happiness, partly through the development of deep interests, and that children ultimately learn what they want to learn. Marks, exams, prize-givings 'sidetrack proper personality development', while 'traditional schooling inhibits a necessary kind of creative play that leads to true learning ... All that any child needs is the three Rs, the rest should be tools and clay and sports and theatre and paint and freedom.'[2] And again: 'all outside compulsion is wrong, that inner compulsion is the only value. And if Mary or David wants to laze about, lazing about is the one thing necessary for their personalities at the moment ... Lazing is abnormal, it is a recovery, and therefore it is necessary when it exists.'

Neill's ideas have filtered through, in greatly diluted form, into mainstream schooling, and we should work to root them more firmly there. A good schooling *should* explore, and help children to develop, the vital balance between compulsion and trust-in-self, duty and creative freedom. It *should* be about doing and finding out, as well as reading, note-taking and imbibing knowledge. Summerhill, now under the leadership of A. S. Neill's daughter Zoë, has, unsurprisingly, faced difficulties with the education authorities. In the late 1990s it was threatened with closure. However, it has stuck to its principles of voluntary student participation and direct encouragement of student democracy, and the latest Ofsted report is glowing, saying that the school provides children with 'outstanding opportunities for personal development'.

Every child has the right to flourish, the right to a serious, well-rounded and stimulating education—not just those lucky enough to be born to parents who can provide it, or pay for it. In his wonderful book *School Blues* the writer Daniel Pennac, who failed at school himself but is now an inspired teacher, likens the effort of getting a child to love learning to that of resuscitating an injured swallow, which eventually

> flies off, still a bit groggy, zig-zagging across reclaimed space, then ... darts south in a straight line and disappears into its future ... We don't always succeed; sometimes we fail to show the way, some of them don't wake up ... But every time we try, we will have tried. They are *our* students ... Neither affection nor sentiment is at stake here. It's a matter of life and death.[3]

In 1962, Paulo Freire, then director of the Department of Cultural Extension at Recife University, taught 300 sugar-cane workers to read and write in just forty-five days. In response to this experiment, the Brazilian government set up thousands of cultural circles across the country.

Does our society really believe that every child deserves a full and rich education? As private-school head Anthony Seldon told me (see Chapter 6): 'We'd be a better, more harmonious society if people had these interests developed when they were young ... the more deprived the background, the less infrastructure at home, the greater the need. If schools aren't going to do these things, who is?'[4] Exactly: but who will provide these opportunities for kids born to families who get by, each year, on the equivalent of the fees for a term or two at Seldon's Wellington College?

Lurking beneath the tough rhetoric about rigour and increased social mobility for the 'disadvantaged' is a different plan, one with uncomfortable echoes of the grammar-school era. The radical academic Danny Dorling is right to raise the suspicion that the powerful 'believe that just a few children are sufficiently able to be fully educated, and only a few of those are then able to govern; the rest must be led'.[5] In this unspoken scheme, a few talented children from poorer homes are deserving of a more rigorous education and a direct route to the prestigious universities. Underneath the rhetoric of 'every child matters'—that suffused New Labour discourse as well as the current Coalition's policies—lingers the belief that children belong in distinct groups. No longer gold, silver or iron, now the distinctions are more likely to be between the 'gifted and talented', the hidden middle, and the struggling.

Current cuts in the education budget, particularly affecting music, arts, and literary projects, as well as one-to-one tuition, are already undermining the right of every child to a broad and balanced education. So does the closure of public libraries, the shutting down of many Sure Start centres and the scrapping of so many school building projects, which, for all their faults, held fast to an ideal that every child deserved pleasant surroundings and first-class facilities. The current government may blame the deficit, but a child from a low-income family is now more likely to receive a narrow and sterile education, in an inhospitable environment, than they were only two years ago.

Some, on the right, think it's not worth the state's effort. They point to the long and rich tradition of working-class self-education, powerfully explored in books like Robert Tressell's *The Ragged Trousered Philanthropists* or in Lee Hall's unexpected West End and Broadway hit play, *The Pitmen Painters*; reflected in the history of skilled mathematicians and enthusiastic scientists among the nineteenth-century miners of Northumberland and

Durham, and present in the literary endeavours of many manual workers and their leaders in the twentieth century, from George Lansbury to Keir Hardie, Ben Tillett to Manny Shinwell. Or the impressive history of the Workers' Educational Association, which celebrated its hundredth anniversary in 2010, honouring the thousands of individuals and local groups around the country who have set themselves the task of seriously engaging with everything from literature to economics, physics to poetry. Many of those most enthusiastically involved in the WEA missed out on a formal schooling, making learning even more precious to them.

Conservative researchers and writers like Ferdinand Mount and James Tooley (both following the trail blazed by E. G. West, one of the first market theorists in education), have suggested that far from facilitating working-class education, the welfare state has betrayed the proud inheritance of working-class self-organisation and culture. Instead, the slow and uneven growth of state education has substituted a culture of condescension, an inferior diet to be digested passively by the masses. Mount sees a distinct lack of rigour in modern culture, the pressure to render everything accessible and a 'panic about the inability of the lower orders to stick at anything difficult'.[6] Ironically, Mount and A. S. Neill share a similar common-sense perspective: knowledge that is won through self-direction will always feel more valuable than learning imposed from on high. This is one of the enduring, very human, contradictions of education—but does it mean that the state should abdicate the role of educator, or that one should write off the education of those who are hardest to reach? On the contrary, it means that we have to keep trying.

Another important principle, deeply embedded within the comprehensive tradition, is not to prejudge our children's ability, or to set their direction in life too early. Professor Ken Robinson is a cogent critic of an increasingly sterile model of education that has taken root in the United States. 'Life is not linear, it's organic. But we are obsessed with this linear narrative, with getting people to college.' When he moved to Los Angeles, he was surprised to hear people say, without irony, 'College begins in kindergarten.' To which he responds, 'No, it doesn't. Kindergarten begins in kindergarten.'[7]

One of the more questionable premises underlying the Knowledge Is Power Programme (KIPP), and associated projects, is that the aim of a good education is to escape. While researching this book, I interviewed a talented and committed Teach First graduate who was critical of this assumption, in his own training and within the Teach First ideology as a whole; the aim, he claimed, was always to get the bright children away from what was presumed to be a dead-end life. In contrast, Gary Phillips, head of Lilian Baylis Technology College, encourages graduates of the school who have gone on to college or university to come back to the school as teachers or mentors or, more broadly, to help effect change within the community from which they come.

One of the most destructive of mainstream educational ideas is that of fixed abilities and pathways. Comprehensive reform itself was partly enabled by the rapid growth of a radical critique of intelligence testing and rejection of the idea of fixed potential.[8] The eleven-plus, the damaging apotheosis of this mindset, was swept away in most parts of the country by popular parental protest. Many successful adults who failed the eleven-plus still feel wounded by it, their self-confidence shaken forever by the state officially telling them they were not good enough. Black parents in the 1960s and 70s objected to the way that intelligence tests, with their cultural and ethnic bias, were used to assign their children to lower-ability groups and in many cases to categorise them as educationally subnormal.[9]

The eleven-plus has largely been eliminated, but intelligence-style testing is still used in many schools as a way of tracking children's progress. Such strategies are understandable, particularly in schools urgently trying to improve results, but they can have unexpectedly negative consequences. Children are frequently required to sit Cognitive Assessment Tests—IQ-style exams—soon after they enter secondary school. Inevitably, the results of such tests risk fixing—and limiting—the way a school thinks about a pupil throughout their school life, and creating an unofficial, inflexible ranking within each class or year group.

Ideally, education should be about the exact opposite: it should not confirm a given truth, or generate a set of IQ-related numbers, but encourage the constant recreation of self through imagination and knowledge and effort. Often, pupils simply need to be given the space, resources and encouragement to push and prove themselves. Add to this the clear links that persist between social class and presumed intelligence—so that middle-class children who have grown up with books, theatre visits, discussion of ideas and so on have an enormous advantage in these tests, as in all schooling —and poorer children lose out yet again.

Challenging the idea of fixed ability can have a surprising impact. At the Wroxham School, a primary school in Hertfordshire, head Alison Peacock has outlawed all discussion and assignation of ability. At Wroxham, the emphasis is on the single idea of *everybody*: everybody is a learner, and learning should involve everybody. The school has developed a wide range of activities, fostering interest and engagement in maths, reading, science and craft-based activities, including innovative ideas like outdoor 'forest schools' and the Learning Bus, the school library that is permanently parked in the playground. The school uses detailed, personalised methods of assessment, but none of them involve the dreaded 'levels'. When Peacock took over the school, it was in special measures. It is now recognised as outstanding in every single area of the curriculum and school management; it is heavily oversubscribed, and has a highly involved and hugely enthusiastic parent body. And, unsurprisingly, very good formal exam results.

The Wroxham school is part of Learning Without Limits, a network of teachers, school leaders and academics that challenges the ideas of 'inborn intelligence' that have been so influential in education in England. It rejects the notion of 'ability ... as a genetic inheritance, a given amount of innate, general cognitive power.'[10] The group argues, instead, for the development of a 'more optimistic view of human educability, one responsive to the natural propensity of human beings not just to learn but to *change* over time' (their emphasis). Schools like Wroxham prove that rejecting 'the fallacy of fixed ability' can work on a practical level, and produce highly successful educational outcomes at primary and secondary level.[11]

A small private day school is doing a project on global poverty; the children are assembling information and images that illustrate what it is like to live on a pound a day; their interest and sympathy are engaged as they cover the whole of one wall of their classroom with photographs of children barefoot or with pleading eyes, sitting with empty bowls before them. In the ensuing discussion, the teacher points out that there are, within a few minutes' walk of their own school, children who exist on a poor diet, with little access to play areas, children who have never seen the sea. In the canteen at a major public school, students are sometimes served soup, or a meat-free meal, to remind them of the more meagre diet of the less fortunate.

Given that all children will learn about the lives of others more or less fortunate than themselves, particularly in today's information-saturated world, what does it matter whether children of different backgrounds and faiths actually learn together? A great deal, as it happens. We know that the failure of public institutions to bridge difference can be disastrous, as the history of sectarianism in Northern Ireland's schools shows, breeding distrust, hatred and violence between the Catholic and Protestant populations. It has taken a long time for the two communities to edge closer to one another, and schooling is clearly going to play an important part in that. Eighty-four per cent of citizens in Northern Ireland now believe that integrated education is important to the continuance of the peace and reconciliation process.[12]

There is also a long history of ethnic segregation in towns like Oldham, and deep mistrust, particularly following the riots of 2001. In the words of one resident, it feels as if 'there isn't a community any more, it's like it's split in two'. But the local authority is now working hard to bring the Asian and white communities together through merging lessons in two previously separate schools—a project that feels of immense importance, not just to the town, but to the country as a whole.[13] Polling regularly shows that many people dislike the idea of separate education based on religion, and worry about the extent to which faith schools harm community cohesion.[14]

Whether we like it or not, schools clearly serve a powerful social function: at their best, binding very different communities together; at their worst, dividing us permanently from each other. Schools offer a unique chance to create powerful early bonds; they encourage children from different classes, ethnic backgrounds and faiths to see each other as human, to recognise the similarities in one another, not emphasise the differences.

Writers from John Dewey to R. H. Tawney have understood that neighbourhood schools provide a place to positively investigate the potential differences between cultures and classes, in order to begin to create a common culture. In *The Uses of Disorder*, Richard Sennett makes a strong case for cities as places of creative possibilities, where we can learn to negotiate our differences, our clashes of interests and identities on a daily basis. In this scheme, he sees neighbourhood schools as a 'focus for conflict and conciliation'. Imagining a bright young girl who attends a neighbourhood school in the inner city, as opposed to a suburb, Sennett writes:

> The little girl sees, every day, that the tensions and friendships in the community or school ... do not create chaos ... People are not sheltered from each other, but their contacts are more explorations of a constantly shifting environment than the acting-out of an unchanging routine. Therefore this little girl grows up in a neighbourhood that does not permit her family or her circle of friends to be intensive and inward-turning. This fact has a liberating power for her as someone who is exceptionally bright.[15]

Sennett's point may be a little sweeping and optimistic, but it is essentially a sound one. How do we begin to learn about others if we never come in contact with them?

A final point about locality. British upper-class education has traditionally been predicated on the idea that excellence requires mobility; up until the late seventeenth century aristocratic young men were sent to other households to live in order to acquire knowledge and worldly understanding. In more modern times, the boarding-school system has served to make 'men' of boys from largely well-off families, wrenched from their parents as young as seven years old; even today, as many as 67,000 children board away from home. Conversely, localism is associated with the immobility of the poor: those without the resources or the encouragement to travel, either intellectually or physically—like the children of the Teach First graduate who had never been on a train. Comprehensives have played their part in unpicking this established association between mobility and intellectual ambition, but the increasing marketisation of our schools has persuaded people, once again, to look further afield for education; children are now travelling further to get to school. The average length of a trip to school for primary and secondary age children has risen by 20 per cent in the last ten years or so—from 1.3 miles to 1.6 miles, and from 2.9 miles to 3.4 miles, respectively, between 1995–7 to 2008.[16] Environmental concerns lend extra force to the argument. School choice often means, in practice, putting children into cars early in the morning for long, exhausting drives across cities and towns; it increases congestion and wastes valuable energy. Why contribute to environmental problems, and needlessly extend the school day, when our children could walk, together, to a local school?

Amid the ever-rising tide of marketisation and increasing fragmentation, we risk losing sight of the crucial role of the state in planning and providing for public services and ensuring their rational and fair distribution. Successive governments have continuously suggested that private enterprise has the monopoly on organisational energy and creativity, while local government tends towards the bureaucratic or inefficient. Contemporary educational market theorists like James Tooley, again utilising the writings of E.G. West, argue that given the natural and entirely proper selfishness of parents, the answer to inadequate education provision lies in the extension of low-cost private education—subsidised by philanthropists for the very poor, or those without family support.[17]

This argument needs challenging on several levels. Firstly, contrary to appearances, the state as currently organised is not backing out of education provision. Far from it: it is colluding in a series of back-room deals with the private sector, enabling and encouraging privatisation at every turn while, at the same time, exercising greater control from the centre. Government has not stepped back from secondary education over the past decades. It has simply shifted control from the town halls to Westminster.

Secondly, however well-meaning or apparently effective, private providers are accountable to no-one but central government, too often cravenly grateful for their high-energy, high-profile interventions. Diane Ravitch, the former education adviser to the Bush administration, has written eloquently of her growing disquiet at the 'billionaires' boys' club' connected to the charter school movement in America. Vast and intricate experiments in schooling have been launched with great fanfare, only to be abandoned a few years later when they hit obstacles. It seems perverse that just when policy makers and politicians agree that low-income children are in need of radically improved education, the state should stand back and hand over control of education, or indeed any other service, to the rich and famous. Our schools are institutions held in common. Building a school requires patient, long-term involvement from hundreds of people over a sustained period of time. New school providers often enter the schools market, bursting with a sense of their own superiority and uniqueness, only to face the same social and practical difficulties as those providers which they have replaced. The philanthropic edu-entrepreneur can always walk away; the state, quite rightly, cannot.

Thirdly, to argue for the state to continue to play a central role in our schools is not to advocate a centralised or rigid model. Here in the UK we have been, and remain, ill-served by top-down prescriptive government, currently run by an impatient elite in alliance with a motley crew of celebrated academics, provocative celebrities and shadowy corporate backers. For schools to function *fairly*, as well as *effectively*, we need a renewed form of local democracy. We have lamentably lost touch with our own history of proud and vigorous municipalism which created so many of our cities, our hospitals, our parks and our schools.

At the same time, the framework for local oversight of schools may need revising and modernising. Some campaigners have put forward alternatives. One suggestion is for a modern equivalent of the old School Boards, directly elected Local Education Councils, whose responsibility it would be to spend their portion of the education budget wisely and effectively, oversee the running of local schools and enable their collaboration.[18] Such Local Education Councils could include representatives of political parties, directly elected members and co-opted experts, including retired head teachers, mental health professionals, community activists, educational administrators, current and ex-students and representatives from local business and enterprise. Such a system would utilise the sorely needed energy and creativity of the thousands of people currently reduced to bystander status, many of them parents with a multitude of interesting ideas for the improved management of schools. They, after all, have direct experience of state education, unlike many of the sponsors who currently run parts of our school estate.

But local government has to become more responsive to local need and more participatory, if we are to bring about the improvements we need. It is time to talk: as a nation, as neighbourhoods. Some councils, as I described in the previous chapter, are beginning to initiate such a conversation. One of the most striking aspects of many of the most successful school systems around the world is not just their robust defence of, and pride in, public (state) education, but the intensive discussions that have preceded every significant structural change. These discussions, among elected officials, school leaders and teachers, continue. Change is a given; it is how we manage it that matters.

What can we learn from other countries? Finland, and the province of Alberta in Canada, are two of the most highly performing entities in international school tests. Both are models of high-quality, non-selective state education systems, with some key features of relevance to us: high levels of trust and autonomy granted to schools and teachers; extensive methods of pupil assessment and teacher collaboration that do not pit child against child or school against school, but help develop each and every learner; greater integration of academic and vocational education.

Alberta offers an interesting alternative model of parental choice to the one traditionally advocated in the UK and US. When US-style charter schools began emerging in Alberta's towns and cities, the school boards and municipal council decided to design a choice system that benefited all children, and in particular revitalised low-income neighbourhoods. They called parents together for a series of area- and school-based meetings, and asked them what *they* wanted to see from their public schools. As a result of this extensive consultation, they introduced *more choice* into state schools; parents and pupils can now decide, within reasonable limits, what kind of learning programme they want to follow, thus creating schools within schools, mixing traditional and free-ranging curriculum programmes.

Compare this to the UK, where parental choice seems increasingly to be confined to one potentially life-changing decision taken before one's child reaches eleven. Given the degree of emotional investment most parents seem to have in their children's education, there should surely be more scope for consultation in how our schools are being run, and debate about their strengths and faults? This is not to detract from the need for strong school leaders, efficient middle management and strongly performing teachers. But a robust local democracy could afford to open the door a crack and ask parents—particularly low-income parents, who tend to have least choice in a market system—for their opinion on the general direction of state education as well as the performance of particular schools? Alberta's school leaders are particularly determined to do their best by, and be accountable to, low-income groups. They will not accept the educational failure of children who come from poor homes.

Alberta's system of choice is combined with a high degree

of school-based autonomy and budget control. In Alberta, an in-school manager deals with all practical and financial questions, leaving heads free to be 'instructional leaders'. At the same time there is intensive co-operation and collaboration between heads and schools. School heads are tenured to the province, not to any one school; they can be moved after as a little as one year, after discussion and consultation. Teaching and learning is rigorously monitored; here, too, a culture of constant collaboration and conversation maintains accountability. As a result, teachers remain 'engaged and excited' about their professional work, and they too seem to develop a loyalty to the schooling system as a whole, rather than to one school. Thanks to these changes, Alberta has seen off much of the charter challenge in the province; several private schools have now chosen to join the state system.

Finland—which regularly tops international test tables, and has the narrowest achievement gap between children of different social or ethnic backgrounds—provides another alternative to market-based systems. In Finland, almost everyone attends their neighbourhood school; choice is inevitably less of an issue, because the quality of schooling is so good. One of the most striking features of the Finnish system is the degree of autonomy and respect granted to teachers. Teachers have high status, and there is intense competition among graduates for places on the teacher training scheme. Every teacher, even at primary level, must be fully qualified in a subject area as well as in general educational and pedagogical theory; in addition, all teachers have a master's degree, displaying specialisation in a particular area relating to children's development or their subject. League tables and SATs-type testing are unheard of. The Finnish teaching day is relatively short, partly because teachers spend a large percentage of their professional time assessing students' work, moderating it among themselves, and personalising their support to students, concentrating on their areas of weakness. In both Finland and Alberta, there is continuous discussion on the national, local, school and classroom levels about how the curriculum is taught and assessed.

*   *   *

The UK is a larger country than either Finland or the province of Alberta, with a greater ethnic and religious mix and far higher levels of economic inequality. Our classrooms are frequently much more challenging places. For all these reasons, we cannot directly read off developments in school systems from other, very different cultures to our own, and apply them wholesale; but neither are they irrelevant.

Finland teaches us that we have to trust our teachers. Over the last thirty years, the tightening of centralised control over the work of the classroom, the constricted nature of the curriculum and the dominance of testing have reduced many of our teaching force to mere technicians. An increasing focus on the role of head teachers and the creation of a new category of super-heads—highly paid, often autocratic school leaders—may have also diminished the potential autonomy and perceived value of classroom teachers, who are increasingly expected merely to deliver results for the greater glory of head and school. If we really want state education to be first-class, we have to foster far greater professionalism and independence of judgement, and permit more creative freedom to our teachers. It is they, after all, who have the closest, most consistent contact with our children. Their quality, as human beings and as professionals, is the greatest guarantee we can have of the quality of our children's education.

The current government is also looking with interest at the Finnish model. It, too, talks a great deal about improving teaching, but many of its proposals risk further reducing the status and significance of the profession. It is interesting that the government has so little to say about Finland's informal classroom culture, with no uniforms, relaxed relationships between pupils and teachers, and far less emphasis on homework and testing: the direct opposite of what is currently being proposed. Government plans to withdraw teacher-training from the universities is another retrograde step. We need not just subject specialists but men and women who have learned to be thoughtful, self-reflective and socially aware. When Afro-Caribbean parents in this country first raised criticisms of the way their children were being pushed into classes and schools for the educationally subnormal, they rejected simplistic solutions such as bringing in more black teachers. What they wanted were teachers who understood the cultural and psychological and political aspects of their children's lives, who recognised how racism operated, and would consciously refrain from insensitivity themselves.[19]

As a 2007 McKinsey report on improving world school systems concluded: 'The quality of an education system cannot exceed the quality of its teachers.' The selection of talented graduates is important. But so is rigorous training. Interestingly, the McKinsey report noted that among the qualities needed in order to select the best candidates for the teaching profession, is a willingness to learn.[20] We need teachers in our classrooms who have not only developed subject expertise but who have been given the space to reflect on the profession they are about to enter, and the context in which they may have to practise it, who are widely read in educational and psychological theory and who understand issues relating to race, gender, culture and class. This is not a 'politically correct' waste of time; it is laying the groundwork for responsible professionals operating in the modern world, preparing men and women for the reality of classes that may contain many children from radically different cultures and backgrounds than their own. Such a grounding is not incompatible with the necessary professional distance and high standards. It does not prohibit teachers from expecting the most from pupils, and it might help them to get it. But in the current political climate the emphasis is on shoving young, bright graduates, or even ex-soldiers, into the classroom as quickly as possible.

Close monitoring of classroom performance is important (but just as important that teachers engage in the process themselves, and become their own best critics), as is continuous professional development. Poor teachers should be quickly spotted, and offered help and support to improve; if they are still failing, they should be moved on. At the same time, the radically differing contexts in which UK teachers work have to be recognised. It is obviously easier to teach fifteen well-rested, well-fed children from well-off homes than thirty teenagers, many of whom are experiencing high levels of deprivation or disturbance outside school. It is unreasonable to expect our teachers to solve—within the school day, or even over a child's educational lifetime—the effect of a multitude of problems in our society, from child poverty to racism, from the commercialisation and sexualisation of childhood to the crasser elements of celebrity culture.

In order to grant our teachers more professional power and autonomy, we need to develop a lighter-touch curriculum. Successive attempts to do so have been consistently blocked from the centre, by politicians who prefer to rank schools in pseudo-academic league order, or to dictate what should be learned from on high. Many commentators believe that the answer to state education is to make it a pale, cheap imitation of the public-school model with a nineteenth-century or at least 1950s mode of teaching, putting everyone into straight lines, drilling them with dates and facts. This idea is behind the times. After all, acclaimed schools like Wellington College use much more imaginative methods, emphasising 'multiple intelligences' and participatory methods of learning.

We need to retain some form of core national curriculum, so that parents can be assured that whatever school their child attends throughout the UK, they will have access to the same broad range of knowledge up to the age of sixteen—even if individual schools and teachers are given greater powers to devise their own approaches and methods of teaching. We should not abandon testing altogether, but far more of this could be undertaken on a class or year-group level, and adapted rather more to the pace at which individual classes, or pupils, progress. There are strong arguments for abolition of current Standard Assessment Tests at age eleven which cause so much stress, choke the enjoyment of learning for so many children in their last year of primary school, and distort the true picture of a school's strengths or weaknesses. When in 2007 the General Teaching Council asked parents about different methods of testing, twice as many parents said they were more likely to trust an individual assessment by the teacher than an exam result. In general they saw teachers as being best placed to assess children, due to their regular contact with them.[21] Given the understandable anxiety about standards, a snapshot picture of school performance could be achieved through regular and random sampling, rather like the PISA system.

For too long, there has been a sterile division between the academic and vocational aspects of education. Children from lower-income families have been pushed down the vocational route, often because it is easier for hard-pressed institutions to stereotype them, and because vocational qualifications have, until recently, boosted a school's rankings in the league tables. Again, we can learn from places like Finland and Alberta who mix and match the vocational and academic with much greater ease, and delay specialisation until later in adolescence. There is no reason why a student who has decided, aged sixteen, to be a plumber or a car mechanic should not also take courses in philosophy or French. Similarly, a student who has chosen to pursue scientific or humanities study should also be able to do cooking or IT. No child should specialise too early.

But if we are seriously to reduce the differential outcomes of the better-off and the poor, we have to move towards a genuinely non-selective system. I have already described how existing degrees of inequality, particularly within our big cities, present a real, but not insurmountable, challenge to policymakers. Interim solutions, such as banding and random allocation (the school lottery) might be necessary in order to create a workable and fair balance within our schools. It is a real pity, then, that the Coalition Government has recently proposed the outlawing of area-wide lotteries. Within schools selected, mixed-ability teaching, for all its challenges, seems to offer the fairest and overall most effective method of learning, certainly in the early years of secondary education. All the highest-performing systems delay setting and streaming to later in adolescence. Similarly, the more poorly performing national systems divide and differentiate their pupils at too young an age.

There are still powerful interests and lobby groups that advocate the return to academic selection in the state system, including the argument that this is the only way to give the private schools a run for their money. However, the evidence of social discrimination and rank unfairness—and the consequent waste of talent among the majority, who are rejected under such a polarising system—is now virtually uncontestable. The existence of so many genuinely mixed, high-performing, 'all-in' schools also provides strong evidence that comprehensive education can work, to the greater benefit of all. Yet we remain in unending political stasis on this issue. No mainstream political leader will condone selection, but none will seriously suggest we phase it out. Why? Quite simply because they fear the fury of established interests, not just the grammar-school lobby, but many within the media, including many of those who benefited from a grammar-school education themselves. As a result, politicians debate schools policy as if selection, in both the state and private sector, simply doesn't exist. Or doesn't exist enough to matter. Or just doesn't matter.

This cannot go on. It may not be for ten, twenty or even fifty years' time, but at some point the political class, and the public at large, will have to face this conundrum head-on. As it is unlikely that they will agree to the country-wide return of academic selection, they will surely have to face the alternative and finally take the steps necessary to create a fair school system for all. With sufficient political momentum, selection could be phased out with relative ease and minimum disruption.

One of the most noticeable changes over my own lifetime has been the larger role that parents now take, and are expected and encouraged to take, in their child's schooling. It was parental engagement and activism, and in particular the setting-up of supplementary schools, that set black families in this country on the road to demanding higher expectations of, and better schooling for, their children.[22] But the current trend seems to be for anxious parents, particularly in poorer families, to hand over their children's education to super-strict institutions which, in return, promise them a college place at the end of it. Charter schools in the USA insist on detailed 'home-school contracts', with parents expected to comply with strict requirements in order to keep their child on the programme. Many of our academies are going the same way.

Surely there are other, less draconian, more long-term and sustainable ways to involve parents in their children's learning, and lives? Sure Start centres, many of which are being closed by the current government, have played a crucial part in improving the learning outcomes of children from poor families. Schemes such as Families and Schools Together work with families in poorer communities to improve inter-family relationships and help parents to help their children at school. So far, the scheme has a high retention rate.[23] Again, there are no easy or quick solutions, especially not in a system as divided as ours: successful parent–school partnerships are usually best developed over the long term. Neighbourhood schools give teachers and other school professionals a chance to meet and get to know the families of the children they teach, and the school can offer extra services from breakfast clubs to after-school care and homework clubs, helping pupils with difficult home lives to keep on track. Pastoral care plays a key role in ensuring a successful education.

And what of the boundaries between private enterprise and government? Education is one of the most important services we provide as a nation—and fund as taxpayers. Yet the practical effect of creeping privatisation means that increasingly, we—as citizens, as well as parents—are passive spectators of an alliance between the private sector and politicians as they step in to 'save' civil society from its failures, including the apparent failure of egalitarianism. We must not let this happen. There is nothing to stop enterprising individuals or companies from offering support to schools; there are many examples of the positive impact of links between schools and businesses, or private or third-sector organisations supplying 'add-ons' to the curriculum. Local businesses should be encouraged to form a relationship with, play a part in and donate to schools, at either a local or national level. The private sector will always have an important voice in the national dialogue about education. But there is no reason why it should be granted such a privileged place—and controlling role—in the management of schools. Quite simply, education is not its business.

Public services should remain within the remit of a dynamic democratic state, at every level. Taxation, of both individuals and corporations, has to remain the crucial component in maintaining proper public provision. One of the glaring contradictions of the academy and free school programmes has been the degree to which public money has facilitated encroaching private control of education, compounded by the readiness of the state to step in and generously finance its favoured schools.

Quality education requires significant investment. That is the prime message of one of the most famous charter school experiments in the USA, the Harlem Children's Zone, which spends far higher amounts than equivalent US public schools in its 'cradle-to-college' care of students (largely thanks to Wall street donations), and which President Obama is now attempting to replicate on a large scale, using federal funds.[24] The OECD has recently highlighted the fact that we in Britain do not concentrate our resources where we need them most. The UK is one of just thirteen countries across Europe where schools with students from poorer backgrounds have similar student–teacher ratios as schools with children from more prosperous backgrounds, and attend schools with the same kinds of teachers and resources. Surely the schools with the greatest difficulties should have the best teachers and proportionally more resources? The proposed pupil premium is, at least currently, an already disappearing drop in the ocean. Whatever benefit it brings will almost certainly be cancelled out by the overall effect of the cuts. So it is back to square one, with another failure to target investment at those schools and those children who need it most.

The current tax subsidy granted to private schools, currently estimated at £100 million, is unjustifiable. This sum could be better used to provide catch-up classes in literacy and numeracy to those who have fallen behind. In the short term, such a move would win popular support. In the longer term, it could play an important part in a much-needed public conversation about the relationship between private and state schools.

Looking at the broader canvas, we need to ask bigger questions about how our nation's finances are spent. While the true cost of the financial crisis will not be known for many years, taxpayer support for UK banks is currently estimated at over £500 billion.[25] Tony Blair came to power and pledged to fund 'education, education, education'. In reality, his government ended up funding war, war, war. Fighting in Afghanistan and Iraq alongside the US has cost British taxpayers more than £20 billion since the 9/11 terror attacks in 2001: £18 billion for military operations, plus the expense of security, overseas development and aid.[26] And this total does not include the salaries of soldiers or paying for their long-term injuries and mental health care, coming on top of a £35-billion annual defence budget. And with the royal wedding coming in at a total cost of £10 million to the taxpayer, plus a further loss to the economy in days taken off, the Crown and Government could have redirected that sum to a local school, for refurbishment, or one-to-one tuition for children who need personalised help with anything from reading to GCSE and A-level preparation.[27]

We could organise our education system along much simpler and fairer lines, and in ways that unify, not divide, the nation. Just imagine, for a moment, an NES: a National Education Service that is held in the same affection and trust, for all its imperfections, as the NHS once was and indeed still is, for all the assaults upon it. A service that allows the poorest family to feel confident that their child will receive a broadly similar educational start in life to their better-off peers, and one that promises to enrich and challenge all. A service based on neighbourhood schools—housed in well-designed, well-equipped, aesthetically pleasing and properly maintained buildings, enjoying plenty of outdoor space—with balanced intakes and a broad, rich curriculum that will allow each child, whatever their talents, temperament or interests, to flourish.

Rather than making schools compete for the easiest to teach or highest-attaining pupils, local collaboration between schools on the crucial question of admissions—overseen by an impartial body, concerned above all with fairness—should ensure that each school has its share of both the most motivated and the hardest to teach. Without this, we will surely continue with the situation we have now, where certain schools are pulled down by the daily battle with the offloaded problems of the wider society, and many of the country's poorest children are educated in a tranche of poorly performing and poorly regarded schools.

Parents, and pupils, should retain their current right to express a preference at secondary transfer. But even the Coalition Government acknowledges that perfect choice cannot operate within state education. To harp on about the shortage of 'good' schools, and then not to implement the very changes that would improve so many existing institutions—and worse, to cut the services of so many of them—is a form of political bad faith. Contrary to all the easy rhetoric on choice and diversity, schools do not operate like shops or businesses, expanding and contracting, opening and closing at will—and parents do not want them to do so. The emphasis should be instead on the creation and consolidation of an enduring, quality public service.

Within such a framework, schools could concentrate on a single vital task: the bringing of rigour and quality to the hour by hour, day by day, learning in our classrooms, be it reception-level art, preparation for GCSE Food Tech, or A-level Latin. I repeat: there are no quick fixes, only a long road of hard and patient work. This does not mean a return to dreary traditionalism in course content or teaching methods. It *does* mean treating the education of every child with the utmost seriousness, and not just that of the more academically talented, or of those with the pushiest or wealthiest parents. For too long, the great unspoken assumption of our elite, and an underlying cause of generations of persistent educational failure, has been that some children do not deserve—or are not worth—a serious education. They should be drilled or trained for work, certainly, but not be taught carefully and seriously in a range of subjects, academic and vocational. Who knows; might our leaders actually fear a larger, more confident, restlessly questioning citizenry?

Change must begin at classroom level. Schools need not necessarily be much smaller; practically speaking, larger institutions can offer a broader range of courses and options. But class sizes should certainly be cut over time, and more generally, learning should aim to be on a human scale. One-to-one and small-group tuition should be used far more, and made available to all children falling behind in key areas of the curriculum.

Pastoral care and the personalisation of learning are two positive developments of modern education, and yet, in practice, these are too often the prerogative of paying customers. Every child within the state sector should be, and should feel, known as a unique being within their school. Each should sense a benign focus on their potential, their progress, their successes as well as their problems, throughout their school life.

Teachers should be trusted with far more freedom than they have at present to implement and vary the curriculum, as and when they see fit, and to track students' progress in more flexible ways. The current state system has nurtured some inspirational and talented head teachers, but whatever freedoms are to be granted from the centre to school managers and leaders—be it to reorganise the school day, or to adapt course content or teaching methods to suit the circumstances—should be offered to all, not just the government's pet projects. Given the existing inequalities in our society, and the disparities in children's readiness to learn, the need for greater resources to be targeted at certain schools and pupils is likely to persist for many years to come.

With these changes, we might begin to consolidate the many gains already made over the last fifty years or more: to move from the important concept of universal education to the even more crucial practice of universal excellence. We might learn collectively to value state education, rather than routinely denigrate it. In Alberta, elected officials, school administrators, head teachers, teachers and pupils appear to take visible pride in their

public (state) schools. Stickers urge citizens to '*Go Public*'; officials and teachers talk about the challenges and achievements of
their schools with sparkling animation. Can we recapture, or even
capture, such pride in our own schools? We urgently need to, in
the interests of all. As Diane Ravitch says of the much-maligned
American public school system,

> our nation's commitment to provide universal, free public education
> has been a crucial element in the successful assimilation of millions
> of immigrants and in the ability of generations of Americans to
> improve their lives ... the market, with its great strengths, is not
> the appropriate mechanism to supply services that should be dis-
> tributed equally to people in every neighbourhood in every city
> and town in the nation, without regard to their ability to pay or
> their political power.[28]

What political leader or significant public figure in the UK has
ever spoken about state education in these rousing terms? It is
time to throw over the fear and cynicism that underlies the new
school revolution—and its very old ideas—and to reassert the
more rational values of the original 'piecemeal revolution'. As
one spirited advocate of comprehensives, the Scottish journalist
Kevin McKenna, recently wrote: 'Thousands among our generation flourished in an environment where there was a presumption
of intelligence and talent. Our teachers were expected to have
the forensic skills necessary to identify gifts in everyone. It was
a system that gave the greatest number of our children the best
chance to gain a robust education.'[29]

    It is time, too, to reclaim the mantle of genuine reform for our
side in the long-running school wars. Genuine comprehensive
reform is unfinished. There is much exciting work still to be done.
The rewards, in terms of better-educated citizens of the future
and greater common ground between communities and religions
and classes, could be enormous. The alternative scenario—of
an increasingly fragmented, mistrustful and divided nation, controlled rather than enlightened, dependent on the unstable whim of
private or religious enterprise—is too frightening to contemplate.

Acknowledgements

Thanks, in various ways, are due to: Leighton Andrews, Jamie Audsley, Christine Blower, Chris Brown, Bridget Chapman, Kevin Courtney, Janet Dobson, Peter Downes, Emily Evans, Gareth Evans, Sue Fennimore, Helen Flynn, Tom Foot, Francis Gilbert, Katy Gough, Paul Goldsmith, David James, Theresa Johnson, Warwick Mansell, Paula Maynard, Gary Phillips, Lorna Scott Fox, Dr Anthony Seldon, Jan Stannard, Henry Stewart, Sarah Sutherland, Nicky Thomson, Ian Whitwham, Sir Michael Wilshaw, Denise Winn, Ruth Winstone, Polly Woodford, and to the staff and students at Mossbourne Academy, Wellington College and Manchester Enterprise Academy who gave very generously of their time. Many thanks are due to the NUT for a generous grant towards research costs. The steering group of *Comprehensive Future*, the board of *Forum*, and the contributors to the *Local School Network*, have all played an important part in shaping my response to the current debates. Thanks too to the teachers, leaders, parents and students of Salusbury School and Queens Park Community School who have inspired me in so many ways over the years.

Stephen Ball, Clyde Chitty, Peter Downes, John Fowler, Mike Hulme, Peter Mortimore, Margaret Tulloch and Anne West all read parts of the manuscript and their comments were invaluable, although in the end all arguments, and errors, are my own. Thanks to Tom Penn of Verso for suggesting I write this book, and for his enthusiasm and many shrewd editorial interventions, and to Faith Evans for her wise advice and constant support. My family and friends, in particular Joshua Benn, Tony Benn, Hannah Benn Gordon and Sarah Benn Gordon, kept me going with their loving encouragement.

This book could not have been written without the help of three people. Dominic Self threw himself wholeheartedly into the research for this project. Full of ideas, enthusiasm and challenges, his different perspective helped sharpen up my own position at every turn. Fiona Millar read several versions of the manuscript, bringing her unrivalled knowledge of school organisation, national education policy, and the wider political world, to the arguments. Last but never least, Paul Gordon gave me unstinting political, practical, literary, grammatical and emotional support throughout.

Notes

Introduction

1 Roy Greenslade, 'It was a considerable cock-up, a seriously misconceived exercise', *Guardian*, 9 July 2001, guardian.co.uk.

2 Roger Graef, 'On the edge of a nervous breakdown', *Guardian*, 27 April 2005, guardian.co.uk.

3 For one example, see Fiona Millar, 'Why I believe, after 18 years as a school governor, it is good heads, teachers, governors and supportive parents that really matter', Local Schools Network, 21 November 2010, localschools network.org.uk.

4 Fraser Nelson and Ed Howker, 'Revealed: the secret war over England's schools', *Spectator*, 28 August 2010, spectator.co.uk.

5 Peter Hitchens, 'Inverted Class War', *Mail Online*, 29 May 2007, hitchens blog.mailonsunday.co.uk.

6 James Delingpole, 'Free Schools: The Stake in the Heart of the Progressive Vampire', blogs.telegraph.co.uk, 6 May 2011.

7 Brian Cox, *The Great Betrayal: Memoirs of a Life in Education*, London: Chapmans, 1992, p. 142.

8 Diane Ravitch, 'The Myth of Charter Schools', *New York Review of Books*, 11 November 2010, nybooks.com.

9 Michael Morpurgo, Dimbleby Lecture, 21 February 2011, michaelmorpurgo. com.

Chapter 1

1 Bryony Gordon, 'Goldie Hawn: "I'm a dreamer, someone who wishes the best for mankind"', *Telegraph*, 2 July 2010, telegraph.co.uk.

2 Camilla Long, 'Michael Gove: the man in charge of children and families', *Sunday Times*, 4 October 2009, timesonline.co.uk.

3 Geraldine Bedell, 'Should parents set up their own state schools? Discuss', *Observer*, 24 January 2010, guardian.co.uk.

4 'Barnardo's calls for fairer school admissions', *BBC News*, 27 August 2010, bbc.co.uk.

5 Nick Britten, 'David Cameron is "terrified" about finding a good London state school for his children', *Telegraph*, 11 July 2010, telegraph.co.uk.

6 John Elledge, 'What's Gove really hiding?', *New Statesman* blog, 9 July 2010, newstatesman.com/blogs; Jessica Shepherd, 'Backbenchers line up to criticise Gove over cancelled school project list', *Guardian*, 9 July 2010, guardian.co.uk.

7 Even the National Grammar Schools Association complains about the Bill, if for a somewhat different reason. It warns grammar schools that if they become academies, they may more easily be turned into comprehensive schools; no longer defined as maintained schools, they might lose the statutory protection of requiring a parental ballot before any change in status.

8 Bookstart, 'Funding update', 20 January 2011, bookstart.org.uk.

9 Save EMA, 'OECD calls on Gove to save EMA', 8 April 2011, saveema. co.uk.

10 Rowan Moore, 'Architects do matter, Mr Gove', *Observer*, 6 March 2011, guardian.co.uk.

11 Polly Curtis, 'Britain "more Thatcherite now than in the 80s" says survey', *Guardian*, 13 December 2010, guardian.co.uk.

12 Adrian Elliott, *State Schools Since the 1950s: The Good News*, Stoke-on-Trent: Trentham Books, 2007, p. 2.

13 Christina Lamb, 'What's wrong with winning?', *Sunday Times*, 15 February 2009, timesonline.co.uk.

14 Zoë Heller, *Notes on a Scandal*, London: Viking, 2003.

15 Sebastian Faulks, *A Week in December*, London: Hutchinson, 2009.

16 Stephen Gorard, 'The international dimension: what can we learn from the PISA study?', in *GENDER in education 3-19: A fresh approach*, ATL, 2004, new2teaching.org.uk.

17 Peter Mortimore, 'A League Table to Worry Us All', *Guardian*, 8 January 2008.

18 Warwick Mansell, 'England joins the elite for maths and science', *TES*, 12 December 2008, tes.co.uk.

19 Warwick Mansell, 'The new national curriculum', *Education by Numbers*, 15 March 2011, educationbynumbers.org.uk.

20 Hansard, House of Commons Debate, 8 February 2011, c. 225.

21 Hilary Wilce, 'Time for a change: how a young woman plans to shake up the school landscape', *Independent*, 12 November 2009, independent.co.uk.

22 Anthony Seldon, 'Free schools are an opportunity, not a threat', *London Evening Standard*, 22 March 2011, thisislondon.co.uk.

23 Press Association, 'UK ranks behind Slovenia in childhood wellbeing', *Guardian*, 3 May 2011, guardian.co.uk.

24 Andrew Anthony, 'Katharine Birbalsingh: "The middle class is disguising the failings of state schools in the inner cities"', *Observer*, 27 February 2011, guardian.co.uk.

25 Andrew Porter and Graeme Paton, 'David Cameron: Tory leader talks to the *Daily Telegraph* about education', *Telegraph*, 6 February 2009, telegraph.co.uk.

26 Fran Abrams, 'Teachers' unions set for row with government', *Guardian*, 19 April 2011, guardian.co.uk.

27 Quoted in Jessica Shepherd and Jeevan Vasagar, 'Swedish-style free schools may increase social divide—study', *Guardian*, 21 July 2010, guardian.co.uk.

28 Francis Gilbert, 'Steiner schools fail to get Free School Funding—for this year at least', Local Schools Network, 6 March 2011, localschoolsnetwork.org.uk.

29 Hansard, House of Commons Debate, 8 February 2011, c. 194.

30 Nigel Gann, 'I recently stood down as chair of governors …', Local Schools Network, 12 April 2011, localschoolsnetwork.org.uk.

31 Warwick Mansell, 'Schools cash in on academy status', *Guardian*, 26 April 2011, guardian.co.uk.

32 Jessica Shepherd, 'How much schools spend varies widely, data shows', *Guardian*, 12–13 January 2011, guardian.co.uk.

33 Polly Curtis, 'Let schools fail to secure reforms, ministers urged', *Guardian*, 11 July 2011.

34 Rachel Williams, '"Savage" cuts to youth spending could rob a generation of chances', *Guardian*, 5 January 2011, guardian.co.uk.

Chapter 2

1 Tony Blair, *A Journey: My Political Life*, New York: Alfred A. Knopf, 2010, p. 579.

2 Board of Education, Report of The Consultative Committee on Secondary Education, with special reference to grammar schools and technical high schools, London: HMSO, 1938, pp. xix–xx, educationengland.org.uk.

3 Quoted in Stephen J. Ball, *The Education Debate*, Bristol: Policy Press, 2008, p. 61.

4 Ross McKibbin, *Classes and Cultures: England 1918-1951*, Oxford: Oxford University Press, 2000, p. 221.

5 Ibid., p. 222.

6 Board of Education, 'Educational Reconstruction', London: HMSO, 1943, p. 6, educationengland.org.uk.

7 Clyde Chitty, *Education Policy in Britain*, Basingstoke: Palgrave Macmillan, 2004, p. 27.

8 Quoted in Nicholas Timmins, *The Five Giants: A Biography of the Welfare State*, London: HarperCollins, 2001, p. 88.

9 Brian Simon, *Education and the Social Order, 1940–1990*, London: Lawrence & Wishart, 1999, p. 115.

10 Dominic Sandbrook, *Never Had It So Good*, London: Little, Brown, 2005, p. 36.

11 Adrian Elliott, *State Schools Since the 1950s: The Good News*, Stoke-on-Trent: Trentham Books, 2007, p. 20.

12 Ibid., pp. 29–59.

13 Michael Fielding, 'Alex Bloom, Pioneer of Radical State Education', FORUM, vol. 47, n. 2, 2005.

14 Abraham Wilson, abrahamwilson.com/page8.htm.

15 E. R. Braithwaite, *To Sir with Love*, London: Vintage Classics, p. 48.

16 Brian Jackson, *Streaming: An Education System in Miniature*, London: Routledge & K. Paul, 1964, quoted in Sally Tomlinson, *Education in a Post-Welfare Society*, Maidenhead: Open University Press, 2005, p. 20.

17 Brian Jackson and Dennis Marsden, *Education and the Working Class*, Oxford: Taylor & Francis, 1986.

18 McKibbin, *Classes and Cultures*, p. 262

19 Ibid., pp. 264-5.

20 Ministry of Education, *15 to 18: A Report of the Central Advisory Council for Education (England)*, London: HMSO, 1959, p. 124, educationengland.org.uk.

21 Ministry of Education, *Half Our Future: A Report of the Central Advisory Council for Education (England)*, London: HMSO, 1963, p. 6, educationengland.org.uk.

22 Quoted in Chitty, *Education Policy in Britain*, p. 28.

23 Simon Jenkins, 'Cameron's historic victory over the gilded myth of grammars', *Sunday Times*, 27 May 2007, timesonline.co.uk.

24 Caroline Benn and Brian Simon, *Half Way There: Report on the British Comprehensive System*, London: McGraw-Hill, 1970, p. 71.

25 Ibid., p. 76.

26 Max Morris, 'The Route to My Comprehensive', in Melissa Benn and Clyde Chitty, *A Tribute to Caroline Benn: Education and Democracy*, London: Continuum International Publishing Group, 2004, pp. 41–52.

27 Robin Pedley, *The Comprehensive School*, London: Penguin, 1963, p. 70.

28 Ibid.

29 Ibid., p. 71.

30 Clyde Chitty, 'The Right To A Comprehensive Education', speech given 16 November 2002, socialisteducation.org.uk/CB2.htm.

31 Jane Shallice, 'In Praise of Sixties Idealism', in Benn and Chitty, *A Tribute to Caroline Benn*, p. 37.

32 Ibid., p. 35.

33 Ibid., p. 37.

34 Leila Berg, 'Risinghill closed quietly. No one broke up the school', *TES*, 3 February 2006, tes.co.uk.

35 Leila Berg, *Risinghill: Death of a Comprehensive School*, Harmondsworth: Penguin, 1968.

36 Gerald Haigh, 'Flutterings from the Tyndale affair', *TES*, 7 July 2006, tes.co.uk.

Chapter 3

1 Clyde Chitty, 'The Right To A Comprehensive Education', speech given 16 November 2002, socialisteducation.org.uk.

2 Caroline Benn and Clyde Chitty, *Thirty Years On: Is Comprehensive Education Alive and Well or Struggling to Survive?* London: David Fulton Publishers, 1996, pp. 24–5.

3 Brian Cox, *The Great Betrayal: Memoirs of a Life in Education*, London: Chapmans, 1992, p. 143.

4 Ibid., p. 145.

5 Ibid., p. 147.

6 Clyde Chitty, *Understanding Schools and Schooling*, London: Routledge, 2001, p. 23.

7 Cox, *The Great Betrayal*, p. 224.

8 Stephen J. Ball, *The education debate*, Bristol: The Policy Press, 2008, p. 73.

9 Simon Jenkins, *Thatcher and Sons: A Revolution in Three Acts*, London: Allen Lane, 2006, p. 116.

10 Ibid., p. 117.

11 Ted Wragg, *Education, Education, Education: The best bits of Ted Wragg*, London: Routledge, 2004, pp. 60–1.

12 Clyde Chitty, *Education Policy in Britain*, Basingstoke: Palgrave Macmillan, 2004, pp. 53–4.

13 Jenkins, *Thatcher and Sons*, p. 177.

14 Benn and Chitty, *Thirty Years On*, p. 468.

15 Chitty, *Education Policy in Britain*, p. 68.

16 Paul Vallely, 'He visited in glory days of '97, but has Blair kept his vow to Aylesbury Estate?', *Independent*, 12 April 2005, independent.co.uk.

17 Wragg, *Education, Education, Education*, p. 50.

18 Blair, *A Journey*, p. 580.

19 Peter Hyman, *1 out of 10: From Downing Street Vision to Classroom Reality*, London: Vintage, 2005, p. 28.

20 Quoted in Melissa Benn and Fiona Millar, 'A Comprehensive Future: Quality and Equality for all our Children', Compass, 2005, p. 17, clients. squareeye.net.

21 Blair, *A Journey*, p. 579.

22 Katy Simmons, 'Reasons to be cheerful: the story of one community school and the New Labour government', FORUM, 2010, v. 52, n.1.

23 House of Commons Education and Skills Committee, 'The Schools White Paper: Higher Standards, Better Schools For All—First Report of Session 2005–06', vol. 1, p. 20.

24 Blair, *A Journey*, p. 281.

Chapter 4

1 R. H. Tawney, *Equality* (first published 1931), London: George Allen and Unwin, 1964, p. 142.

2 All figures above are sourced from the 2010 edition of 'Education and Training Statistics for the United Kingdom', education.gov.uk.

3 Hansard, HC, Parliamentary Written Answers for 28 April 2008.

4 Kathryn Torney, 'Northern Ireland grammar schools 11-plus intake revealed', *Belfast Telegraph*, 25 June 2009, belfasttelegraph.co.uk.

5 Maggie Taggart, 'Grammar school academic selection an "annual charade"', BBC News, 27 May 2011, bbc.co.uk.

6 Anushka Asthana, 'Early starts for the children desperate to pass their 11-plus', *Observer*, 11 October 2009, guardian.co.uk.

7 House of Commons Hansard Written Answers, 26 April 2011: Col. 288w.

8 David Willetts, Speech to CBI Conference, 16 May 2007, accessed 22 March 2011 on news.bbc.co.uk.

9 Quoted in Fiona Millar, 'Fairer admissions for poor children? Let's start by ending selection', *The Truth About Our Schools*, 14 September 2010, thetruthaboutourschools.com.

10 *Unlocking the gates: Giving disadvantaged children a fairer deal in school admissions*, Barnardo's report, August 2010, p. 8, barnardos.org.uk.

11 Sir Martin Harris, *What more can be done to widen access to highly selective universities?* Office for Fair Access, April 2010, offa.org.uk.

12 Polly Toynbee, 'Faith schools: now even the church admits they're unfair', *Guardian*, 22 April 2011, guardian.co.uk/commentisfree.

13 Trevor Fisher, 'The Death of Meritocracy: Exams and University Admissions in Crisis', FORUM, 2010, vol. 52, n. 2.

14 James Crabtree, 'Oxford race row just the start', *Financial Times*, 14 April 2011, ft.com/cms.

15 Simon Baker, 'Willetts mulls quota-free recruitment of self-funding UK students', *THES*, 7 May 2011, timeshighereducation.co.uk.

16 Jo Blanden et al., 'Intergenerational Mobility in Europe and North America', Centre for Economic Performance, 2005, suttontrust.com.

17 Tim Luckhurst, 'Meritocratic deficit', *Sunday Times*, 28 August 2005, timesonline.co.uk.

18 Iain Martin, 'Large Hole in Miliband's Social Mobility Speech', *Wall Street Journal*, 4 February 2011, wsj.com.

19 Blanden, 'Intergenerational Mobility in Europe and North America', p. 14.

20 'Study: Comprehensive schools do not reduce social mobility', University of Oxford, 3 March 2011, ox.ac.uk/media/news_stories; Vikki Boliver and Adam Swift, 'Do comprehensive schools reduce social mobility?', *British Journal of Sociology*, vol. 62, n. 1 (2011): 89–110, onlinelibrary.wiley.com.

21 David Raffe et al., Centre for Educational Sociology, University of Edinburgh, 'Social Class Inequalities in Education in England and Scotland', May 2006, ces.ed.ac.uk.

22 Stephen Glover, 'I'm sure the bishop means well, …', *Mail Online*, 25 April 2011, dailymail.co.uk.

23 For example, see Comprehensive Future's 2009 pamphlet, 'Ending Rejection at 11: See how it can be done', comprehensivefuture.org.uk.

24 Lynsey Hanley, *Estates: An Intimate History*, London: Granta, 2007.

25 I am very grateful to a private briefing paper by Janet Dobson for Comprehensive Future in setting out the background main issues on this subject.

Chapter 5

1 Irena Barker, 'Clint and me: Mossbourne head says school leaders are "lone heroes"', *TES*, 18 February 2011, tes.co.uk.

2 Statistics collated by Hackney Learning Trust.

3 Catalyst / Public World, 'Academy Schools: Case Unproven', 2006, pp. 46–50, nasuwt.org.uk.

4 Francis Beckett, *The Great City Academy Fraud*, London: Continuum, 2007.

5 Local Government Association, 'Local freedom or central control?', July 2010, p. 3, lga.gov.uk.

6 Jon Slater, 'Enemies of the state in retreat', *TES*, 4 April 2003, tes.co.uk.

7 Kevin Farnsworth, 'Business in education: a reassessment of the contribution of outsourcing to LEA performance', *Journal of Education Policy*, vol. 21, n. 4 (2006).

8 David Woods and George Gyte, 'Advice to the Secretary of State on the

application from the Birkenshaw, Birstall and Gomersal Parent Alliance and Serco for consent to publish proposals for a new 11–16 Trust School in Kirklees', March 2010, dcsf.gov.uk/schoolorg.

9 Melissa Benn, 'What kind of future is this?', *Guardian*, 23 October 2007, guardian.co.uk.

10 Blair, *A Journey*, p. 578.

11 Stephen Machin and Joan Wilson, 'Academy schools and pupil perform-ance', *CentrePiece*, Spring 2009, p. 8, cep.lse.ac.uk.

12 Andrew Curtis et al., 'The Academies Programme: Progress, problems and possibilities', The Sutton Trust/Institute of Education, December 2008, suttontrust.com.

13 As I posted on the Local Schools Network, January 2011, localschools network.org.uk.

14 William Stewart, 'Gove's favoured academies are failing to meet his own standards', *TES*, 25 February 2011, tes.co.uk.

15 Stephen J. Ball, 'Privatising education, privatising education policy, pri-vatising educational research: network governance and the "competition state"', *Journal of Education Policy*, vol. 24, n. 1 (2009): 96–7.

16 CBI, 'Fulfilling potential: the business role in education', September 2010, highereducation.cbi.org.uk.

17 ATL, 'England's Schools: not open for business', September 2010, atl. org.uk.

18 Melissa Benn, 'Economic uncertainty spreads to education', *guardian.co.uk*, 12 October 2008, guardian.co.uk/commentisfree.

19 Rebecca Smithers, 'Failed academy has not got better, says Ofsted', *Guardian*, 20 March 2006, guardian.co.uk.

20 Chris Irvine, 'Sponsor may back out of academy school', *Telegraph*, 10 October 2008, telegraph.co.uk.

21 Martin Waller, *The Times*, 27 April 2011.

22 David Cohen, 'Hedge fund star: My plan to turn round London schools', *London Evening Standard*, 7 March 2011, thisislondon.co.uk/standard.

23 Hilary Wilce, 'Swedish lessons: Are new "free" schools the answer?', *Independent*, 22 April 2010, independent.co.uk.

24 Rebecca Allen, 'Replicating Swedish "free school" reforms in England', Research in Public Policy, Summer 2010, bris.ac.uk.

25 Molly Mulready-Jones, 'No such thing as a "free school" for Hackney', Hackney Citizen, 14 March 2011, hackneycitizen.co.uk.

26 Diane Ravitch, 'The Myth of Charter Schools', *New York Review of Books*, 11 November 2010, nybooks.com.

27 Centre for Research on Education Outcomes (CREDO), Stanford University, 'Multiple Choice: Charter School Performance in 16 States', June 2009, credo.stanford.edu.

28 Richard D. Kahlenberg, 'Myths and realities about KIPP', *Washington Post*, 4 January 2011, voices.washingtonpost.com.

29 Gary Miron, Jessica L. Urschel and Nicolas Saxton, College of Education and Human Development, Western Michigan University, 'What Makes KIPP Work? A Study of Student Characteristics, Attrition, and School Finance', March 2011, ncspe.org.

30 Ravitch, 'The Myth of Charter Schools'.

31 Francis Gilbert, 'Why do our politicians think American charter schools are so great?', 30 April 2010, francisgilbert.co.uk.

32 Leighton Andrews, 'Welsh Labour's education promise', *WalesOnline*, 28 April 2011, walesonline.co.uk.

33 Michele Hanson, 'Compare and contrast', *Guardian*, 11 June 2009, guardian.co.uk.

Chapter 6

1 Graham Greene, (ed.), in *The Old School: Essays by Divers Hands*, Oxford: Oxford University Press, 1984, p. 8.

2 Brian Cox, *The Great Betrayal: Memoirs of a Life in Education*, London: Chapmans, 1992, p. 1.

3 Peter Wilby, 'The pursuit of happiness', *Guardian*, 29 May 2007, guardian. co.uk.

4 Simon Jenkins, 'Oh come, come, headmaster—private schools are pretend charities', *Sunday Times*, 20 January 2008, timesonline.co.uk.

5 Gillian Sutherland, 'Education', in F.M.L. Thompson (ed.), The Cambridge Social History of Britain 1750–1950, Volume 3: Social Agencies and Institutions, Cambridge: Cambridge University Press, 1990, pp. 119–69.

6 Quoted in Nicholas Timmins, *The Five Giants: a biography of the welfare state*, London: HarperCollins, 2001, p. 75.

7 Quoted in Michael Shaw, 'Class act', *TES Magazine*, 14 January 2011, tes.co.uk.

8 Timmins, *The Five Giants*, p. 87.

9 George Monbiot, 'Unsentimental Education', 22 January 2008, monbiot. com.

10 Chris Ryan and Luke Sibieta, 'Private schooling in the UK and Australia', Institute for Fiscal Studies, 2010, ifs.org.uk.

11 Anthony Seldon, 'Free schools are an opportunity, not a threat', *London Evening Standard*, 22 March 2011, thisislondon.co.uk/standard.

12 Warwick Mansell and Polly Curtis, 'Top private school dumps "too easy" GCSEs', *Guardian*, 4 March 2009, guardian.co.uk.

13 The Sutton Trust, 'Private-school pupils 55 times more likely to go to Oxbridge than poor students', December 2010, suttontrust.com.

14 One glaring example is posted by Fiona Millar in 'Watch out for private school spin and dodgy statistics', 16 August 2010, thetruthaboutourschools. com.

15 Francis Green et al., 'The Changing Economic Advantage From Private Schools', Centre for the Economics of Education, April 2010, cee.lse.ac.uk.

16 Independent Schools Council, 'Private schools—perceptions of the sector 97–06', March 2007, isc.co.uk.

17 Simon Head, 'Children of the sun: David Cameron, Nick Clegg and the Conservative party elite', *Guardian*, 2 October 2010, guardian.co.uk/ books.

18 Monbiot, 'Unsentimental Education'.

19 Barbara Ellen, 'Who declared class war among our teens?', *Observer*, 16 November 2008, guardian.co.uk/commentisfree.

20 Private communication.

21 Alex Derber, 'Eton and the masses', *guardian.co.uk*, 14 March 2010, guardian.co.uk/commentisfree.

22 Quoted in Richard Garner, 'Lord's prayer: Andrew Adonis on why he still has faith in academies', *Independent*, 1 May 2008, independent.co.uk.

23 Ibid.

24 'Academy truancy among UK worst', *This Is Kent* website, 21 January 2001, thisiskent.co.uk.

25 Chris Woodhead, 'Analysing the Parties' Policies', *Attain*: the official magazine of the Independent Association of Prep Schools (IAPS), Spring 2008, attainmagazine.co.uk.

26 Anthony Seldon, 'An end to factory schools: An education manifesto 2010– 2020', Centre for Policy Studies, March 2010, cps.org.uk.

27 Irena Barker, 'Top public schools: state staff fail to inspire', *TES*, 1 October 2010, tes.co.uk.

28 Jenkins, 'Oh come, come, headmaster'.

29 Civil Society, 'David Miliband calls for private schools to lose charitable status', 23 June 2010, civilsociety.co.uk/governance.

Chapter 7

1 Craig Woodhouse, 'Michael Gove's department "is shambolic and chaotic"', *London Evening Standard*, 21 March 2011, thisislondon.co.uk/standard.

2 Stephanie Northern, 'What became of the bog-standard comprehensive?', *Guardian*, 15 February 2011, guardian.co.uk.

3 Quoted in Richard Garner, 'The free school revolution: Behind the scenes at the first parent-led secondary', *Independent*, 17 March 2011, independent. co.uk.

4 Fiona Millar, 'Amendment to Education Bill hints at Tory backbench campaign to bring back selection', Local Schools Network, 6 April 2011, localschoolsnetwork.org.uk.

5 Melissa Benn and Fiona Millar, 'A potential killer blow to the comprehensive ideal', *Guardian*, 19 April 2006, guardian.co.uk.

6 Susanne Wiborg, 'Learning Lessons from the Swedish Model', FORUM, vol. 52, n. 2 (2010): 279–84.

7 'Segregation in charter schools, research shows', Pennsylvania State University, 17 February 2011, physorg.com.

8 Katy Simmons in 'Selection at 11—what it does to children and schools', Comprehensive Future Parliamentary Seminar, 9 May 2006, comprehensive future.org.uk.

9 Sharon Wright, 'A rather unchristian school admissions policy?', *Guardian*, 20 September 2010, guardian.co.uk.

10 David Marley, 'Academy sponsor in talks over "super-chain"', *TES*, 18 March 2011, tes.co.uk.

11 Ibid.

12 Innovative Schools website, innovativeschools.co.uk.

13 'A million UK children "lack access to computers"', BBC News, 28 December 2010, bbc.co.uk.

14 Stephen Ball, 'Back to the 19th century with Michael Gove's education bill', *Guardian*, 31 January 2011, guardian.co.uk/commentisfree.

15 Letter to Julian Taylor, 7 March 2011, whatdotheyknow.com.

16 Caroline Scott, 'Inner-city academy that's a blueprint for the future', *Telegraph*, 16 May 2011, telegraph.co.uk.

17 Mike Baker, 'MPs warn of risks of academies expansion', 27 January 2011, mikebakereducation.co.uk.

18 David Moberg, 'How Edison Survived', *Nation*, 15 March 2004.

19 Molly Mulready-Jones, 'There is no such thing as a "free school" for Hackney', *Hackney Citizen*, 14 March 2011, hackneycitizen.co.uk.

20 Peter Wilby, speaking to 'Radical Education and the Common School' conference at the Institute of Education, 18 March 2011.

21 Interview with Peter Wilby, 18 March 2011.

22 Daniel Boffey, 'Free schools: private firm Cognita "milked profits"', *Observer*, 10 April 2011, guardian.co.uk.

23 James Croft, 'Profit-Making Free Schools: Unlocking the Potential of England's Proprietorial Schools Sector', Adam Smith Institute, April 2010, pp. 7–8, adamsmith.org.

24 Fiona Millar, 'There is another way', Local Schools Network, 6 May 2011, localschoolsnetwork.org.uk.

25 William Stewart, 'Teachers doubt reforms will boost lot of disadvantaged', *TES*, 22 April 2011, tes.co.uk.

26 A complete list of the Anti Academies Alliance's campaigns is available at antiacademies.org.uk.

27 Warwick Mansell, 'Is academy status being foisted on schools?', *Guardian*, 15 March 2011, guardian.co.uk.

Chapter 8

1 Richard Pring, 'A Comprehensive Curriculum for Comprehensive Schools', speech given 13 November 2004, socialisteducation.org.uk.

2 Summerhill School Website, summerhillschool.co.uk.

3 Daniel Pennac, *School Blues*, London: Quercus, 2010, p. 260.

4 Interview with Peter Wilby, 'The pursuit of happiness', *Guardian*, 29 May 2007, guardian.co.uk.

5 Daniel Dorling, *Injustice: Why Social Inequality Persists*, Bristol: Policy Press, 2010, p. 1.

6 Ferdinand Mount, *Mind The Gap: The new class divide in Britain*, London: Short Books, 2004, p. 227.

7 Ken Robinson, 'Bring on the learning revolution!', speech to TED, February 2010, ted.com.

8 Brian Simon, *Intelligence Testing and the Comprehensive School*, London: Lawrence & Wishart, 1953.

9 Brian Richardson and Bernard Coard, *Tell It Like It Is: How Our Schools Fail Black Children*, Bookmarks, 2007, p. 91.

10 Susan Hart, *Learning Without Limits*, Maidenhead: McGraw-Hill International, 2004, p. 6.

11 Ibid., and forthcoming publication, September 2011.

12 'Parents and Public continue to back Integration Education: The Millward Brown Report 2008', Northern Ireland Council for Integrated Education, nicie.org.

13 'Oldham merges schools segregated by race', *BBC Online*, 5 August 2010, news.bbc.co.uk.

14 For example, see the results of a YouGov poll commissioned by the Accord Coalition in 2009: yougov.co.uk/archives/pdf/RESULTS per cent20for per cent20Accord per cent20Coalition per cent20(School per cent20Worship).pdf .

15 Ibid.

16 Office for National Statistics, 'Social Trends', no. 40, Palgrave Macmillan, 2010, statistics.gov.uk.

17 James Tooley, 'From Adam Swift to Adam Smith: How the "Invisible Hand" Overcomes Middle-Class Hypocrisy', in *The Common School and the Comprehensive Ideal*, Richard Pring and Mark Halstead (eds), John Wiley and Sons, 2008.

18 Francis Beckett, *The Great City Academy Fraud*, London: Continuum, 2007, p. 172.

19 Richardson and Coard, *Tell It Like It Is*, p. 100.

20 McKinsey & Company, 'How the world's best-performing school systems come out on top', September 2007, mckinsey.com, p. 19.

21 Caroline Roberts, 'What parents think of schools', Research and Information on State Education, June 2010, risetrust.org.uk.

22 Richardson and Coard, *Tell It Like It Is*.

23 See the website of 'Families and Schools Together', familiesandschools. org.

24 Sharon Otterman, 'Lauded Harlem Schools Have Their Own Problems', *New York Times*, 12 October 2010, nytimes.com.

25 National Audit Office, 'Maintaining the financial stability of UK banks: update on the support schemes', December 2010, nao.org.uk.

26 'Cost of wars in Iraq and Afghanistan tops £20bn', BBC News, 20 June 2010, bbc.co.uk.

27 'The 2.9bn pound Royal Wedding bank holiday', The FactCheck Blog, Channel 4 News, 23 November 2010, blogs.channel4.com.

28 Diane Ravitch, *The Death and Life of the Great American School System: How Testing and Choice are Undermining Education*, New York: Basic Books, 2010, p. 241.

29 Kevin McKenna, 'Stop knocking comprehensives. They work', *Observer*, 8 August 2010, guardian.co.uk/commentisfree.

Index